Rawls and the Environmental Crisis

The liberal political theorist John Rawls, despite remaining largely silent on 'green concerns', was writing during a time of increasing awareness that the ecological stability of the earth is being compromised by human activity. Rawls's reluctance to engage with such concerns, however, has not stopped several scholars attempting to 'extend', or 'expand', his works to incorporate this newfound fear for the ecosystems that support human life. But why Rawls? What is to be gained from developing the ideas of a theorist whose primary aim was to establish a system of justice for contemporaneous, rational, and reasonable citizens of a liberal polity?

This research monograph offers a critical consideration of the contextual framework within John Rawls's *Political Liberalism* and considers its compatibility with the conceptual process of 'greening'. *Rawls and the Environmental Crisis* argues that Rawls's perceived neutrality on green concerns is representative of a widespread societal indifference to environmental degradation and describes the plurality of methodological and ethical approaches undertaken by green political theorists in analyzing the contribution Rawls's theory makes to environmental concerns.

Addressing a series of key debates within contemporary political philosophy regarding a wider frustration with liberal theory in general, *Rawls and the Environmental Crisis* will be of great interest to researchers in contemporary political philosophy, environmental ethics, green political theory, stewardship theory, and those interested in renewing existing conceptions of deliberative democracy.

Dominic Welburn is a Lecturer in Politics at Oxford Brookes University.

Routledge Explorations in Environmental Studies

For a full list of titles in this series, please visit www.routledge.com

Contemporary Perspectives on Ecofeminism
Mary Phillips and Nick Rumens

Culture and Conservation
Beyond anthropocentrism
Eleanor Shoreman-Ouimet and Helen Kopnina

The Governance of Sustainable Rural Renewal
A comparative global perspective
Rory Shand

Disasters and Social Resilience
A bioecological approach
Helen J. Boon, Alison Cottrell and David King

Fairness and Justice in Natural Resource Politics
Edited by Melanie Pichler, Cornelia Staritz, Karin Küblböck,
Christina Plank, Werner Raza and Fernando Ruiz Peyré

Environmental Justice in India
The National Green Tribunal
Gitanjali Nain Gill

Socioeconomic Evaluation of Megaprojects
Dealing with uncertainties
Edited by Markku Lehtonen, Pierre-Benoît Joly and Luis Aparicio

High Speed Rail and Sustainability
Decision-Making and the Political Economy of Investment
Edited by Blas Luis Pérez Henríquez and Elizabeth Deakin

Rawls and the Environmental Crisis
Dominic Welburn

Rawls and the Environmental Crisis

Dominic Welburn

First published 2017
by Routledge
2 Park Square, Milton Park, Abingdon, Oxon OX14 4RN

and by Routledge
711 Third Avenue, New York, NY 10017

Routledge is an imprint of the Taylor & Francis Group, an informa business

© 2017 Dominic Welburn

The right of Dominic Welburn to be identified as author of this work has been asserted by him in accordance with sections 77 and 78 of the Copyright, Designs and Patents Act 1988.

All rights reserved. No part of this book may be reprinted or reproduced or utilised in any form or by any electronic, mechanical, or other means, now known or hereafter invented, including photocopying and recording, or in any information storage or retrieval system, without permission in writing from the publishers.

Trademark notice: Product or corporate names may be trademarks or registered trademarks, and are used only for identification and explanation without intent to infringe.

British Library Cataloguing in Publication Data
A catalogue record for this book is available from the British Library

Library of Congress Cataloging in Publication Data
Names: Welburn, Dominic, author.
Title: Rawls and the environmental crisis / Dominic Welburn.
Description: Abingdon, Oxon ; New York, NY : Routledge is an imprint of the Taylor & Francis Group, an Informa Business, [2017] | Series: Explorations in environmental studies
Identifiers: LCCN 2016031109 | ISBN 9780415721721 (hbk) | ISBN 9781315859026 (ebk)
Subjects: LCSH: Rawls, John, 1921–2002. | Environmentalism—Political aspects. | Environmental justice. | Environmental ethics.
Classification: LCC JC251.R32 W45 2017 | DDC 333.701—dc23
LC record available at https://lccn.loc.gov/2016031109

ISBN: 978-0-415-72172-1 (hbk)
ISBN: 978-1-315-85902-6 (ebk)

Typeset in Bembo
by Apex CoVantage, LLC

Printed and bound by CPI Group (UK) Ltd, Croydon, CR0 4YY

To my parents

Contents

Preface		*viii*
Acknowledgements		*x*
	Introduction	1
1	Rawls and political liberalism	16
2	Rawls on green concerns	35
3	A green critique of Rawls	55
4	A second green critique	88
	Conclusion	121
	Bibliography	136
	Index	143

Preface

This monograph is based on my PhD thesis entitled: *Darkening Green Liberalism: Towards a Rawlsian Stewardship Ethic*, which was completed at the University of Hull in the summer of 2012. Following numerous revisions, this work has sought to bring together, for the first time, key works on the environmental implications of John Rawls's later vision of political liberalism.

The original PhD thesis suffered from two significant defects, the correction of which hopefully explains at least part of the time lapse between then and the publication of this monograph now. The first was the incorrect ordering of the thesis that sought to find an ethic, or theory, of environmental justice that best complemented Rawls's notion of justice as fairness. The problem with this method is that it affirms, rather uncritically, his own view of the correct configuration of humanity's relationship to wider nature in *A Theory of Justice* (1971). Simply put, and as explored in Chapter 2 in the work that follows, Rawls believed that his partially comprehensive liberalism would naturally reflect a true environmental ethic that, once found, offered a substantive vision of humanity's wider place in the cosmos. This would have meant Rawls was seeking to uncover a universal – and fundamentally liberal – ordering of humanity's relationship to wider nature, *sub specie aeternitatis*. Rawls would later come to subtly revise this idea, along with other excessively ambitious doctrinal aims. Instead, this monograph now seeks to expose a tension within his mature theory that justice between contemporaneous rational and reasonable humans is 'but one part of the moral view', and that once we attempt to extend justice to entities who are neither rational nor reasonable, beyond the here and now, we have to acknowledge the more conservative elements of his work. The drawback in the original thesis, with hindsight, was that Rawlsian theory was merely applied to vague notions of the environmental crisis. Although this reflected Rawls's own preferred method of extensionism, it overlooked the nuances of the relationship between both the liberal and the more conservative elements of his theory. It wrongly (and again, uncritically) identified Rawls's notion of a 'well-ordered society' as an outright *good* of justice, to be bequeathed from one generation to the next. The case was then made that his theory inevitably produced a substantive community of liberal justice united around uniform, normative principles. Rawls, of course, was explicit that there was no *summum bonum* to be found in his freestanding, political and overlapping consensus, as it was rather the case that citizens deeply divided by a reasonable plurality of views of the good would agree to a political consensus for reasons specific to their own doctrines. As such, this second attempt to provide an overview of the environmental implications of Rawls's thought looks to the idea of a well-ordered society as a much more limited 'good' of intergenerational justice only, and one that requires certain virtues of citizenship if it is to be maintained. It will then be argued that justice as fairness can be seen as more of an enduring political agreement characteristic of modernity, as opposed to a metaphysical higher good.

The overall aims of both works, however, remain the same. First, the book attempts to offer an overview of what we may call the *green critique* of Rawls that can (potentially) serve as a coherent methodological body of work alongside other schools of thought, including multiculturalism, feminism, and the more fashionable recent 'realist' turn in political theory. Second, that Rawls's separation of 'strict' justice from environmental justice does not automatically denote a political indifference towards the plight of non-human species and future generations at risk from declining ecological conditions. Third, that his later political liberalism embodies the key tenets of a traditional theory of stewardship when his principle of 'just savings' is considered in more detail. Fourth and finally, that it is perhaps not so prudent to dismiss the liberal-conservative undertones of Rawls's theory of intergenerational justice, as he reminds scholars to look beyond the language of the inviolable rights and opportunities of the individual when addressing significant moral and political dilemmas.

Dominic Welburn
Oxford Brookes University, 2016

Acknowledgements

There are several people without whom this work would not have been possible. First and foremost, I would like to express my sincere gratitude to my then PhD supervisor, and now colleague, Professor James Connolly, for his patience, good humour, and unwavering support that meant that the thesis came to fruition. Professor Derek Bell of Newcastle University, the external examiner of the original thesis, has offered invaluable advice and timely guidance throughout the whole process of turning the work into a coherent monograph. I thank Professor Bell for both his time and support. Professor Noël O'Sullivan, University of Hull, has acted as a mentor and a source of great academic wisdom over the past few years, and he has taken time out of what should have been his peaceful retirement to help me (along with several fellow research students at Hull), and for this I am incredibly grateful. Dr Derek Edyvane at the University of Leeds has been a brilliant mentor during my time at the School of Politics and International Studies there, and has provided excellent feedback on an early draft of this work. Those mentioned above have all demonstrated the supreme academic virtue of patience.

The School of Politics, Philosophy and International Studies at The University of Hull was kind enough to award me an 80th Anniversary Research scholarship allowing me to commit to my doctoral studies full time. I am incredibly grateful to the School also for providing a research-intensive environment for doctoral students.

The Political Theory and Cultural Values research seminar at the University of Leeds provided a perfect setting for testing the water with my conclusions on Rawls and environmental thought, and I am indebted to the helpful comments from my then colleagues – and now friends – Dr Graham Smith and Dr Jonathan Dean.

I would also like to extend my gratitude to the team at Routledge, including Kelly Watkins, Rebecca Brennan, and Margaret Farrelly, whose untiring help and support in completing the manuscript has been invaluable.

My partner, Elizabeth, has been an eternal source of calm reassurance throughout this long process, and I cannot thank her enough for being so encouraging and optimistic during the darker moments of writing.

Finally, and perhaps above all, I would like to extend a heartfelt thank you to my parents, John and Maureen, to whom this book is dedicated, for their inexhaustible patience and kindness over the many years that they have had to put up with me. You are both simply wonderful.

Introduction

The liberal political theorist John Rawls, despite remaining largely silent on 'green concerns', was writing during a time of increasing awareness that the ecological stability of the earth is being compromised by human activity. Rawls's reluctance to engage with such concerns, however, has not stopped several scholars attempting to 'extend', or 'expand', his works to incorporate this newfound fear for the ecosystems that support human life. But why Rawls? What is to be gained from developing the ideas of a theorist whose primary aim was to establish a system of justice for contemporaneous, rational, and reasonable citizens of a liberal polity? Immediately, two problems present themselves. Even if we can successfully reconcile Rawlsian liberalism with green concerns, what use is this endeavour for societies facing grave environmental threats? Presumably, Rawls's theory of justice is seen as an apologia for the theoretical under-pinnings of modern liberal polities, and so if his ideas can indeed be 'greened', then the inference is that so, too, can a liberal society in the 'real world'. The literature under review in the following chapters, however, does not make this link clear, predominantly because very vague, and abstract, notions of 'the' environmental crisis are used to condemn or condone Rawlsian liberalism. So the second problem, if indeed Rawls's theory is to be seen as ripe for greening, is to investigate the competing extensionist methodologies employed by green political theorists. The aim of this introduction, then, is to set the scene for how Rawlsian liberalism has come to be embroiled in wider debates regarding the supposed un-ecological implications of liberal thought.

Beginnings

The vituperation of the political thought of John Rawls (1921–2002) has come in many different forms. Indeed, since the publication of his seminal *A Theory of Justice* (*TJ* hereafter) in 1971, there have been several tides of criticism that have washed up against his central idea of 'justice as fairness'. These have included the so-called idea of communitarianism; the Cambridge revolution in the history of political thought; agonal theory; discourse theory; multiculturalism; feminist political thought; and the more recent 'realist' turn to name but a few. There is, however, a largely overlooked – but

2 Rawls and the Environmental Crisis

equally fascinating – body of scholarly work that has engaged with his version of liberalism on the subject of environmental thought that can be referred to as *the green critique of Rawls*. Rupert Read has rather derogatorily described this 'sub-sub-discipline' as something of a 'growing cottage industry' (2011: 81), whereby the key precepts of Rawlsian liberalism are theoretically developed so as to incorporate a number of competing conceptions of environmental or ecological justice.[1] This, it should be pointed out, happens in a number of ways. Predominantly, and whether one is either scathing of, or indeed sympathetic towards his ideas, it is because Rawls's political liberalism is widely recognized as the most influential version of liberalism to have emerged in the second half of the twentieth century. For the more serious critics of Rawls, his ideas amount to something altogether more insidious; namely, that he has become a figurehead for a neutral, liberal system of politics and economics that has promulgated rampant consumerism and brought the planet to the edge of ecological ruin. Even those who are sympathetic towards Rawls's theory argue that his liberalism possesses only a minimal commitment to taking green concerns seriously. The principal aim of this monograph is, for the first time, to offer an in-depth overview of key elements of the green critique of Rawls. The second aim is to then highlight a tension between the liberal and conservative elements of his mature thought by tracing a subtle – yet significant – development within the critique that sees Rawlsian thought progressing from the embodiment of a *shallow instrumentalist* approach to green concerns, to a more *enlightened* (yet still anthropocentric) theory of environmental justice. Simply put, although his theory of justice is built on the political recognition of the inviolable (and thoroughly modern) liberty and equality of the individual, once our duties to future generations and wider nature are involved, his 'principle of just savings' dictates that successive generations are to first inherit, and then bequeath, the just institutions of a well-ordered society from one generation to the next. This calls upon citizens to adhere to what he calls the 'great political values' and thus, it will be argued, they are to act as *liberal stewards* of both an intergenerational and enduring human search for justice in a secular world.

Before we begin to consider whether or not the green critique represents a coherent body of work akin to, say, feminist or communitarian analyses of Rawlsian liberalism, why have several theorists turned, in the first instance, to a thinker who had so little to say about the grave threats to humanity posed by environmental crises? The short answer is that, again, Rawlsian liberalism is often seen as an extended *apologia* for modernity – a *post-hoc* philosophical justification of the principles that underpin liberal societies that, in fetishizing individualism and the free market, has led humanity to the brink of ecological catastrophe. For many, the abstraction of human progress from the ecological systems upon which such growth depends is the true *crisis of modernity*. Yet this statement is merely an inference, as will be demonstrated from the in-depth discussion of the key literature in the chapters that follow, and it is therefore necessary to address the assumed link between Rawlsian liberalism and modernity, given that theorists working in this area tend to focus on his explicit dualism between human justice and a concern for wider nature (or what will later be identified as 'the separation argument') as symbolic of a genuine crisis of modernity. The suggestion here is that Rawlsian liberalism serves as an influential reinforcement of the idea that green concerns should been treated as secondary in importance to contemporaneous human justice. The separation argument is then used to either condemn or condone Rawls. If we condemn Rawls, we strike a blow against modernity, but if we can demonstrate that his theory is well placed to absorb green concerns, then there is an assumed hope that our liberal societies can change their un-environmental ways whilst continuing along the path of human progress. The key theme that emerges throughout the literature surveyed is that Rawls's particular theory of justice is seen to underpin the normative, political aspirations of most liberal democratic societies. This statement is, again, not uncontroversial and will itself be challenged in what follows, yet our starting point is that Rawls's theory represents a sort of ethical laboratory for testing the perceived incongruence between liberalism and green concerns.

In providing a new and comprehensive overview of the way in which environmental crises have been utilized to reappraise the work of Rawls, the competing methods used by green political theorists working in this area will be examined in greater detail. The green critique is split into two camps, representing the two different directions this body of work has taken. The first camp argues that Rawlsian liberalism embodies a limited, shallowly instrumentalist – but theoretically significant – conception of environmental justice. The second part of the critique, covering the latest research in this area, opens up new possibilities for the greening of Rawls in the form of a liberalized theory of environmental stewardship. Again, though, this forms only one front upon which a wider tension between liberal political thought and green concerns reveals itself. First, a little more background is needed on how exactly Rawls has become embroiled in discussions that were once quite separate from the idea of liberal justice.

Liberalism versus green concerns?

Most, if not all, individuals hold what we may call *green concerns*. That is, they will inevitably possess views about how humanity should interact with wider nature, and the non-human world, beyond their relations with fellow contemporaneous citizens. These could range from fleeting anxieties about sourcing their next meal from a company with high animal welfare standards through to more metaphysical concerns about humanity's alienation from the ecosystems upon which their very existence depends. Even if an individual may claim not to consciously possess a single regard for wider nature, there is no doubt that at some point he or she will have contemplated, and even worried about, the future of the planet. Whether motivated by a fear of global pandemics, natural disasters, climate change, rising sea levels, pollution, overpopulation, or threats

4 Rawls and the Environmental Crisis

to a stable supply of food, it is unlikely that a citizen has never held even a fleeting green concern.

For some, these concerns do not need to go so far as to become part of a philosophical discourse about humans *in* nature, and merely represent a common sense approach to sustainable living. Put slightly differently, humans should not live beyond their ecological means for if they do, they risk destroying the conditions for life on earth. For the less instrumentally minded, however, their green concerns will become something closer to what Aaron Lercher (2006) has called an *ecological conscience*, meaning that their beliefs are verging on the doctrinal, on a par with religious or spiritual conceptions of the good life.

It would be illogical for humanity to destroy the ecosystems upon which life on earth depends, and so although taking a range of green concerns seriously appears uncontroversial, we soon encounter a problem when it is a liberal democratic society that has to incorporate these concerns into the realm of 'the political'. Given that they will more often than not form part of timeless questions about the human condition, and humanity's place in the world, there is a sense for liberals that they should be kept separate from the inner workings of a conception of a just political order. Very generally speaking, and since the European religious wars of the sixteenth and seventeenth centuries, liberalism, in both theory and practice, has tried to prevent societies from slipping into civil conflict via a policy of containment regarding the more contentious doctrinal disagreements. To do this, it has sought to privatize the most controversial and divisive views of the good by keeping them out of the public–political sphere. Should green concerns therefore, as part of a wider discourse surrounding the correct conception of humanity's relationship with wider nature, take their rightful place outside of the political for the sake of agreement and the avoidance of civil strife?

An interesting development in recent decades has been the *politicization* of these concerns as they become less-straightforwardly green, and more aligned with the conceptual methods and language of contemporary political philosophy. Although attentive to an impending environmental crisis, these concerns look to the effects of ecological degradation on groups and entities traditionally excluded from liberal justice. Specifically, this area of the green critique looks beyond the confines of contemporaneous, rational agents willing to relegate their conceptions of the good to the private, or background, public sphere, for the sake of political agreement. What of future generations not born yet, or environmental refugees fleeing from natural (or man-made) disasters? And what of non-human – but sentient – beings not privy to the establishing of liberal principles of justice? Questions such as these do not actually rely on a notion of the environmental crisis for their existence, and could of course be forced onto the political agenda via any number of anthropogenic crises. The point to make here is that included within an array of green concerns, in addition to an ecological conscience, many citizens may adhere to a more comprehensive theory of *environmental* or *ecological justice* that talks of extending rights, duties, obligations, entitlements, or liberties to individuals or groups who have historically been excluded from the discourse of political justice. The umbrella term of *green concerns*, then, contains within it a plurality of reasonable concerns about humanity's relationship with wider nature from fleeting anxieties about sustainability, through to the reflective possession of an ecological conscience, and even to the more politically minded who see the need for the formal representation of excluded groups, at risk from deteriorating environmental conditions, within the discourse of justice. The focus of this monograph is on politicized green concerns and the ability of Rawlsian liberalism to accommodate such views.

Prima facie, any theory of liberalism seems at odds with green concerns, with the latter seeking to limit the excessive individualism of the former. Marcel Wissenburg and Yoram Levy (2004), however, present a compelling case for thinking that liberal political thought – Rawlsian or otherwise – can successfully 'absorb' green concerns. The fact that there is a waning interest in these particular concerns amongst European and American publics forms part of a wider bureaucratization of all things green, as well as a reduction of once controversial and metaphysical environmental issues to the level of procedural, technical, and policy problems (1–3). In their words: 'there are good grounds for believing that green concerns are being addressed in, and have been successfully incorporated into, everyday politics and political thought . . . there seems to be no reason why environmentalism as an independent school of thought should continue to exist' (2–3). Wissenburg and Levy, however, remain suspicious of the etymology of 'endism' in the social sciences, as it can serve as a teleological goal, or as a more historical, and presumably less successful, 'end-point' when something ceases to exist (4–5). In other words, green concerns as reflected in the catch-all ideology of 'environmentalism' could be considered as either an outright failure or as a critique that has now run its course. Yet even the use of the concept of endism assumes a strong link between liberal political thought and the actual functioning of liberal democratic states in practice. By focussing on the 'alleged pacification of environmentalism from the perspective of political *theory*' (3, emphasis in original) we again arrive at the key challenge of establishing the link between the greening of established ideas and the practical ability of liberal societies to take green concerns seriously.

Wissenburg and Levy's thesis may, however, have been somewhat premature. As will be demonstrated in the chapters that follow, the idea of incorporating green concerns into Rawlsian liberalism is far from straightforward. If, as Chapter 1 argues, Rawls's mature liberalism represents the search for political unity on basic principles of justice within societies characterized by competing visions of the good, then the idea of an environmental crisis can serve either as an outright threat or as a blessing in disguise. The green critique is one of the lesser-known fronts upon which Rawlsian liberalism – and indeed liberalism more generally – comes under scrutiny. This body of thought utilizes a plethora of ideas that serve as new *tests* for the validity of the Rawlsian project. With the politicization of green concerns, or what Martha Nussbaum (2007)

6 *Rawls and the Environmental Crisis*

has called the 'new frontiers of justice', including the role of non-human species, future generations, and citizens or groups that fall outside of the scope of traditional theories of justice, the green critique under scrutiny highlights how in recent decades there has been a merger between the discourse of liberal justice, contemporary political philosophy, and the concept of sustainability. Andrew Dobson (1999) argues that where there was once a belief that green concerns were of only secondary importance to debates surrounding justice and perhaps even represented a mere indulgence for the affluent West, notions of the environmental crisis and a greater recognition of the need for sustainable economic growth have moved to the forefront of contemporary political thought (1–4). The moral significance surrounding the plight of non-human species, environmental refugees, and future generations most at risk from deteriorating ecological conditions has, again, become increasingly politicized. Rawls himself was clear that this was an appropriate direction for the discipline to take, and he was open to the idea of developing the green implications of his thought, in particular, within his much later version of *political* liberalism. Although the traditional relegation of green concerns to the peripheries of political thought now seems archaic, the process of 'absorption' has certainly not been as plain sailing as Wissenburg and Levy would have us believe.

Dobson (2007) pinpoints three key areas where this unification of once distinct bodies of thought (that is, liberalism, justice, and green concerns) has taken place. The first is that the 'environmental' *is* the political, so to speak. As boundaries of what we term 'the political' have expanded in line with Nussbaum's above argument, debates surrounding deteriorating environmental conditions and the unequal distribution of environmental goods (and bads) have become politicized. The second is the extension of political concepts, including justice, rights, democracy, etc., to incorporate those entities traditionally excluded from justice between contemporaneous moral agents. The third area considers the 'greening' of theorists and their related theories. This final area is a broad church: from Plato to Rawls, Aristotle to Arendt, and Spinoza to Heidegger, there is no shortage of thinkers from the canon of Western thought to which green political theorists can look for normative resources in addressing unprecedented environmental challenges. A more straightforward overview of this project is to invoke Anthony Weston's description of 'extensionist environmental philosophy' (Weston, 1999) as it sits more comfortably with Rawls's own view of green concerns. To reiterate, although he 'leaves these problems of extension and focus[ses] on . . . the fundamental question of political justice', Rawls by no means rules out the possibility of extending justice as fairness to future generations and non-human species (Rawls, 2005: 21). Indeed, in a seemingly obscure footnote, Rawls states that 'these questions may become ones of constitutional essentials and basic justice once our duties and obligations to future generations and others societies are involved' (246, fn.35). These statements from Rawls will be considered, in more detail, in Chapter 2.

There is, then, a sense in the wider literature that the once convenient orthodoxy of keeping green concerns distinct from political justice is not just outdated, but also morally untenable. Dobson (1998) even goes so far as to make the claim that if a notion of political justice fails to consider the needs and interests of non-human species, it amounts to a 'second-division' political theory (174). Tim Hayward (1998), too, reaches a similar conclusion stating that political theorists 'cannot justifiably remain neutral or agnostic on the question of the moral considerability of nonhuman beings' (150). Similarly, future generations and those beyond the scope of traditional justice most at risk from deteriorating environmental conditions cannot be overlooked within theories of political justice. Rawls, who is clearly in Dobson's sights, has even been charged with the outright offence of 'speciesism' insomuch as his theory excludes all non-human considerations from the outset and therefore represents a weak green, shallow instrumentalist, and arrogant theory of environmental justice in and of itself (Garner, 2003). Here, however, it is Dobson's claim that we are engaged in 'bad' political theory if we abstract *political* justice from *environmental* or *ecological* justice ('the separation argument', or more grandly, the true crisis of modernity) that will be central to the analysis of the green critique as it is presented in the following chapters.

Viewing the 'extension' (Weston, 1999), or 'expansion' (Dobson, 2003), of Rawls's political thought to include politicized green concerns is an essential component of wider attempts to analyse the compatibility of liberal thought, as the great ideological product of modernity, with theories of environmental or ecological justice. How can liberal thought, which appeals so much to the importance of an individual's self-authorship of the good life, warm to beliefs that highlight the need for individual self-restraint and sacrifice? Can the curtailing of individual freedoms, in the interests of environmental protection, be justified? Liberalism is seen as part of the problem because critics, like Mark Sagoff (1988), round on the idea that it is an ideology born of the Enlightenment. Dobson echoes this sentiment by describing the very spirit of the age of Enlightenment as an anathema to ecological stability: the 'world had been made for human beings and that in principle, nothing in it could be kept secret from them' (7). Reinforced politically under the guise of liberalism, humanity has developed a hubristic attitude of domination over wider nature fostered and encouraged by the separation argument, and the divorcing of human progress from green concerns.

Two themes, therefore, can be distinguished within the wider literature on green political theory. The first has already been covered; namely, that liberal political theory is to be considered 'second-class' if it is to remain neutral on the subject of environmental thought. The second key theme is that many strains of liberal thought claim to be able to 'absorb' green concerns. Yoram Levy and Wissenburg (2004), again, put forward the assertion that liberal democracy, embodying the key tenets of liberal political thought, has largely incorporated the challenge from environmentalisms arguing, 'the alleged pacification of environmentalism is, for the greater part, not skin-deep but quite deep – and not yet deep enough' (195). Levy and Wissenburg continue: 'there are good grounds to believe that environmental and liberal democratic values can cohere within a pluralist conception of a reasonable, just and green society' (ibid.). This is the view that a liberal appeal to self-interest and the good of human flourishing requires a commitment to a minimal set of environmental standards that are necessary for individuals to pursue their own conceptions of the good life. In order to 'pacify' green concerns (if this combative terminology is indeed appropriate), Levy and Wissenburg have to distinguish weaker, lighter green 'environmentalism' from a stronger, darker green 'ecologism'. In doing so, Levy and Wissenburg do not take us very far beyond Dobson's telling conclusion that: '[m]y own view is that the compatibility question depends entirely on one's terms of reference: environmentalism and liberalism are compatible, but ecologism and liberalism are not' (2007: 165). To reiterate, Rawlsian liberalism is just one particular front upon which this departure – or attempted reconciliation – takes place.

Wissenburg (2006), again, arrives at a similar impasse regarding the greening of liberalism stating that there remain 'differences of opinion between liberal and ecologist political thinkers, yet most of these are no longer fundamental challenges – they no longer force us to ask *whether* but only *to what degree* liberalism can be green' (31, emphasis in original). Like Dobson, he offers a vision of liberalism 'transformed' and 'strengthened' in response to deteriorating environmental conditions. Wissenburg's view is that environmental limits place corresponding restraints on individual preferences and visions of the good life. Now such limits are perfectly acceptable in line with the classic liberal 'harm principle' outlined by John Stuart Mill. Liberalism, for Wissenburg, has always had to limit the range of admissible conceptions of the good life in order to allow for a range of competing views to flourish. This is an uncontroversial political condition for liberal thought but the problem facing theories of justice is how can this be separated from prescriptive, thicker conceptions of the good? Or, as Wissenburg, puts it: the imposition of a 'correct' and 'substantive ideal of the good life is definitely incompatible with liberal neutrality' (25). So at what point do green concerns become *a threat* to liberalism by promoting a more controversial vision of the green good?

Light versus dark green political theory

Following on from both Wissenburg's and Dobson's claims that the issue of compatibility is dependent upon the 'type' of green concern held, and as a means of assessing the degree to which Rawls's ideas can themselves be greened, it is necessary to consider the difference between *light* and *dark* versions of such concerns. John Barry (1999) draws such a political distinction between environmentalism and ecologism beginning with the notion that a multitude of views fall under the banner of 'environmentalism'. First, there are light green concerns that offer a purely political solution to perceived environmental crises. Liberal environmentalisms (or environmental theories of justice) become a balance, or a compromise, between competing views of the green good. Not only this, but environmental concerns must also compete with other equally valid societal issues. Liberal systems of justice, in theory, aim to distribute political, economic, and social resources impartially, favouring no particular concept of the good life, whether environmental, religious, political, or otherwise. Liberalism can allow for a plurality of anthropocentric visions of the green good thanks to the fact that it would be inherently *illiberal* to fail to secure the requisite environmental conditions necessary for individuals to flourish or to act as self-authors of the good life. Wider nature, therefore, is merely a provider of goods/resources for humans now and in the future – it is instrumentally valuable.

Ecologism, or *deep* ecology, denotes a series of *darker* green concerns, proposing a much stronger critique of human progress. Proponents of such doctrines (theories of ecological justice) ask us to fundamentally reconsider our relationship with wider nature and attempt to impress upon us a distinctively sceptical and less anthropocentric worldview. Owing to what Wissenburg explains as the fact that the 'environment' is a problematic term and cannot be universally accepted as it means different things to different people, there is hence 'a future not for environmentalism but for *environmentalisms*' (Wissenburg, 2004: 71, emphasis added). Wissenburg continues that 'Where once "environment" served as a practical container concept, through which environmentalists . . . and ecologists could join forces and make political progress, we now see that ecologist demands that do not fit into the container are being left behind' (65). Wissenburg is highlighting a distinctive process at work here; namely, that ecologisms are deemed too radical – too controversial – to be incorporated into mainstream political, economic, and social policy. Environmentalisms (or any lighter green concerns) advocate a more reformist agenda in arguing that liberalism, as the dominant theory behind modern Western democracies, can be modified to embrace fundamental *light* green concerns. It is thus on these grounds that Wissenburg and Levy argue that liberalism can absorb lighter green concerns and environmentalisms by incorporating non-humans and future generations for shallowly instrumental reasons.

The way in which wider nature is valued plays a pivotal role in determining whether or not a citizen holds an environmentalist, light green theory of the good or an ecologist, darker green comprehensive doctrine. Light green concerns are characterized by their instrumentalism – a reductivist ethic that assesses relations between humans and the non-human world (including non-human species, natural processes, features, etc.) purely in relation to the utility value (whether economic, moral, or aesthetic) it generates for humans. It is, therefore, anthropocentric instrumentalism under scrutiny. The ownership of, or access to, certain non-human species and natural features can bring not only financial gains to humans, but also immaterial rewards, such as a greater appreciation of natural processes that widen the human understanding of the world. The essential feature, however, is that such value is instrumental to human ends: the non-human species or natural feature in question possesses no value in and of itself but only as a means to contemporary human ends. As Arne Naess puts it: 'environmentalists who approach issues . . . with

10 *Rawls and the Environmental Crisis*

human values and interests as paramount, tend to treat natural things in an instrumental way' (Naess, *in* Smith, 1998: 14) and hence he identifies such environmentalists as *shallow ecologists*. For Naess, 'shallow ecologists' are juxtaposed to 'deep ecologists', a distinction that starts to reveal a spectrum of green concerns including both environmentalisms and ecologisms. Instrumentalist approaches, therefore, fall on the lighter side of a spectrum of green concerns and consequently, those who hold such an ethic, when politicized, could be deemed as light green environmentalists, adherents to an environmentalism, or holders of a theory of *environmental justice*. As will become clear in later chapters, Rawls's political liberalism can be seen to reflect a position somewhere between shallow and deep theories of ecological justice – or what will be called *light green enlightened environmental justice*.

In considering the idea that nature could be valued beyond its instrumental use to humans, we can bring in the view from *darker* green concerns, or *ecological justice*, and explore the notion that nature possesses some form of intrinsic value. Non-anthropocentrism provides an alternative, non-instrumentalist means of valuing nature. Dobson (2007) states that 'ethical non-anthropocentrism will underpin responsible behaviour to the non-human natural world' by valuing nature for its intrinsic ends and properties, beyond human subjective concerns (36). This reflects O'Neill et al.'s (2008) belief that intrinsic value is an end in itself, and thus it follows that nature can be valued for its own sake. In effect, this becomes a deontological position placing faith in the inherent value of a natural species or process that is *irreducible* to human interests, preferences, and assessment (Harlow, 1992: 20; Wissenburg, 1998: 92–3).

For Wissenburg, as already seen, such value is external and intrinsic only to the human valuer (Wissenburg, 2001: 96). So can a non-anthropocentric, non-instrumentalist ethic really provide a realistic alternative to weak green, shallow instrumentalism? Wissenburg concludes that humans are free to pursue their own unique conceptions of the good life only, again, until harm is caused to wider nature in such that manner that prevents other humans from doing the same. Humans, therefore, can measure their own well-being with regards to their treatment of nature. The key point to make here is that notions of weak intrinsic value, although darker on our spectrum of green concerns, are unable to escape anthropocentrism but can, and do, offer an *enlightened* critique of shallow, arrogant, or human-chauvinistic attitudes towards wider nature (67). In later chapters, it will again become clear that the green critique of Rawls concludes that Rawlsian liberalism is trapped into valuing non-human species and natural processes anthropocentrically yet, as Dobson notes, there is room for manoeuvre in the extent to which anthropocentrism (combined with strong instrumentalism) can be rejected in favour of less chauvinistic, less shallow, and more enlightened forms of the term. As Dobson asks: 'Will human-prudential reasons do the job for the environment that is asked of them?' (2007: 45–6). For many green liberals this is the ultimate objective: incorporating green concerns into a human-centered system of environmental justice. For *liberal* greens (that is, greens who also happen to be liberal), mere reconciliation is not up to the job, and a widespread metaphysical shift in valuing nature is required. So although intrinsic value rejects neutrality on such matters, it is unable to lead us out of our present theoretical conundrum. How can ideal liberal theory admit holders of darker green theories of ecological justice into the political sphere without *illiberally* rejecting shallow instrumentalist views? How is Rawlsian liberalism to navigate a spectrum of competing views born of rival, politicized, and normative environmental ethics?

It seems difficult, therefore, to disagree with Dobson's 'terms of reference' argument. It is also nigh on impossible to circumvent the fact that green political theory can be often reduced to the question of *value* in nature. In turn, this question tells us something of the relationship between humanity and wider nature, and this is the subject of later chapters, when the analysis of reconciling Rawls with green concerns begins in earnest. If we are right to imagine a continuum, or even a spectrum, of green concerns from light green, very shallow environmentalisms at one end through to darker green, stronger ecologisms at the other, then what we are essentially doing, in assessing the green critique, is attempting to locate Rawlsian liberalism somewhere on this spectrum. In turn, this will inform the view that the green critique, by and large, limits his theory to the lighter shades of environmental justice.[2] Again, and not insignificantly, this monograph will conclude that his concept of 'justice as fairness' embodies a theory of environmental justice that moves us subtly away from a shallow instrumentalist position on wider nature towards a slightly darker green, and more enlightened, form of anthropocentrism.

Outline of the book

Chapter 1 sets out to underpin the uniqueness of Rawls's political liberalism and his move from a more comprehensive, Kantian form of liberalism to a freestanding and independent theory of justice. Rawls's mature theory started to appear in the mid-1980s when he sought to develop a political agreement built on ideas to be found in the public political culture of democratic societies. With regards to green political theory, this is significant, not least because it moves us away from a key impasse, as outlined in previous sections, that liberalism's worship of individualism makes it incompatible with any notion of a wider, green common good. The chapter proceeds to outline how the historical origins of political liberalism throw up a perennial problem of political thought; namely, that any agreement on principles of justice that are capable of governing the just institutions of a 'well-ordered society' must tread carefully between being too thick so as be considered non-comprehensive on one side, but too thin so as to be rendered meaningless on the other. The key aim is to offer a conception of justice that is capable of sustaining loyalty within a citizenry. It is to this problem that Rawls himself looked, in addition to the narrative of the fallout of the European Reformations of the sixteenth and seventeenth centuries, as he sets the scene for his idea of political unity based on reasonable principles of justice. Again, though, such unity can only be

12   *Rawls and the Environmental Crisis*

built on key precepts already agreed upon by citizens of democratic states. The chapter seeks to demonstrate that not only is Rawls's mature liberal thought aiming at something quite different to the more deontological liberalism targeted by greens, but that it also sets its sights on addressing an enduring conceptual problem of modern political theory: how can societies, which have removed any notion of divine guidance, establish a well-ordered and stable polity grounded on the latent beliefs of a citizenry?

Chapter 2 outlines the role green concerns play in Rawls's theory, and brings together his somewhat fragmented justification of the separation argument. Rawls claims that 'justice is but one part of the moral view', and suggests that his theory is right to leave green concerns outside of the political. In other words, if citizens wish to debate the value of wider nature, or humanity's place within it, then they are to leave such matters to the scope of public discussion or the 'background' culture, as they are too controversial for political agreement. If we are to agree on a political conception of justice that recognizes the freedom and equality of individuals, then controversial views of the green good or environmental comprehensive doctrines must be kept out of the domain of the political. This reluctance to engage directly with green concerns, understandably, has led several scholars to view Rawls's theory as dismissive of grave environmental threats.

The separation argument is entrenched by the centrality of the 'original position' to Rawls's notion of justice as fairness. In order to arrive at the concept of justice as fairness, Rawls establishes a heuristic device that places representatives of citizens behind the 'veil of ignorance' so that they can reach agreement on principles independently of their particular visions of the good. His notion of justice as fairness arises from ideal conditions of fairness. The principles to which we would agree, when ignorant of the religious or political doctrines we hold, represent a *freestanding* conception of justice that would govern the basic structure and constitutional essentials of a well-ordered society. The problem is that, at best, any green concerns held by a citizen would be merely one view of the good amongst others. Yet the main motivation that compels individuals to hold green concerns is that protecting wider nature, and thus the ecosystems that sustain human life on earth, is a fundamental prerequisite of justice. How can human societies engage in the practice of political cooperation if the stable conditions provided by wider nature, which make human life tolerable, are absent?

The story of Rawls and green concerns, however, does not end there, as Chapter 2 also outlines four areas of his thought that invite the green political theorist to extend his ideas to those beyond the traditional scope of justice, and call for a stronger commitment to the protection of wider nature, albeit indirectly. Rawls's attitude towards the incorporation of green concerns into his theory, it could be argued, is one of ambivalence. Clearly, Rawls did not condone the ceaseless exploitation or human dominion of wider nature for human gain, especially on the subject of animal rights. Politically, green concerns could be presented reasonably in democratic deliberations, something

Rawls argues would not be too difficult. He is adamant, however, that such concerns are not an appropriate subject for the sphere of political justice and what he calls the 'basic structure' of society. The green critique largely sees this as symptomatic of an insidious indifference to the plight of those at risk from deteriorating environmental conditions. Even those theorists within the green critique surveyed in the following chapters, who are more sympathetic to his political liberalism, see the perceived indifference of the separation argument as problematic in that it privileges human flourishing above any concerns for wider nature.

The aim of the chapter, then, is to provide an extensive account of the four roles Rawls assigns to green concerns within his theory by exploring the idea of his heuristic original position; the notion of sentientism as an ethic capable of protecting non-human species; his own approach to extensionism; and the idea of preserving institutions via a principle of 'just savings'. By putting together a more systematic approach to the subject and introducing a framework of analysis for judging the efficacy of Rawls's theory, the chapter poses an important question that will shape the direction of discussions to come; namely, that if the separation argument is to remain intact, how can questions of justice between citizens be isolated from fundamental issues of humanity's dependence upon wider nature? Put slightly differently, would a political indifference towards green concerns for the sake of consensus encourage a post-political, individual attitude of disregard for wider nature within a citizenry?

Chapters 3 and 4 present two sides of the green critique of Rawls. Centred on the separation argument, Chapter 3 offers an overview of the critique and focusses on the idea that amongst the theorists working in this area, there is a consensus that Rawls can only take us so far with regards to the incorporation of green concerns into liberal theories of justice (that is, not beyond *shallow instrumentalist* attitudes). Not only this, but the problem is that each thinker covered appears to apply their own 'test', and their own idea of the environmental/ecological crisis, when appraising the green credentials of Rawlsian liberalism. Chapter 3, despite these contingent assessments, attempts to bring the thinkers together to strengthen the case that the green critique operates as a stand-alone critique of Rawls. The problem identified in this chapter, which potentially complicates the presentation of a unified critique, is the relatively vague manner in which 'the' environmental, or 'the' ecological, crisis is again used to test Rawls's political liberalism. The waters are further muddied by the opposing – and often absent – reasons given by theorists for the selection of Rawls as a candidate ripe for greening. The *Why Rawls?* question, as will be highlighted, is never definitively answered.

For the sake of clarity, the first critique itself is divided into subsections. First, the idea of a new environmental, or ecological, principle of justice being added to Rawls's famous two principles of justice (an equal scheme of liberties, and the equality of opportunity) so as to promote green concerns to the forefront of his concept of the political. The second section delves into the

14   *Rawls and the Environmental Crisis*

belief that Rawls's theory already embodies a very light green conception of environmental justice. Although not directly encouraging of the exploitation of wider nature, Rawlsian liberalism cannot move us very far towards a more meaningful theory of environmental justice. The third section of the chapter looks to those theorists who have sought to correct and thereby significantly modify Rawls's political liberalism in order to either improve its green credentials or expose its inherent light green, shallow instrumentalist intentions. The section opens up the green critique to the hope that the separation argument can work in the interests of green concerns, provided we are willing to look beyond the language of rights when it comes to our duties towards wider nature, and especially non-humans. The fourth section of the chapter focusses on those theorists who are adamant that Rawls's notion of justice as fairness is but a smokescreen for an exploitative, capitalist economic system that is ecologically ruinous. Chapter 3 thus concludes with the idea that the series of tests applied to Rawlsian liberalism by the green critique leads us to believe that his theory, for better or for worse, is unable to transcend a very light green, shallow instrumentalist theory of environmental justice.

Chapter 4 looks to a seemingly disparate body of work that, when welded together, invites a much more favourable reading of justice as fairness as a light green, but *significantly more enlightened* theory of environmental justice. It also leads us to a definitive statement of how a schism appears between the inviolability of individual rights and liberties and a language of duties and obligations beyond these liberal values. The chapter will ultimately argue that this tension is most pronounced between the inherent liberalism of Rawls's two principles of justice and the more conservative vision of stewardship that accompanies a commitment to the idea of an intergenerational polity. Commencing with a discussion of the break from its Christian roots, the chapter charts the development of a new *liberalized* theory of environmental stewardship. The key challenge faced by any theory of stewardship is the fact that it has traditionally been seen as an ethic of human dominion and thus unfit to serve as a contemporary theory of either environmental or ecological justice. The breakdown of a tripartite relationship between God, humanity, and wider nature has been a central feature of modernity, and stewardship was once defined by the idea that humans were entrusted by God to rule over nature. A liberalized theory of environmental stewardship needs to replace this lost source of accountability with an entity, or concept, *for whom* which wider nature is to be preserved. Again, however, the focus is on the fact that some citizens' interests will exist beyond the here and now and will therefore be dependent upon the preservation of elements of wider nature beyond their immediate wants and needs. This second green critique is therefore tasked with a much clearer extension of liberal thought to a plurality of green concerns for both instrumental *and* non-instrumental reasons. The result is that this seemingly unconnected series of works develops *a theory of liberalized environmental stewardship* that not only maintains the separation argument inherent to Rawlsian liberalism, but one that simultaneously offers a much stronger theory of environmental justice.

Both parts of the green critique, however, lack a strong conception of citizenship capable of motivating citizens to look beyond mutual disinterest in favour of what can be identified as 'transpolitical' goods. The conclusion, therefore, sets out the case for a new theory of Rawlsian environmental stewardship, as a response to the complex and far-reaching implications of ecological crises for liberal polities. If we are to address the tension between the liberal and conservative aspirations of Rawls's political liberalism, then it means embracing the view that liberal theory is committed to a much more profound and ongoing search for justice in the name of humanity. Further to this, we again see the need for a greater commitment to an idea of citizenship (in this case, *stewardship*) that motivates citizens to fulfil their duties and obligations to the intergenerational project of justice. This reconciles the inviolable liberty of the individual with a more conservative appreciation for the transpolitical good of the 'well-ordered society' providing the very conditions for the flourishing of liberal principles of justice.

Notes

1 This is despite Read not engaging with *any* of the array of articles published in said 'cottage industry'.
2 Compare with David Heyd's (2009) conclusion that green political theorists engaged in this endeavour (especially with reference to future generations) will be led to a point whereby '[t]hree alternatives seem then to suggest themselves regarding the extension of justice . . . either modify the conception of the circumstances of justice, or establish intergenerational justice on non-contractarian grounds, or, finally, admit that intergenerational relations are in their nature not subject to judgements of justice at all (but rather to moral principles or duties of another kind)' (169). This monograph looks to challenge Heyd's thesis that these three possibilities are mutually exclusive.

1 Rawls and political liberalism

The introduction has identified the perceived incompatibility between liberal thought and green concerns and the origins of the green critique that has sought to further explore this incongruity with reference to Rawls's unrivalled contribution to liberalism in the second half of the twentieth century. Rawls has clearly come to be seen as a figurehead for liberal thought, and so it would seem that his theory is taken to be a legitimation – and even a post-hoc explanation – of how liberal societies operate in both theory and practice. Yet this link, that his theory represents an extended apologia for liberalism, and indeed potentially for the epoch of modernity itself, becomes more tenuous if it can be shown that there is a real tension between his argument for liberal principles of justice (an equal scheme of liberties for all, and the equality of opportunity) and the conservative implications of his intergenerational 'well-ordered society', which emerges once green concerns are introduced. As such, this chapter seeks to highlight the central, perennial question that has dogged theories of political liberalism since the European Reformations of the sixteenth and seventeenth centuries; namely, how can first principles of justice, capable of motivating citizens towards unity, be found in societies that are characterized by a deep-rooted, yet reasonable, plurality of comprehensive and doctrinal visions of the good life? Given that this is the question Rawls's mature political thought sought to answer, it is necessary to explain in greater detail the significance of his move from a partially comprehensive Kantian liberalism to a much more limited notion of political liberalism. It will then be possible to not only investigate how the 'separation argument' manifests itself in his heuristic 'original position', but to again highlight the uneasy relationship between a classical liberal commitment to the inviolability of individual liberties and the more conservative idea of citizens as stewards of the well-ordered society that is central to his mature works on political liberalism. We are thus faced with the question as to what room there is left for green concerns given the importance of the separation argument to Rawls's notion of 'justice as fairness'.

Rawls's political liberalism

What is so *political* about Rawls's mature liberalism? Rawls initially set out to construct a means of assessing the extent to which the institutions of a society's basic structure could be considered just, hence his opening claim in *TJ* that 'justice is the first virtue of social institutions, as truth is of systems of thought' (*TJ*: 3). The aim was to establish an Archimedean point – a view of ideal objectivity – to be then used to determine the principles of justice that will come to govern the main political, social, and economic institutions of a well-ordered society. In order to construct such principles, according to Rawls, we must mediate between the model-conceptions of the well-ordered society (a society which is 'effectively regulated by public principles of justice'; Rawls, 2005: 66) and the notion of society as being composed of the free and equal 'moral person' so as to 'depict certain general features of what a society would look like if its members publicly viewed themselves and their social ties with one another in a certain way' (Rawls, 1980: 308). As such Rawls presents us with his original position (the OP, hereafter), 'a thought-experiment for the purpose of public- and self-clarification' (Rawls, 2001: 17). Rawls elaborates:

> Thus if the original position suitably models our convictions about these two things (namely, fair conditions of agreement between citizens as free and equal, and appropriate restrictions on reasons), we conjecture that the principles of justice the parties would agree to (could we properly work them out) would specify the terms of cooperation that we regard – here and now – as fair supported by the best reasons.
>
> (ibid.)

Although the significance of the OP would change slightly in later writings, parties (who represent individuals) within this hypothetical situation are always to be placed behind a 'veil of ignorance' that prevents them from knowing 'the social position of those they represent, or the particular comprehensive doctrine of the person each represents' (Rawls, 2005: 24). For Rawls, this ensures that no citizen, or comprehensive doctrine for that matter, can monopolize political power so as to promote their own social standing or natural talents. These conditions of fairness represent a philosophical view of impartiality, leading to his central conception of *justice as fairness*. Crucially, parties in the OP are 'artificial' representatives of citizens who 'ignore persons' inclinations to be envious or spiteful, or to have a will to dominate or a tendency to be submissive, or to be peculiarly averse to uncertainty and risk' (180), and such parties represent both the reasonable and rational citizen (reasonable in their capacity to possess a sense of justice, and rational in their ability to hold a conception of the good life).

The principles chosen behind a veil of ignorance, and under conditions of ideal fairness as modelled by the OP, can then be used to establish a constitution, whilst at the same time assessing the justice of social institutions. According to Rawls, rational parties representing rational persons in his heuristic OP, ignorant of their life plans and conceptions of the good, would agree to his two well-known principles of justice:

> (a) Each person has the same indefeasible claim to a fully adequate scheme of equal basic liberties, which scheme is compatible with the same scheme

18   *Rawls and the Environmental Crisis*

of liberties for all; and (b) Social and economic inequalities are to satisfy two conditions: first, they are to be attached to offices and positions open to all under conditions of fair equality and opportunity; and second, they are to be to the greatest benefit of the least-advantaged members of society (the difference principle).

(2001: 42–3)

The ideal conditions of deliberative fairness within the OP result in a corresponding sense of justice within the well-ordered society, hence Rawls's notion of *justice as fairness* (see Rawls, 2001: §13).

Rawls would, however, come to describe his earlier efforts, those of *TJ*, as 'a comprehensive doctrine of liberalism designed to set out a certain classical theory of Justice – the theory of a social contract – so as to make it immune to various traditional objections' (Rawls, *in* Freeman, 1999: 617). Simply put, Rawls recognized that such principles were unsustainable given that they would lead 'reasonable' persons to confirm a specific liberal comprehensive doctrine. The right, as the saying goes, became congruent with the good. By the mid-1980s, he would attempt to avoid such 'claims to universal truth, or claims about the essential nature and identity of persons' and instead, 'apply the principle of toleration to philosophy itself: the public conception of justice is to be political, not metaphysical' (Rawls, 1985, *in* Freeman, 1999: 223). Rawls now sought a much more limited and *freestanding* political agreement on the above principles, or at least a shared conception of justice (an 'overlapping consensus'), supported by citizens deeply divided by reasonable pluralism – a conception adhered to by competing comprehensive doctrines for reasons specific to their code of beliefs (Rawls, 2005: xxx). The feasibility of this project relied on the formation of a stronger – yet less contingent – principle of toleration that would transcend a mere *modus vivendi*. Simply put, such a concept must be *thin* enough to motivate most citizens who view themselves as both free and equal, but not so *thick* that it would border on the comprehensive, thus making it unpalatable to the majority of reasonable citizens. Simultaneously, it must not become too *thin* so as to lack meaning and coherence.

It was Book III of *TJ* that would lead to a breakdown of Rawls's early work. The central problem was again that justice as fairness became synonymous with the good, or at least his own version of the good. The arguments are well known and there will be no attempt to add to this understanding of *TJ*, but it is important to stress that Rawls's later, refined political liberalism acknowledged the instability of basing first principles of justice on both a Kantian and Aristotelian view of the self. The Kantian influence (that the individual is subordinate to the supreme good of justice and the moral law) is clear enough, but it was in §§64–5 of *TJ* that would prove the most controversial as this was where the Aristotelian notion of human flourishing came to the fore. If the higher good of flourishing encased in a unified, planned, and rational conception of the good life, imported from Aristotle's writings, was to be the apotheosis of human existence, then it would require the formation of a stable and just society, governed by Rawls's above two principles. The *good* of human life (to adhere to a rational and unified plan as a vehicle of human flourishing) would be protected, and even nurtured, by the *right* of a Rawlsian well-ordered society. Combined with a capacity for a sense of justice, individuals would recognize that their only chance for a life of meaning and personal development would lie in loyalty to the shared, cooperative endeavour offered by a just liberal polity. Rawls had originally hoped that the stability of these arrangements would lay in individuals' deferral to the initial agreement of the OP: the conditions of perfect fairness that would remind them that the resultant *justice as fairness* was the most appropriate moral arrangement compared to other major systems of political thought. Justice as fairness, if one valued the liberal good of rights and opportunities to flourish, would be the most reasonable option. The good of human flourishing was enshrined in a system of justice – a system that would best reflect the *telos* of human life.

Again, by the mid-1980s, Rawls would drop the excessively Kantian and Aristotelian foundations of his theory and seek instead to develop a freestanding and independent meta-political *ideal* (note, not *good*) as the basis for a well-ordered and just society. This, he argued, was the key aim of political liberalism and culminated in his second great work of the same title *Political Liberalism* (1993/2005, *PL* hereafter). Proponents of this version of liberalism, of which Rawls is the most prominent figurehead after his abandonment of a comprehensive and doctrinal theory, represents a thoroughly modern search for a unifying political ideal built on agreement. Political liberals seek consensus on ideals to be found within inherent notions of the free and equal self rather than in controversial philosophical or religious comprehensive doctrines that came before the modern period. As Shaun Young (2004) observes, it hopes to 'achieve something that has not been achieved', but it is here where the uncomfortable concept of neutrality enters the arena, as various thinkers, beyond Rawls, offer subtly different political variations on a theme. For Young, political liberalism treads a normative ground between two extremes of liberalism: somewhere between a Hobbesian *modus vivendi* on one hand, and pure moral neutrality on the other.

Although political liberalism is firmly rooted in the idea of toleration, its key break is from a sole reliance on the Enlightenment ideal of individual autonomy and flourishing, a phenomenon encapsulated in Rawls's own break from comprehensive liberalism in the period between the publication of *TJ* and *PL*. Charles Larmore (1990) notes that individualism, neutrality, and autonomy, as characterized by Lockean or Millean classical liberalism, have all 'piggybacked' onto political liberalism's search for freestanding, non-doctrinal first principles of justice. Yet the concept, as Bruce Ackerman reminds us, 'is not merely the name of a book by John Rawls' (2004: 79). Rather, it has been described as a 'normative framework' or a 'strategy' (Moon, 2004) that makes political cooperation possible. The aim, then, is to achieve political unity around a normative ideal of enduring human cooperation that comprehensive, doctrinal, and *classical* liberalism has failed to achieve. Herein lies

20 *Rawls and the Environmental Crisis*

the key to political liberalism: it seeks a non-doctrinal agreement on publicly shared values. Despite this political optimism, there is a clear sense of reality on the conditions of disagreement in society, hence Rawls's claim that it is to be 'realistically utopian' (Rawls, 2001: 4–5). Political liberalism, in its most recognizable form, aims at 'finally solving the great problem of *e pluribus unum*, of presenting a "freestanding" political doctrine both independent and yet acceptable from the point of view of a plurality of incompatible comprehensive doctrines' (Forst, *in* Young, 2004: x).

So, political liberalism sets itself two important tasks. The first is to remain freestanding and independent between competing religious, spiritual, and political conceptions (comprehensive, doctrinal, or otherwise) of the good. The second task results from a successful completion of the first: how can an ideal, freestanding political conception of justice, agreed upon by a significant number of both rational and reasonable individuals, come into being? Can it remain suitably *thin* so as to gain adherents but not too *thick* so as to border on being doctrinal? Simultaneously, how will it avoid becoming too *thin* so as to render it a hollow, meaningless concept of 'anything-goes' neutrality? The question, then, is what will be agreed *upon* by a diverse and incompatible array of competing visions of the good? Put in the language of political liberalism: what will the *e pluribus unum* be? Chapter 2 will begin an assessment of Rawls's own answer to this last question, in the form of the relationship between the value of liberty and the notion of the well-ordered society.

The Reformations as the birth of political liberalism

So far we have offered a preliminary sketch of Rawls's work that has focussed on his own break from an earlier classical form of liberalism, and its commitment to autonomy, as mirroring the wider project of political liberalism. Yet it is important to look to the historical narrative of post-Reformation modernity, as Rawls himself did, so as to set the scene for his own unrivalled contribution to political thought. By the late seventeenth century the religious unity of the Middle Ages was all but lost. Religious *authority*, perhaps, is the more appropriate term as the Renaissance and the Reformation(s) had dismantled the self-declared universal influence of the Catholic Church and the papacy in Western Europe. Such leadership, however, had not been confined to spiritual or religious realms: advances in politics, science, geography, metaphysics, and astronomy could all be corroborated through knowledge of the Scriptures. The political fallout of this process, as Reinhart Koselleck aptly states, was that 'the subsequent split in religious authority had thrown man back upon his conscience, and a conscience lacking outside support degenerates into the idol of self-righteousness' (1988: 28). The 'outside support', the overarching belief in the salvation of mankind through the worship of Christ, and the divine knowledge of humanity's place in the world, would never return to Western intellectual thought.

Koselleck's words are pertinent here insomuch as his diagnosis of modernity's ills is that it is an age of perpetual crisis (and critique, of course). He argued that in a world devoid of religious authority, and thus outside support, humanity has come to rely on the very term 'crisis' so as to denote the arrival of a critical time in human history requiring urgent action. The notion of an environmental crisis, according to Koselleck, is just one such crisis that potentially 'illustrates a widespread manner of speech rather than contributing to the diagnosis of our plight' (2002: 12). Yet interestingly, Koselleck himself would later recognize that if ever there was to be a point of genuine crisis it is indeed *now*. Our own period of modernity, given 'the potential of autonomous humanity for self-destruction has multiplied many times' and the fact that 'a kind of final resolution of conflict, has retained a better chance of realization than at any time previously' (22). This 'resolution' as either a Christian term for final judgement, the catechism, or in its non-Christian meaning, 'indicates an increasingly urgent set of circumstances, the meaning of which mankind seems unable to escape'. Clearly, this meaning is the possible extinction of humanity due to overpopulation and ecological degradation.

Rawls, however, believed it possible to replace this long-lost 'outside support' and religious authority with a moral and, later, a specifically *political*, agreement salvaged from the ensuing post-Reformation degeneration into the 'self-righteousness' of the individual. In the decades prior to the publication of Rawls's *TJ* in 1971, the stultification of any such 'grand' theories of politics had featured heavily in the discourse of political thought (Skinner, 1985: 4). It was widely believed that due to the dramatic events of the European Reformations, any quest to uncover a unity or systematic truth in morality and politics was at best nonsensical and, at worst, dangerous. Theories in the period immediately prior to Rawls's *magnum opus* had further suffered as a result of a wider hostility to politics brought about by the horrors of the two World Wars and the ensuing Cold War. As Judith Shklar at the time declared: '[p]olitics, in short, have become futile' (1957: viii). Faith had been lost in politics and associated theories of politics. Such attitudes also lead to near-famous proclamations such as '[f]or the moment, anyway, political philosophy is dead' (Laslett, 1967: vii). Laslett, for one, did not particularly share Shklar's pessimism regarding general politics as a practice, or an art form, but instead argued that politics was too serious a business for the likes of philosophers and other associated gadflies. So it was during this period that political philosophy was at risk of becoming a second-order, excessively naval-gazing sub-discipline of ethics. With Rawls, however, would come the rebirth of a grand and systematic slant to political thought and, later, the search for agreement in the form of a philosophical basis for consensus in deeply divided societies.[1]

Yet the sheer ambition of the early Rawlsian project, which endured in some form in his later works, means it has also been placed within a much older timeline of political thought that articulates a traditional search for a *summum bonum* of morality in Western philosophy. The following introductory lines from John Stuart Mill's *Utilitarianism* summarize this endeavour: 'From the dawn of philosophy the question concerning the *summum bonum*, or, what is the same thing, concerning the foundation of morality, has been accounted the

22   *Rawls and the Environmental Crisis*

main problem in speculative thought, has occupied the most gifted intellects, and divided them into sects and schools, carrying on a vigorous warfare against one another' (1972: 1). Or, in Isaiah Berlin's assessment of the state of political thought: 'The attempts, from Plato to our own day . . . to found objective sciences of ethics and aesthetics on the basis of universally accepted values, or of methods of discovering them, have met with little success; relativism, subjectivism, romanticism, scepticism with regard to values, keep breaking in' (1962: 148). Leo Strauss's notion of the *summum bonum*, when applied politically, was better described as a search for 'transpolitical goods', goods that give politics its 'dignity' (1989: 162–3). For the Ancients, it was philosophy accessible only to philosophers themselves; in the pre-Reformation period, the transpolitical was to be found in divine revelation; and finally, post-Reformation liberalism looked to the idea of the inviolable and the equal rights of humanity. If early Rawlsian liberalism can indeed be placed within this ancient search for the *summum bonum*, then the transpolitical value in *TJ* was inherently liberal, and modern. Crucially, though, Rawls sought to avoid establishing political unity amongst a diverse citizenry through coercion and oppression, as had been the case in medieval period. Skinner therefore sees Rawls as representative of a return to this much older tradition of 'grand' political philosophy that espoused normative and comprehensive theories based on universal truths.

Rawls's particular interest in the European Reformations lay in questioning the efficacy and stability of a mere *modus vivendi* between competing conceptions of the good life and doctrinal truths. He would, in his later works, look beyond this resultant Lockean-esque 'principle of toleration as a modus vivendi' that 'came about following the Reformation: at first reluctantly, but nevertheless as providing the only alternative to endless and destructive civil strife' (*PL*: 159, and Rawls, 2001: 192). Catholics and Protestants in this period, according to Rawls, 'both held that it was the duty of the ruler to uphold the true religion and repress the spread of heresy and false doctrine. In this case, the acceptance of the principle of toleration would indeed be a mere modus vivendi: should either faith become dominant, the principle of toleration would no longer be followed' (*PL*: 159). Toleration, as the cornerstone of classical liberalism, signifies a compromise and a political way out of the bloodshed of the European wars of religion that followed the Reformations. What was needed, according to Rawls, was a stronger conception of tolerance; one that would 'apply the principle of toleration to philosophy itself' (Rawls, 1985: 223). Questions of longer-term stability in the first decades of liberal thought, and notions of unity or external authority, were peripheral compared to the pressing need for order and peace. So the key to understanding the Rawlsian project is to appreciate that it looks to a lost tradition of unity that had disappeared, along with the doctrinal coercion of Christianity following the split in the Catholic Church, and one that would go beyond the classical liberal compromise of a *modus vivendi*.[2]

Rawls's mature political philosophy, articulated principally in *PL*, was much more focussed on this period arguing: 'thus the historical origin of political liberalism . . . is the Reformation and its aftermath, with the long controversies over religious toleration in the sixteenth and seventeenth centuries' (*PL*: xxiv). For Rawls, this is a period that witnessed the birth of the liberty of conscience, and the freedom of thought, that would come to characterize modernity. The question that his version of political liberalism sought to answer was as follows: 'How is it possible that there may exist over time a stable and just society of free and equal citizens profoundly divided by religious, philosophical, and moral doctrines?' (*PL*: xxv). He then immediately issues the following self-limiting caveat, however, distancing himself from a wider search for the *summum bonum* of morality: 'This is a problem of political justice, *not a problem about the highest good*' (emphasis added). Two things stand out here. The first is that Rawls outlines the possibility of both a 'stable' and 'just' society. It is this notion of a well-ordered society, with its just institutions, that will provide the basis for a subsequent green reinterpretation of Rawls's theory in the chapters that follow. This, it will be argued, is at odds with his own rejection of the *summum bonum*, as a well-ordered society potentially embodies a good in itself and offers normative resources to those concerned with environmental or ecological justice. The second point to make is that Rawls then separates *the good* from *the political* by arguing that his mature liberalism occupies an independent domain freed from competing, and controversial, comprehensive doctrines and visions of the good life. This is significant not least when exposed to green concerns. Is it possible for Rawls's theory to remain both outside of, and independent to, the realms of comprehensive doctrinal theories of environmental or ecological justice, whilst remaining truly political in scope when talking of the stable, just and well-ordered society?

With Rawls's works firmly located in the ongoing political fallout of the Reformation, the modern period saw the rise of what he called the enduring 'fact of reasonable pluralism' ('a phenomenon new to historical experience, a possibility realized by the Reformation', *PL*: xxv). From the diverse range of competing visions of the good life to the irreconcilable differences between comprehensive moral and religious doctrines, there could no longer be agreement on a singular notion of the good life, the political good, or of humanity's wider place in the world. Yet the hope of establishing a feasible, but limited, political theory of justice remains central to the Rawlsian project. Despite the liberty of religious conscience unleashed by the European Reformations, he maintains that 'the success of liberal constitutionalism came as a discovery of a new social possibility of a reasonably harmonious and stable pluralist society'. So out of the religious disorder the potential for order, in the form of political liberalism, becomes possible. At this point, liberalism splits into two: *classical* and *political* liberalism. Classical liberalism forms one comprehensive doctrine among others, but political liberalism pursues what it again calls a freestanding, independent conception of justice beyond a mere *modus vivendi*. To reiterate, Rawls's works encapsulates this difference, as he abandons his earlier efforts to forge agreement around a comprehensive doctrine of human flourishing (classical liberalism).

Early political liberalism

Political liberalism, since the Reformations, has looked to the question of whether or not a *communitas communitatum*, united by first principles of political justice, is indeed feasible or even desirable. Can a unity, or a consensus on shared values, beyond the divisions of everyday life be found externally, or even internally, within this plurality of competing conceptions of humanity's place in the world? The Reformations did not immediately silence voices that sought to return to the relative stability of the increasingly tenuous Salvationist creed of the Catholic Church. David Ogg is careful to remind us that during this period of schism between (and within) Catholic and Protestant camps, many influential thinkers, for example, Calixtus, Erasmus, and Grotius, clung to an Augustinian idiom that somehow it was 'better to suffer all things than to violate the unity of the Church' (1952: 545). Ultimately, the hegemonic shift brought about by the European Reformations was a 'dispute between the two opposed interpretations of Christianity . . . fought on grounds of history and scholarship, and so long as the discussion was confined to these grounds there was no chance of reconciliation' (547). There is, therefore, a permanency to this split; an intransience that is still being felt today in modern societies divided by competing political and spiritual visions of the good life, afar from the original quarrels over religious truth. Rawls would again identify this legacy as being that of reasonable pluralism whereby individuals, devoid of external authority and empowered by self-righteousness, hold competing and irreconcilable comprehensive religious, political, and spiritual doctrines or sincerely held conceptions of what it means to lead a good life. Ultimately the central questions remain unchanged: in a world devoid of a singular doctrinal creed, can any form of unity or meaningful consensus be built on first principles of justice? Are such principles enough to generate meaningful political obligations, and perhaps even sacrifice, from a given citizenry? These two related questions, now nearly four centuries old, continue to form the centrepiece to theories of political liberalism.

Rainer Forst (2004) offers several examples of early explorations into political liberalism and a search for a 'moral-political consensus' that predates the modern period, for example, Nicholas of Cusa's notion of *una religio in rituum varietate* and Erasmus of Rotterdam's *Christiana philosophia* (ix). Later, early-modern proposals for a proto-political liberalism would come from the likes of Pierre Bayle and Baruch de Spinoza. Forst's argument that '"political liberalism" is the name for a project that both has a very long history and marks a truly innovative turn in political philosophy' highlights how it embodies an ongoing search for principles of unity within societies rife with discord between competing conceptions of the good. Forst's point is a very specific framing of the problem, or rather a far-reaching interpretation of the conditions of the project of political liberalism. It is, however, defensible. The first reason for adopting this approach is that it is the narrative to which Rawls himself looked, as previously stated. The second (which is the focus of the

remainder of this chapter) is to agree with Forst in identifying how the param-
eters of the problem faced by post-Reformation liberal thinkers has remained
broadly the same: how can first principles of political justice, or a conception
of unity, remain suitably *thin* so as to gain the loyalty of adherents, but not too
thick so that it borders on the comprehensive and thus, could not be agreed
to by the majority of reasonable citizens? Simultaneously, it must not become
so *thin* as to become meaningless and tokenistic. Interestingly, even debates
within green political theory, when considering the role of liberalism in light
of an all-consuming environmental crisis, will continually run into this same
question. That is, are there any first principles of *environmental*, or *ecological*,
justice that can be agreed to by a significant number of reasonable individuals? If so, again, can they remain suitably *thin* so as to gain the loyalty of most
citizens but not too *thick* that they border on being doctrinal and thus could
not be agreed to by the majority of reasonable citizens? Simultaneously, they
must not become too *thin* so as to lack motivational force.

The break from Forst's central question comes only in the form of maintaining a distance from his assertion that 'no "neutral" ground had been found'
in the literature on proto-political liberalism (ibid.). Indeed, it is the very
term 'neutral' that has caused the biggest headache for Rawls, as critics rallied
against his so-called neutralist liberalism. Again, the fact that Rawls's mature
political liberalism sought to establish principles of justice on ideas that he saw
as being latent, or dormant, in the public political cultures of Western societies
means that it cannot straightforwardly be considered as neutral in and of itself.
But to reiterate, it is Forst's evaluation that early-modern efforts to articulate
consensus through reduction failed to achieve a *thinness* composite with a widely
held, moral–political agreement whilst at the same time preserving a sufficient *thickness* so as to marshal loyalty and commitment within a citizenry. As
will be made clear in what follows, this is the very same question that besets
searches for agreement on principles of environmental or ecological justice.
In particular, attempts to green Rawls's political thought have yet to reconcile
the idea of non-doctrinal agreement with comprehensive notions of a green
common good.

To tidy up the discussion so far, it is useful to acknowledge the central challenges faced when concluding what, if any, contribution Rawls can make to
green political thought. His mature work was firmly geared to answering the
enduring question of political liberalism that again, in his words, could be
stated as follows: 'How is it possible that there may exist over time a stable and
just society of free and equal citizens profoundly divided by reasonable though
incompatible religious, philosophical, and moral doctrines?' (*PL*: xviii). One
fundamental question, so far left largely unanswered, is whether or not it is
appropriate to view Rawls's political liberalism as an *apologia* for an unsustainable model of human progress in both theory and practice. If we are to take
the greening of Rawls seriously, then it is vital that we abandon the strain
of thought that associates his work solely with the Kantian, Enlightenment-
inspired self-authorship of the good life, characteristic of his earlier thought.

26 *Rawls and the Environmental Crisis*

His political liberalism asks something quite different as, in addition to this, he asks how can freestanding – almost transpolitical – principles of justice be found that are capable of uniting a diverse and pluralistic liberal society? As Chapter 4 will argue, it seems that a resurgence of the ideas of environmental stewardship could potentially offer a more robust greening of Rawlsian theory. The success of reconciling the two approaches, however, will depend on whether or not environmental stewardship can also address the conceptual problem of political liberalism, and the hope of a unity around principles that, although thick enough to garner popular support, refrain from bordering on the comprehensive.

It should be clear now that we have the germ of the problem. Rawlsian liberalism has become embroiled in a wider, far-reaching debate surrounding the incompatibility of liberalism (in theory and practice) and green concerns. As this chapter has so far demonstrated, however, Rawls's mature thought represents a unique, and historical, politically liberal approach to questions of enduring disagreement in modern societies. This is significant, not least because it begins to distance itself from more comprehensive, and highly individualist accounts of liberal theory that are commonly blamed for the un-environmental attitudes that are at the root of environmental crises. Despite this, Rawls's own work adhered to the separation argument, and so he held the view that questions of political justice should be abstracted from doctrinal, controversial, and metaphysical interpretations of the correct relationship between humanity and wider nature. It is this that has led to his political liberalism being branded as a reflection of a hubristic disregard for green concerns, and the fate of those who are most at risk from deteriorating ecological conditions, including non-human species and future generations. It could be inferred that his work is often viewed as little more than a defence of modernity and the self-righteousness of the individual. His mature work on political liberalism, however, hints at the more conservative values of duty and obligation that extend well beyond the primacy of the self-authorship of the good life. The concluding chapter will return to this final point by introducing the traditional liberal versus conservative paradigm of modern political thought in a manner that encapsulates this tension within Rawls's political liberalism.

The original position

Having outlined the main aim of Rawls's mature political philosophy, and its claim to be freestanding between competing comprehensive doctrines, what room is there left for green concerns? Due to their urgency, should notions of an impending environmental crisis 'trump' the demands contemporaneous rational agents make of each other? Or do controversial green concerns have to stand separately to a politically freestanding overlapping consensus, in joining non-green comprehensive conceptions of the good? The plan here is to start with the fundamental aims of Rawls's theory, and the belief in the possibility of political agreement in a period of late modernity, before introducing the green critique. This will allow for an approach that sees it as a stand-alone body of works that has developed alongside – but mostly in isolation from – the vast literature on Rawls, offering fresh insights into his theory of justice.

From the literature surveyed, the extension of justice as fairness comes down to a question of timing, insomuch as the green critique focusses on the point at which the inclusion of non-contemporaneous entities (elements of wider nature, future generations, non-human species, etc.) can potentially occur. More often than not explorations into extensionist Rawlsian theory begin and end with an analysis of his heuristic OP, and the compatibility of green concerns with what Rawls calls 'strict justice'. Although noticeably less prominent in later works, his faith in the inherent connection between justice and fairness is best explained by the OP. Exploring the separation argument – that is, the divorcing of strict justice from green concerns within his political liberalism – warrants a more detailed explanation of the relationship between the OP and the idea of a freestanding political conception of justice.

Citizens, as represented in the OP, are to be viewed as both *rational* and *reasonable*. Although the reasonable is not a direct development of the rational, the two are not entirely divorced. This is not to say, however, that what is reasonable for an individual may be derived directly for what he or she views as being rational. It is rather the case, Rawls argues, that the reasonable is the public aspect of our behaviour and, specifically, our motivation with regards to the political sphere and principles of justice. Rational, self-interested desires and opinions remain something non-public: they are the manner in which a citizen develops, revises, and pursues self-defined ends (*PL*: 49). The reasonable becomes much broader in scope than the rational, and relates to a form of moral consideration 'that underlies the desire to engage in fair cooperation as such, and to do so in terms that others as equals might reasonably expected to endorse' (*PL*: 51). As well as the reasonable citizen's 'willingness to propose and honor fair terms of cooperation', he or she will also accept 'the burdens of judgement' (*PL*: 49). To clarify, being reasonable becomes a virtue of political life: a necessary component of a citizen's civic life when engaging and cooperating fairly with other individuals. The reasonable citizen desires a stable polity and recognizes that all citizens must bear the sacrifices necessary for social cooperation to flourish. Not only this but any principled agreement on a framework of justice must gain the support of all such reasonable citizens. Reasonable pluralism as characterized by a plethora of competing and incommensurable conceptions of the good is, then, a standard outcome when individuals act rationally within a modern democratic society.

It is well documented that Rawls's later political liberalism was in part a response to several waves of refutation by numerous scholars, and stressed that the chief aspiration of justice as fairness was in fact to establish a perspective that evaluates competing conceptions of justice – including, potentially, environmental and ecological justice – as opposed to unearthing timeless, nascent principles of justice. Rawls acknowledged that his version of justice as fairness will stand as one of a family of liberal conceptions, but it will, nonetheless, be

28   *Rawls and the Environmental Crisis*

the most reasonable. Although one does not have to hold a liberal comprehensive doctrine, it is the acceptance of liberal principles of justice that allows all reasonable citizens to pursue their unique conceptions of the good, doctrinal or otherwise. The acceptance of society as a fair system of cooperation is the end result. Rawls concludes:

> Justice as fairness aims at uncovering a public basis of justification on questions of political justice given the fact of reasonable pluralism. Since justification is addressed to others . . . we begin from shared fundamental ideas implicit in the public political culture in the hope of developing from them a political conception that can gain free and reasoned agreement in judgement.
>
> (*PL*: 100–1)

A political conception of justice is no longer grounded in any controversial metaphysical claims, or Koselleck's notion of 'outside support' in the form of a divine order long since lost in our age of modernity. Instead, political principles are to be built upon 'implicit' and 'shared fundamental ideas' that citizens already share. Political principles are not discovered through some form of philosophical revelation. Rather, the notion that we are free and equal beings capable of political agreement is derived from ideas shared in the pubic political culture.

In order to justify this agreement, citizens' judgements, at all levels, must become coherent following a process of deliberation, so as to achieve what Rawls calls 'reflective equilibrium', reached when discussion on citizens' interpretations of their established moral judgements (for example, considering the just or unjust nature of a policy or law) combined with their uncertain expression of wider principles of justice, no longer produce incongruities with the general conception of justice (*PL*: 28). For Rawls, assessing how a citizen's broader view fits in with their inherent moral judgements provides a test for establishing a narrow equilibrium. To advance from a narrow to a *wide* reflective equilibrium, three aspects of judgement must be brought into unity: citizens' established judgements; broad principles of justice; and, most important, citizens' moral convictions concerning the nature of humanity, society, rationality, and the like. It is this wide reflective equilibrium, as will be discussed in due course, which will lead to the formation of an 'overlapping consensus'. Any theory of justice, acceptable to all reasonable citizens, is contingent upon a unification of the three aforementioned elements: personal judgement, general principles of justice, and the inherent background views possessed by citizens (*PL*: 101). This is the normative framework of judgement-based political constructivism by which Rawls deduces his theory of political liberalism. To reiterate, justice as fairness is grounded on principles already shared by citizens, as opposed to the imposing of a controversial outside ideological, divine, or moral order upon a citizenry.

What makes Rawls's constructivism specifically political is the scope of his concept of justice as fairness. Rather than applying to all the possible moral decisions that a citizen (as a moral agent) could face, justice as fairness is reduced to guiding the basic structure of society, including the main political, social, and economic institutions in existence (*PL*: 223). It is citizens' *political*, not their ethical or moral, identity, that is of interest to political liberalism. Rawls seeks to avoid any metaphysical or analytical assumptions about human motivation and agency by attempting to generate agreement on the existing fundamental makeup of political culture within established democratic societies. Political liberalism now becomes something more situated, and uncontroversial, with the OP teasing out a latent view of the citizen and their reasonable desire to cooperate for the good of a well-ordered society.

How is a political agreement to be reached? The OP is a hypothetical bargaining process whereby parties that represent citizens are stripped of all knowledge of their future position, sex, or conception of the good in society by a 'veil of ignorance'. The actors involved in this thought experiment are to be both rational and reasonable, as well as *mutually disinterested* in one another's preferences. The OP, therefore, becomes a model of how actors orientated towards justice would act in a rational choice situation. Despite this, representatives in the OP will not act out of pure selfishness but rather will merely tolerate others whilst remaining unwilling to lose out against them (in terms of the distribution of public goods and resources). Mutual disinterest, as a form of toleration, is the primary motivating force behind justice as fairness.

In *PL*, as already noted, this thought experiment becomes less central and instead becomes much more representative of the recognition of latent – and publicly shared – fundamentals of political association. In *TJ*, the OP was constructed so as to establish 'a unanimous choice of a particular conception of justice', or, in other words, to force its participants to accept Rawls's view of what is most reasonable for society, determined by a subjective view of the self (*TJ*: 141). It was, therefore, a partially (if not fully) comprehensive and classically liberal view of justice. The OP, as a representative and hypothetical construct in *PL*, serves to reinforce the various stages of Rawls's vision of a political conception of justice as fairness. The stages include a *modus vivendi* born out of a liberal conception of justice; a constitutional consensus; and finally, an overlapping consensus.

The first stage is a akin to a *modus vivendi* which, as previously mentioned, is more of a compromise between competing parties (who represent citizens in the OP) with the aim of ending what is the ongoing conflict between competing conceptions of the good (*PL*: 159–63). This is characteristic of the early, and dominant, form of post-Reformation liberalism. Rawls explains: 'liberal principles of justice, initially accepted reluctantly as a modus vivendi and adopted into a constitution, tend to shift citizens' comprehensive doctrines so that they at least accept the principles of a liberal constitution' (*PL*: 163). It is these 'liberal principles' that ensure fundamental 'political rights and liberties and established democratic procedures for moderating political rivalry' are established as well as 'determining issues of social policy'. He identifies this stage as a 'constitutional consensus' or, put another way, a procedural

30   *Rawls and the Environmental Crisis*

consensus. This is because there is now agreement on the way in which society should procedurally deal with conflict ('simple pluralism', *PL*: 164) and a shared desire to expel controversial disagreement, for example religious conflict, from the domain of the political. For Rawls, this stage is where most contemporary Western societies find themselves, as states governed by a liberal procedural system that guarantees basic liberties and establishes the rules and regulations that will manage political conflict.

What makes this procedural consensus specifically liberal? Rawls explains that 'the most reasonable political conception of justice will be, broadly speaking, liberal' (*PL*: 156) due to the fact that it is only a broad conception of political liberalism that gives priority to liberty and equality; removes the most controversial issues from the political agenda; and thus ensures a greater degree of social cooperation. Rawls views these features as 'fundamental ideas we seem to share through the public political culture' (*PL*: 150). These political virtues are already displayed by citizens of liberal democratic societies in the form of toleration, fairness, mutual respect, and, crucially, reasonableness that together makeup the 'political capital' of society (*PL*: 157). These 'great political values' are what make consensus not only possible but also *enduring*, from one generation to the next.

At this point Rawls alludes to how an overlapping consensus can come into being, but is keen to stress that such a conception is yet to be realized by any contemporary polity. The procedural consensus transforms into an overlapping consensus by creating a substantive and meaningful conception that inspires a degree of loyalty amongst a citizenry, whilst remaining purely political in nature. The driver of this change is the fact that more and more groups will attempt to form majorities around specific political issues and, significantly, 'move out of the narrower circle of their own views' (*PL*: 165). As more and more groups enter into the political arena, the fact that their views must adhere to the limits of public reason means that their ability to communicate and reason with other groups engaged in similar work is imperative. As a result of this process, a prevailing sense of common endeavour becomes apparent whereby citizens – now no longer individuals – within the political sphere enter into dialogue with one another in order to debate and discuss previously conflict-ridden and troublesome issues (*PL*: 164–8).

Throughout this political progression Rawls argues that most citizens will possess comprehensive doctrines that are, as yet, fully developed. A citizen's moral doctrine influences and shapes their conception of the good whether fully or only partially comprehensive (*PL*: 152 fn.17). Rawls assumes that a comprehensive doctrine is an unfinished project because it 'allows scope for the development of an independent allegiance to the political conception that helps to bring about a consensus' (*PL*: 168). Combined with increasing knowledge from previous experience that other citizens will comply and engage equally in fair terms of cooperation, the political conception becomes feasible as citizens 'gain increasing trust in one another' (ibid.).

It is Rawls's concept of the political that forms the crux of his mature liberal thought and is primarily juxtaposed to the 'metaphysical' (*PL*: 10). If a conception of justice lays its claim to superiority out of a comprehensive analysis of human reason, subjectivity, or view of the good, then it is metaphysical. He does not, however, then go on to label such metaphysical views as incorrect or misinformed, but merely states that these positions are too controversial, and too unstable, for a modern political conception of justice. The fact that a metaphysical view is so entrenched in substantive comprehensive moral doctrines means that it will only be acceptable to those who already adhere to such a position. Justice as fairness, therefore, no longer rests upon any assumptions that could reasonably be rejected by citizens. Hence, the political is *freestanding*, built as it is on key values latent within liberal democratic societies. It seeks to forge a political – yet still moral – agreement on principles of justice against a background of reasonable pluralism. In Rawls's words, 'reasonable comprehensive doctrines can adhere to it as they endure in a society regulated by it' (*PL*: 145).

Again, Rawls himself admits that his earlier work and the position he put forward in *TJ* was that of a partially comprehensive doctrine in that it argued for the superiority of justice as fairness over other comprehensive or partially comprehensive moral doctrines. The stability of *TJ*, therefore, depended upon the 'fact of oppression' (*PL*: 37). Rawls elaborates: 'If we think of political society as a community united in affirming one and the same comprehensive doctrine, then the oppressive use of state power is necessary for a political community'. It is for this reason that *TJ* contradicted itself, because in putting forward what he defines as a 'partially comprehensive doctrine' (*PL*: 59), any state endorsing it would have to act illiberally to enforce it, and herein lies the internal problem of his earlier work. *PL*, therefore, was deliberately self-limiting by arguing for a political conception of justice in order to avoid the metaphysical assumptions of *TJ*.

In summary, a political conception of justice and the ensuing overlapping consensus is 'not a compromise between those holding different views but rests on the totality of reasons specified within the comprehensive doctrine affirmed by each citizen' (*PL*: 170–1). Rawls lists the fundamental components of such a political agreement: it is to be endorsed by holders of all reasonable comprehensive doctrines; it is to provide social harmony as a political conception; it is stable for the right reasons; and it transcends a mere *modus vivendi* (*PL*: 134). Again, it is freestanding and reliant upon a prevalent sense of justice amongst a democratic citizenry. The consensus does not represent the triumph of a comprehensive doctrine to which all citizens must adhere, and instead confers a 'political conception [that] is at best but a guiding framework of deliberation and reflection which helps us reach political agreement on at least the constitutional essentials and the basic questions of justice' (*PL*: 150).

The manner in which an overlapping consensus will gain acceptance is that it will be supported for different reasons specific to individual comprehensive doctrines. This is not to say that justice will be intrinsic to all doctrines, and indeed for some liberal justice will be at best instrumental to their own comprehensive ends. Crucially, however, Rawls claims that the consensus will be internally stable 'for the right reasons' because, as previously stated, a *modus*

32   *Rawls and the Environmental Crisis*

vivendi is liable to change as groups or individuals rise to prominence in societies characterized by a balance of power (*PL*: 388).

Rawls believed that justice as fairness, articulated within such a consensus, has the advantage over other theories in that it steers citizens away from any such controversial contest in the first place. Instead, Rawls's justice as fairness insists on remaining impartial between such competing conceptions of the good, allowing citizens to cooperate politically as free and equal persons. From this angle, citizens must 'bracket' or marginalize what they believe to be the truth when dealing with constitutional essentials and matters of basic justice just as their representatives would in the hypothetical OP. Justice as fairness no longer triumphs over other theories of justice and is not incompatible with other conceptions of justice found in a multitude of other moral doctrines. It can be said to be freestanding insomuch as it is intended to constitute a sphere beyond the 'narrowness' of comprehensive doctrines, and one which amounts to a form of positioned – or specific – impartiality rather than neutrality.

There are, therefore, three distinguishing features of Rawls's political conception of justice that, as will become clear in the next chapter, are relevant to green concerns. First, his political liberalism refers to the 'basic structure of society'; that is, it concentrates not only on 'constitutional essentials', but also on the main political, social, and economic institutions that allow for the existence of a coherent system of cooperation that endures from one generation to the next (*PL*: 11). Thus, the very scope of his political liberalism is self-limiting and applies simply to the basic structure of government, the political process, and the formalizing of basic liberties and equality of opportunities (*PL*: 227). This point is particularly pertinent when it comes to the question of separating the basic structure of a liberal society from background discussions surrounding green concerns (the separation argument). The question that now follows is whether or not this implies that environmental or ecological justice will always be of secondary concern to political liberalism?

Secondly, Rawls's political concept attempts to defend itself without any appeal to values, views, and subjective concerns that are both controversial and metaphysical. It should be stressed that Rawls's political ideal does not deny any idea of the good (*PL*: 12–13). It is more the case that justice as fairness represents the political virtue of citizens coming together, unified in a common enterprise to agree upon principles of justice as a moral obligation in itself, in a way that transcends a mere *modus vivendi*. The principles they will agree to, however, will not be born out of individual and subjective claims to the truth. The key question for the green critique is, again, the extent to which a 'freestanding', impartial political sphere can be supported by greens if it sees their concerns as purely second-order preferences and as peripheral to the search for justice between contemporaries. In other words, what role is there for a spectrum of light and dark green concerns within such a political conception?

Thirdly, Rawls's justice as fairness takes its inspiration from 'fundamental ideas . . . implicit in the public culture of a democratic society', and included in these 'ideas' is a belief amongst its citizens that society is 'a fair system of cooperation over time, from one generation to the next' (*PL*: 13–14). As will be demonstrated in the following chapters, a transpolitical good begins to emerge here in the form of an enduring, modern faith in human cooperation, to which the political is sometimes only instrumental. So although Rawls attempts to build a freestanding political conception of justice, it is born of ideas already latent in the public–political culture. The immediate question that springs to mind is the extent to which this conception could include green values that may exist within a polity. Central to this is the fact that Rawls highlights how justice as fairness does not manifest itself as a compromise between competing conceptions of the good that exist at any one time. If it were to do this it would be drawing upon a 'political conception that strikes some kind of balance of forces between them' (*PL*: 39). Contrary to relying on such pragmatism, which would lead us back to a *modus vivendi*, Rawls's OC is established via a deductive form of reasoning which combines three factors to reinforce his argument. First, there is the aforementioned idea of society as a fair system of cooperation. Second, there are what Rawls sees as equally important ideas such as viewing goodness as rationality; the significance of political virtues ('values of equal political and civil liberty; fair equality of opportunity; the values of economic reciprocity; the social bases of mutual respect between citizens' (*PL*: 139); and the good of the well-ordered society (*PL*: 176). Third, and crucially to understand Rawls's political conception of justice, is the notion of primary goods, including basic rights and liberties, freedom of movement and association, powers and opportunities of office, wealth, income, and the social bases of self-respect (*PL*: 187–90). These assumptions, when combined, form the foundations of a broad consensus that would appeal to holders of all reasonable comprehensive conceptions.

Rawls recognizes that disagreements will naturally linger within what he identifies as the 'background culture', and thus that his overlapping consensus can 'bypass religion and philosophy's profoundest controversies', but he concludes that agreement on a regulative system of justice is possible on the basis of a citizen's moral sense of justice, intrinsic to his or her own comprehensive doctrine (*PL*: 152). Debates surrounding green concerns, because they unearth profound questions of humanity's place in the world, are no doubt examples of such controversies. As Rawls notes: 'citizens themselves, within the exercise of their liberty of thought and conscience, and looking to their comprehensive doctrines, view the political principles as derived from, or congruent with, or at least not in conflict with, their other values' (*PL*: 11). In effect, Rawls stipulates that any citizen would be unreasonable, even asocial, if he or she were to reject a politically liberal conception of justice that guarantees his or her freedom to rationally pursue, modify, and develop his or her own conception of the good (doctrinal or otherwise). Despite acknowledging the criticism that his vision of may appear utopian, Rawls alludes to a political philosophy that is both humanistic and political in believing that politics 'becomes the defence of reasonable faith in the possibility of a just constitutional regime' (*PL*: 172). Further, this returns us back to the idea of a much stronger transpolitical good

34   *Rawls and the Environmental Crisis*

of an enduring, intergenerational timeline of human cooperation in the modern period. Again, though, it also represents the beginnings of a problematic tension between the idea of a political unity based on tolerance and mutual disinterest (the freedom and opportunities needed to pursue a self-authored vision of the good life), and the idea of an agreement that is to be preserved from one generation to the next, well beyond the relatively fleeting life of the citizen.

With these three key features in mind (that the political focusses on the basic structure; it is to be freestanding; and that it is to be built upon ideas latent in the public–political culture), it is necessary to now consider the role Rawls himself assigned to green concerns, both within and beyond the OP. At first glance, the freestanding nature of his political liberalism would seem to suggest a very thin moral view that is neither *inclusive* nor *exclusive* of such concerns – a fact not missed in the green critique outlined in Chapters 3 and 4. He seemed to recognize the probable charge of neutrality that could be leveled at this theory on the subject, and the next chapter will elucidate his own justification for this inconclusiveness. Much of the green critique revolves around the separation argument, and his own limited treatment of green concerns is reflected in the constraints of the OP. Quite uniquely, Rawls himself eventually became Rawlsian with regards to green concerns, and by the time we reach his later works he engages openly in extensionism by developing justice as fairness to apply to those who fall beyond the traditional scope of justice in the areas of both international politics and health care. The green critique, by and large, sees such a Rawlsian method of extensionism as being capable of invoking only very light green, shallowly instrumentalist reasons for protecting wider nature.

Notes

1 See Vincent (2004) for a rebuke of the idea that, prior to Rawls, political philosophy had died a death.
2 It is worth stressing further the significance of the Reformations in dashing hopes for political unity within deeply divided societies. The Reformations did not merely result in the flourishing of religious toleration. As John Neville Figgis stressed, 'political liberty, as a fact of the modern world, is the result of the struggles of religious organisms to live . . . Religious forces, and religious forces alone, had the sufficient influence to ensure practical realisation for political ideas' (1960: 6–7). Figgis, as a historian-turned-preacher, was concerned with the transposition of Church and state from the medieval to the modern period, a period within which we see the development of classical liberalism. From within this plurality of religious views, therefore, came the political good of liberty embodied in what, by the eighteenth century, had become known as liberalism. The root of the term Protestantism was, after all, from the word 'protest'.

2 Rawls on green concerns

Chapter 1 has argued that political liberalism, since the Reformations, has set out to face the conceptual problem of agreement, and even unity, on the shared political ideas of the free and equal citizen. A second question now occupies the green political theorist if they are to consider the implications of what we have called 'the separation argument'; that is, the abstraction of political justice from green concerns. If the two areas operate in isolation from one another, does a theory of political justice that deals solely with contemporaneous, rational human agents automatically downgrade green concerns to the periphery? This chapter will further explore Rawls's own justification for this separation, and the particular aspects of his theory that address this central challenge. It will also offer an initial assessment of how far Rawlsian liberalism can proceed along our spectrum (or continuum) of green concerns, from light to dark green, as outlined in the introduction. We are, however, left with a vexing question that if the separation argument is to hold, then to what extent will it influence the ideas and behaviours of citizens beyond the OP? Would a politically impartial stance on green concerns encourage an attitude of indifference in a well-ordered society at large – in the 'background culture'? Put another way, if the main political and economic institutions of a society are unwilling to engage in the controversies surrounding humanity's relationship to wider nature, or the sustainability of a polity, does it follow that individual citizens themselves in the non-political public and private spheres, are excused from taking green concerns seriously? The key aim of this chapter, therefore, is to highlight the key tenets of Rawls's own position on green concerns. Further, it is important to start to address the argument, prevalent in the green critique, that his own justification of the separation argument represents a shallow instrumentalist (that is, unenlightened), light green theory of environmental justice in and of itself. In order to achieve this, it is necessary to outline the fact that despite the move to a more freestanding political liberalism, the idea of the 'well-ordered society' remains, and can be considered as a transpolitical good of intergenerational justice capable of motivating citizens for reasons other then mutual disinterest.

36   *Rawls and the Environmental Crisis*

Sentientism

Although our primary interest lies in Rawls's mature political liberalism, it is worth paying attention also to his early, partially comprehensive theory as it reinforces what would become a reasonably consistent attitude towards green concerns throughout his career.[1] There are four key passages, or general ideas, from *TJ*, *PL*, and elsewhere that summarize his own view of the appropriate relationship between green concerns and justice as fairness: sentientism; the justification of the separation argument; the metaphysical concept of human/non-human relations; and the just savings principle. These four areas will now be considered in more detail prior to outlining an analysis of the green critique of Rawls in the following two chapters. The first two areas under investigation in this chapter (sentientism and neutrality) present grounds for a *prima facie* incompatibility between justice as fairness and green concerns, whereas the proceeding two areas (a metaphysical view of human and non-human relations, and the just savings principle) have come to represent a more hopeful means of greening Rawls.

In an often-quoted line from *TJ*, with regards to the plight of non-human species and wider nature, Rawls is keen to stress that a 'conception of justice is but one part of the moral view' adding that whilst a capacity for a sense of justice is not the only prerequisite to being owed the 'duties of justice . . . it does seem that we are not required to give strict justice anyway to creatures lacking this capacity' (*TJ*: 448). Strict justice, then, is the preserve of those who possess Rawls's two moral powers: a conception of the good life and a capacity for a sense of justice – the *rational* and the *reasonable*, respectively. It seems, then, that this would also exclude future generations and those beyond the reach of contemporaneous liberal justice. Rawls continues: 'certainly it is wrong to be cruel to animals and the destruction of a whole species can be a great evil. The capacity for feelings of pleasure and pain and for the forms of life of which animals are capable clearly imposes duties of compassion and humanity in their case'. In a similar vein, and prior to *TJ*, Rawls had written that we 'do not normally think of ourselves as owing the duty of justice to animals, but it is certainly wrong to be cruel to them. Their capacity for feeling pleasure and pain for some form of happiness, is enough to establish this' (1963: 114). As such, 'it does not follow that there are no requirements at all in regard to them, nor in our relations with the natural world'. Rawls remains adamant, though, that his 'considered beliefs', here, 'are outside the scope of the theory of justice, and it does not seem possible to extend the contract doctrine so as to include them in a *natural* way' (*TJ*: 448, emphasis added).

As with any enquiry regarding 'our relations with the natural world', the separation argument is defends the exclusion of those who fall beyond the scope of 'strict' justice. Again, does this reluctance to engage substantially with green concerns reflect an existing political and social indifference to the plight of sentient beings and as yet, non-existent future generations, most at risk from environmental degradation? A personal ethic of sentientism is certainly discernible here; a form of *pathocentrism*, whereby moral consideration is to be attributed to sentient beings according to a Benthamite, utilitarian philosophy of the pleasure/pain calculus (see Wissenburg, 1998: 53). What is missing, according to Rawls, is a *natural* means of extending his theory of justice to those who happen to lack a capacity for a sense of justice.

In an early rummage into political psychology, Rawls had come to the conclusion that a capacity for a sense of justice is part of the natural constitution of humanity. Those bereft of this capacity are 'also without certain natural attitudes and certain moral feelings of a particularly elementary kind . . . one who lacks a sense of justice lacks certain fundamental attitudes and capacities included under the notion of humanity' (Rawls, 1963: 111). To be human is to be capable of being just. Again, it is increasingly apparent that Rawls's *political* continually departs from his earlier-stated *ethical* view, insomuch as justice as fairness does little to promote or even defend a widespread societal disposition toward his own preferred notion of sentientism. There is a certain distance between a clear moral duty to animals and an account of environmental justice that politicizes such a concern. Having said this, his interest in the concept of *humanity* makes a reappearance in Chapter 4 as a potential means of conferring stronger duties towards wider nature.

Rawls's troublesome obeisance to green concerns here is limited to the inclusion of non-human sentient beings as opposed to a more general notion of an environmental crisis, or a metaphysical conception of 'our relations with the natural world'. Yet these brief statements, and the idea of extending a conception of liberal justice *naturally*, are the source of many of the tensions between Rawlsian liberal greens and greens (liberal or otherwise) more generally. The unequivocal separation of justice from green concerns has come to cost Rawls dearly in the subsequent critique. It is, so to speak, his original environmental sin, according to critics. Those who seek to green Rawlsian liberalism are, unwittingly or otherwise, trying to clear his name from charges of providing an *apologia* for environmental neglect. Again, the clear sense of moral duties towards non-human sentient beings present in his writings suggests that it is seems intuitively unfair to accuse his work of being an outer reflection of an inner disregard for all things green. What it is fair to say is that the separation of strict, political justice from these concerns is the root cause of the discourse discussed in the remaining chapters, as human justice is firmly separated from any notion of environmental and/or ecological justice. So far then, to extend justice as fairness beyond the realm of contemporaneous humans (who are both rational and reasonable) means proceeding in a manner that Rawls believes should be, rather ambiguously, *natural*.

The justification of the separation argument

Following the divorcing of 'strict', contemporaneous human justice from those who fall beyond its scope, including future generations and non-human species, the impartiality of Rawlsian liberalism to green concerns is compounded by a second statement found in Rawls's later work regarding the limits of

38   *Rawls and the Environmental Crisis*

public reason and human and non-human nature relationships. Rawls begins, 'Yet we want a political conception of justice to be complete: its political values should admit of a balance giving a reasonable answer to for all or nearly all fundamental questions' (*PL*: 244). He then states that 'several "problems of extension," . . . may seem answerable from within a political conception.' The four areas of extension are 'our duties to future generations'; 'political relations between peoples – the traditional *jus gentium*'; 'the principles of normal healthcare'; and finally, 'our relations to animals and the order of nature'. Rawls believes that the 'justice as fairness can be reasonably extended to cover the first three problems' (*PL*: 245). The process of expansion 'begin(s) by taking for granted the full status of adult persons in the society in question (the members of its citizen body) and proceed from there: forward to other generations, outward to other societies, and inward to those requiring normal healthcare . . . to obtain a reasonable law'. The starting point for any extension of justice as fairness, then, is the acceptance of the modern idea that the individual is able to act as a self-author of the good, and also that the individual can be said to possess a mutual disinterest in his or her fellow citizens' freely chosen ends.

For now, the focus is on the pre-extensionist separation of political liberalism from questions of humanity's relationship to wider nature. Rawls frames the issue as thus: 'suppose our attitude toward the world is one of natural religion: we think it utterly wrong to appeal solely to those values, to determine our relations with the natural world' (*PL*: 245). Rawls continues: 'the status of the natural world and our proper relation to it is not a constitutional essential or a basic question of justice . . . it is a matter in regard to which citizens can vote their non-political values and try to convince other citizens accordingly' (*PL*: 246). By the time we reach *PL*, therefore, there is even less room for an ethic of sentientism. Within a politically liberal society, it would be unthinkable to allow any doctrinal – and thus controversial – theory of environmental or ecological justice to form the basis of shared values. It would be wholly unreasonable, say, to base institutional first principles on an attempt to reestablish the Earth's homeostasis following James Lovelock's Gaia theory (see, for example, Lovelock, 2001). The following example, again from *PL*, illustrates this point: if some citizens happen to believe that 'human beings should assume a certain stewardship toward nature and give weight to an altogether different family of values' (*PL*: 246), then they are said to hold a comprehensive view on green concerns; a natural religion-esque ecologism as it were, drawing their argument from a comprehensive doctrine (akin 'to those who reject abortion on theological grounds'). These kinds of views must wait until after constitutional essentials have been decided upon, and until they can be presented politically (or non-politically) beyond the OP. A reasonable law – normative or legislative – can then be established.

At the risk of employing the term *neutral*, a label Rawls himself identified as 'unfortunate'; a 'stage-piece' to be 'avoided',[2] the above passage from *PL* reinforces a perceived apathy towards the fate of wider nature in respect to impending environmental crises. Although neutrality and apathy are two different things, with the former denoting a sense of impartiality and the latter, a form of disinterest, they are presented as synonymous within the literature on green concerns. Dobson has arguably been one of the leading figures in green political thought occupied in what he himself calls 'the full frontal assault on what many continue to regard as a jewel in liberalism's crown: its commitment to neutrality as far as 'comprehensive doctrines' are concerned' (Dobson, 2003: 161). Dobson's 'immanent critique' of liberal neutrality demands that the liberal state, in both theory and practice, must embrace a darker green version of ecological justice that preserves nature not for its intrinsic value, but because 'a structured bequest package amounts to a wider range of options from which to choose good lives' (168). We see here a repeat of the argument that a much stronger commitment to the protection of wider nature is not doctrinal but *pre-political*, so to speak, and forms a material prerequisite to justice as fairness.

Combined with the first point on sentientism, and the language used here – with it being 'utterly wrong' to appeal to doctrinal environmentalism or ecologism – it does seem that a theoretical impasse is soon reached. If the basic structure and the constitutional essentials of society are the subject of political justice, and 'justice is the first virtue of social institutions', then Dobson's adage is that a system of political thought that relegates a concern for wider nature to second place is in itself a 'second-division' political theory. If green concerns were to be manifested in, say, green regulations or citizenship policies within a liberal polity, whose citizens had agreed to 'a family' of politically liberal values, then at any point such regulations or policies could be outweighed by first principles of liberal justice. Secondary in the ordering of justice, therefore, implies secondary in moral importance. For critics of Rawls there is simply no sense of rumination in his works when confronted with dismal notions of environmental crises that are anything but of secondary importance, especially given that they threaten the essential conditions necessary for an individual's self-authorship of the good.

The metaphysical concept of human/non-human relations

A third feature of Rawls's work pertinent to the search for a coherent Rawlsian view on green concerns is an unremarkable footnote in *PL*, made immediately after the previous section's discussion of the separation argument, within which Rawls puts out what seems like an invitation to the green political theorist who, dissatisfied with the separation argument, may wish to extend his conception of justice as fairness. Although, as previously stated, Rawls himself leaves non-human species and future generations firmly off the political agenda, he adds that: 'these questions may become ones of constitutional essentials and basic justice once our duties and obligations to future generations and other societies are involved' (*PL*: 246, fn.35. See also, *PL*: 20–21). Rawls puts forward the assertion that 'we want a political conception of justice to be complete: its political values should admit of a balance giving a reasonable

40 *Rawls and the Environmental Crisis*

answer for all or nearly all fundamental questions' (*PL*: 244). How does this tie in with his admittance that justice is 'but one part of the moral view'? To be 'complete' is surely to answer fundamental questions of human relations not just in a contemporary setting but also with regards to 'our relations with the natural world'. The language used is more confusing than contradictory but what Rawls seems to be arguing is this: taking justice as fairness forward, or outward, or inward to identify a reasonable law, must mean that it is reflective of a 'correct' configuration of human and non-human relations.

The green critique, however, pushes for the recognition that a looming universal environmental crisis *cannot now be anything other than a fundamental question of justice*. Without a stable ecological system, citizens of a political society could not even hope to agree on principles of justice, yet alone provide the political liberties necessary for the individual pursuit of the good. Moderate scarcity would become just scarcity, as the 'the normal conditions under which human cooperation is both possible and necessary' (*TJ*: 109) are lost. The question remains, however, as to when and where this extensionism (or the taking of justice 'forward', or 'outward') is to take place. For Simon Caney (2005), there should be no separation of environmental rights and duties from similar political or economic obligations; that is, a theory of political justice must not be devised in 'isolation' from environmental justice (763). The location of extensionism again primarily revolves around the role of the OP, and whether the inclusion of green concerns takes place at a pre or post-OP deliberative stage (that is, with or without knowledge of one's conception of the good life).

Rawls himself reveals where he would start this process by identifying four key 'problems of extension' in *PL*: international law; universal healthcare; non-human species; and future generations (*PL*: 21). Turning to the subject of international justice in his *The Law of Peoples* by seeking an 'extension of a general social contract idea to a Society of Peoples' (Rawls, 1999b: 4), he addresses what he sees as ideal theory; that is, that both liberal societies and non-liberal (but 'decent') peoples would adhere to the 'reasonably just Law of Peoples' (5). In addition to this, he also considers non-ideal theory and in particular, non-compliant regimes (for example, the hypothetical 'Kazanistan') that refuse to adhere to a reasonable Law of Peoples.[3] In a similar vein, Rawls takes an extensionist approach to the idea of universal medical care. Clearly, he has in mind here the problem of health care in the United States. He adopts Rawlsian first principles of justice to act as a guide for assigning medical resources within a liberal society, and effectively steps outside of his own theory to do so. There is no internal modification of his OP and no change to the scope of his idea of political liberalism.[4] Rather, the difference principle decided upon is to influence the distribution of resources to those 'normally cooperating members of society whose capacities for a time fall below the minimum' (Rawls, 2001: 173). Crucially, the incorporation of health care comes at a post-OP and post-constitutional, legislative stage of deliberation, when one is no longer behind the veil of ignorance. The extension (or the establishing) of a reasonable law occurs not in the political sphere, but more in the political–public domain, where although the influence of the basic structure remains strong, it is still not a 'fundamental' of political justice.

This is interesting not least because it offers a blueprint for those wishing to extend the first principles of justice decided upon behind the veil of ignorance (in this case, the difference principle, and the extension of a general social contract idea) for post-OP citizen deliberations when knowledge of one's physical and mental attributes becomes known. But can this be done *in a natural way*, as Rawls himself stipulates? The loosely defined concepts of environmental or ecological justice are based on a general merging of theories of justice (liberal or otherwise) and green literature, arguing again, very broadly speaking, that ecological degradation has led to new circumstances of justice, bringing into question the distribution of resources and opportunities to previously excluded groups. They should, therefore, surely be seen as matters of basic justice and constitutional essentials. Will the 'least advantaged' in society be able to adapt to changing natural environments and temperatures as effectively as the wealthier in society? Will the health of society's most vulnerable suffer? This avenue of thought will not be pursued until a later stage, but needless to say several theorists have attempted to state that the severity of the changing circumstances of justice are enough to render Rawls's notion of 'moderate scarcity' redundant. Rawls appears to reserve final judgement on how successful political liberalism would be in progressing forward, outward, or inward so as to generate extended first principles of environmental justice to cover the plight of non-human species.

Of assistance here is the approach taken by Rawls in *TJ* that suggests his method of extensionism remained largely consistent throughout his career. An intriguing statement, which has been picked up on by several theorists in this area (see, for example, Barry, 1999), is made by Rawls immediately after the points he raises in the first section of this chapter regarding sentientism. He writes that a 'correct conception of our relations to animals and to nature would seem to depend upon a theory of the natural order and our place in it. One of the tasks of metaphysics is to work out a view of the world which is suited for this purpose; it should identify and systemize the truths decisive for these questions' (*TJ*: 448–9). Rawls adds, rather ambitiously,'[h]ow far justice as fairness will have to be revised to fit into this larger theory it is impossible to say. But it seems reasonable that if it is sound as an account of justice among persons, it cannot be too far wrong when these broader relationships are taken into consideration.' Rawls seems to suggest here that his philosophy not only establishes a stable political order between citizens, but that it will naturally capture the essence of justice between humans and wider nature, and presumably, offer a vision of humanity's 'relations with the natural world'. Contemporary justice, encapsulated in the just institutions of the well-ordered society, will mirror a more metaphysical 'order of nature' – or what we may have once called the 'great chain of being' (*PL*: 245).

The above statement throws up significant barriers to the reasonable extension of a coherent theory of environmental justice. The obvious problem is

42 Rawls and the Environmental Crisis

that there will be little room for extensionism because, for Rawls, it will only strengthen the philosophical basis for his idea of justice as fairness. This is representative of his wider search for a more universal and comprehensive liberalism; a search endemic to his earlier works, and, as we have seen, a position from which he would later try to distance himself. We are to 'systemize' the metaphysical quest for truths in the makeup of the natural order. Put another way, Rawls's normative political theory on the subject of justice between humans is at the mercy of a meta-ethical search for a 'correct' configuration of human and non-human relations within wider nature.

Rawls does indeed maintain this idea, albeit subtly, in *PL*, as it is clear he believes that the key tenets of justice as fairness can be applied to the new frontiers of political theory. We need only to take his principles forward, outward, or inward to wherever they are needed. Yet there are two possible interpretations of Rawls's above statement in *TJ*. The first is that his suggestion is disquieting: once a single 'true' notion of the environmental crisis is agreed upon, and the means by which we are to deal with it become politically, morally, and scientifically unequivocal, then much contemporary political theory (including his own) could very likely be rendered useless. A meta-ethical 'theory of the natural order' could be an act of self-sabotage. Although Rawls is hopeful that his theory of justice between humans will not be 'too far wrong' when extended to, say, the protection of non-human species and future generations at risk from deteriorating ecological conditions, is he too optimistic that a similar meta-ethical view on the natural order of things can be found? Surely such an argument could have the perverse effect of doing away with liberal theories on spurious grounds. In some ways, Rawls was being unintentionally prophetic in acknowledging that his theory would be subject to the scrutiny of a much more profound search for a more symbiotic relationship between humanity and wider nature. In *PL*, and although the phrasing is altered, this view is at odds with the idea of a freestanding political liberalism.

The second interpretation comes from a different angle. Those, like Pier Stephens (2001a), who view the ecological crisis as a 'metaphysical crisis', and so who wish to discover '[t]he natural order and our place in it' need look no further than the idea of justice as fairness, as Rawls suggests that it will be well on its way to uncovering our role within the cosmos. In order to discover the role humanity should assume within wider nature, the starting point seems to be liberalism. We thus extend justice as fairness to those beings beyond the scope of justice, as it will not 'be too far wrong'. A Rawlsian concept of environmental justice, then, will be anthropocentric and modelled on reason. This statement epitomizes a thoroughly modern, liberal, and ambitious theory of environmental justice (outlined in detail in Chapter 4) whereby humanity attempts to uncover its duties to wider nature without reference to any form of outside support. Although it seems that Rawls himself quietly dropped the bolder elements of *TJ*, the link between liberal principles and a theory of environmental justice holds firm in *PL*.

The principle of just savings

In taking justice 'forward', *TJ* is often credited with providing one of the first substantive discussions on the rights of future generations. Whilst the difference principle deals with *intragenerational* justice, his principle of 'just savings' attempts to resolve the idea of justice *between* the generations. Intergenerational justice is not *ipso facto* the preserve of green politics and environmental philosophy, and yet what we find in Rawls's treatment of the subject is a commitment to ensuring a political transfer of justice from one generation to the next, a fact that inevitably incorporates transgenerational environmental challenges. When analyzing this principle, one option is to assume the same distance Rawls himself took when he extended his idea of justice as fairness to international law and universal health care; that is, adopting a Rawlsian-inspired theory of intergenerational justice by applying fairness to a separate aspect of public–political morality, or a new frontier of justice. An alternative method is to assess the totality of the Rawlsian project, the 'well-ordered society', as being a good of intergenerational justice in and of itself. The concluding chapter will consider the merits of viewing these seemingly mutually exclusive methods as one and the same.

For now, the question of an appropriate distance to take from Rawls's theory, and the degree to which his work is to be internally modified, varies significantly within the green critique. In seeking to avoid any substantial alteration of his theory, the danger of presenting an uncritical *apologia* of Rawlsian moral and political philosophy is ever-present. What would be more uncritical, however, is to blindly accuse Rawls as being complicit in a body of intellectual thought responsible for deteriorating environmental conditions in many quarters of the world. The problem is, however, that the green critique has rarely examined the often-contradictory theories of environmental and ecological justice being used to condemn or condone justice as fairness (see Bell, 2004a: 290–3; Caney, 2005: 748).

The principle of just savings is often understood as a restatement of a self-contained shallow instrumentalist Rawlsian theory of environmental justice, as already suggested by the separation argument, and the 'application' of justice as fairness to the problems of extension. Derek Bell argues that any internally coherent theory of environmental justice that moves from mere commentary to a more systematic theory of extensionism can be divided into three straightforward sections: *who*, *what*, and *how* (a: 290–3). A given society, therefore, taking into consideration the needs of future generations, must decide on *who* are those that are to be the subject of justice; *what* goods (or 'bads') are to be distributed; and finally, *how* the principle of distribution is to proceed. Edward Page (2007) approaches the subject in a similar way by asking what is to be the 'scope' of justice, what is the 'pattern' of such justice, and what is to be the 'currency of advantage' within such a system of distribution. Page's 'scope' of justice refers to Bell's 'who' and his 'pattern of justice' to Bell's 'how'. In Page's own words 'a complete theory of intergenerational justice involves us

44 *Rawls and the Environmental Crisis*

specifying *which entities* should receive a certain *level of benefit* as calculated in terms of some credible *conception of advantage*' (2007: 453, emphasis in original). Our point of departure, however, will be to focus on Bell's objects or goods (the 'what') of justice, but not Page's 'currencies'. To be sure, when working through the details of what is actually to be bequeathed to future generations, there exists a two-stage process. The first stage is to deliberate upon the object or good of intergenerational justice – the *thing(s)* of value to be bequeathed to future generations (in what follows, this will be identified as being the just institutions of Rawls's well-ordered society). The second stage involves assessing Page's 'level of benefit' within a 'credible conception of advantage', and thus refers to the interpersonal evaluation of Bell's 'what'; that is, the criterion by which we measure the comparative advantage to persons of distributing such goods intergenerationally (see Welburn, 2013). Caney, too, proposes a similar framework of analysis. He argues that a conception of environmental justice demands that the distribution of environmental burdens and benefits, when applied to the potential plight of future generations, should be done according to a timeless principle of justice as relevant to future persons as it is to us now (Caney, 2005: 749). Taking the *how, what,* and *who* of the just savings principle, in turn, strengthens the case that Rawls's political liberalism is often already seen to embody a comprehensive, but light green, vision of environmental justice, built on a justification of the separation argument, that requires very little extension. Or, put slightly differently, it sees justice as fairness being taken forward and applied to the potential plight of future generations.

How does Rawls's 'just savings' principle, as the pattern of intergenerational justice, proceed? The main aim of Rawls's notion is to establish just 'how far the present generation is bound to respect the claims of its successors' and, moreover, that the 'the principle of just saving holds *between* generations, while the difference principle holds *within* generations' (Rawls, 2001: 159, emphasis added).[5] Any savings, within the intergenerational setting, are to preserve the basic structure for no other reason than that of justice, although understandably there will be other reasons for citizens to save for future generations well beyond the scope of justice (that is, 'imperfect duties'). Rawls's political liberalism deals with *intragenerational* justice by utilizing the difference principle (see Rawls, 2001: 61–6) and addresses the issue of justice *between* generations via the principle of just savings. Rawls is unable to sideline the issue of what we bequeath to future generations owing to the central aim of his political theory; namely, the need 'to establish and preserve a just basic structure over time' (159–61). As such, 'society is to be a fair system of *cooperation between generations over time*' and thus, 'a principle governing savings is required' (160, emphasis added). This is stating the obvious: any valid theory of justice seeks to establish fair terms of cooperation that will endure over time, yet Rawls's approach allows us to look at the issue of intergenerational justice in a new light. In one way, it serves to provide a hypothetical method of reasoning as to what resources we value now and why, but the very fact that we are forced to deliberate on what we are to bequeath to future generations allows for the inclusion of a substantive discussion of green concerns.

How would Rawls's just savings principle work in practice? Rawls has in mind three applications. The first aim of such a principle, according to Rawls, is 'to encourage a wide and far more equal dispersion of real property and productive assets' in order to regulate 'bequest and inheritance' (160–1). In keeping with his commitment to liberty and equality, Rawls hopes that the equitable distribution of both material and cultural goods will uphold the notion of intergenerational justice. Rawls adds that the onus on paying tax is on those receiving such goods rather on those bequeathing them. Progressive taxation is thus aimed at developing intergenerational justice at the point of receiving. Rawls avoids advocating for a progressive taxation on the accumulation of wealth in order to avoid the creation of a disincentive to those citizens seeking to generate assets for the benefit of future generations. Secondly, and further to the first aim, the implementation of a progressive tax may not be necessary in the first place. Rawls argues that progressive taxation should only be used to prevent the amassing of wealth, a process that is detrimental to background justice.[6] Thirdly, he stipulates that any form of income taxation could be replaced by regulating consumption in the form of a proportional tax (161). In effect, a consumption tax would mean citizens are to pay for the goods and services they use rather than having to pay for the wealth they contribute to society's total capital. Such a proportionate tax can also be adjusted so as to guarantee a social minimum – a minimum level of wealth to allow society's 'least advantaged' to develop their two moral powers within a system of fair cooperation. The 'least advantaged' Rawls stresses, are 'not identifiable apart from, or independently of, their income and wealth' (59 fn.26). To be sure, Rawls does not state that they are to be defined as such owing to their ethnicity, race, gender, or nationality. He notes, however, that 'there may be a tendency for such features to characterize many who belong to that group'. In effect, Rawls is stating that there is a natural tendency for societies to favour some groups over others, a fact that can be countered by justice as fairness as all citizens are guaranteed rights and liberties. The least advantaged possess the lowest expectations of income and wealth over a complete life.

So the principle of just savings must not contradict the difference principle that guarantees a basic level of welfare for the least advantaged. This principle is concerned with equity across generations insomuch as it seeks to ensure that each successive generation is bequeathed the institutions that govern the basic structure of society in such a way that individuals from within it are able to pursue their two moral powers. Any savings beyond those required to secure just social institutions are superfluous. Central to the just savings principle, however, is that it shifts the burden of taxation onto consumers as opposed to savers of goods. It would seem, therefore, that Rawls was an early advocate of modern green taxes based on the 'polluter pays' principle. In addition to this, both savers *and* beneficiaries require a sense of duty and obligation to

46 *Rawls and the Environmental Crisis*

work on behalf of the wider intergenerational and enduring good of human cooperation.

Rawls does not say a great deal more on this matter, and it is rather the case that the process of deliberation with regards to what we are to bequeath is 'the problem of extending justice as fairness to cover our duties to future generations, under which falls the problem of just savings' (*PL*: 20). The ultimate end of the just savings principle, as the pattern or 'how' of intergenerational justice, is to achieve a steady-state phase whereby just institutions are preserved from one generation to the next. Once the just institutions within the basic structure of society are secured, the net accumulation rate of saving falls to zero. The onus is, again, on both those who are saving as it is on those receiving the benefits of such savings, and this will be significant when we move to the second part of the green critique in Chapter 4, and the idea of humanity as a whole engaged in an intergenerational project of cooperation. This leads us neatly to the issue of what exactly is meant by 'just social institutions' that are to be secured by the just savings principle. Are such institutions a legitimate 'good' or resource (that is, the 'what') of justice between generations?

We are led to a distinct difficulty in identifying the exact nature of the intended 'what' of intergenerational justice to be distributed in Rawlsian liberalism. Recall his objection to advocating for any form of *summum bonum* that would represent a comprehensive view to be agreed upon by all citizens. What, exactly, is to be bequeathed? Is it the liberty to choose one's green conception of environmental justice, or the extent to which one holds an ecological conscience, or is it the outcome of this freedom; the chosen conception itself, that is to be included within a system of justice, and the domain of the political? A straightforward means of assessing Rawlsian liberalism's accommodation of green concerns is to sideline controversial views by including only supposedly 'reasonable', light green, and instrumental reasons for protecting wider nature at the post-OP stage (akin to Rawls's earlier views on sentientism and the duties of humanity). These freely chosen green conceptions of the good or comprehensive doctrines are therefore not the actual goods (the 'what') of intergenerational justice, and so we must explore the process of self-authorship as a means by which these outcomes are reached. To resolve this matter, we must consider the different stages of Rawls's political liberalism. In the initial stage, parties in the OP are initially unaware as to what their respective conceptions of the good will be once the veil of ignorance is lifted. In order to secure their interests, they will seek a society that guarantees the all-purpose means of achieving these ends. As such, these conceptions do not represent a stand-alone good, as it is rather the case that 'the choosing' of the good is what is of value in a politically liberal order. For Rawls, is it the capacity of citizens themselves to devise, develop, and revise their unique conceptions of the good, green or otherwise, that is inherently valuable? At the constitutional stage, the parties then design institutions that ensure the just distribution of the primary goods required to pursue their freely chosen conceptions of the good. Yet it is the outcome of such self-authorship that a political society must work with, and, as such, Rawls seeks to develop a well-ordered society, built on reasonable principles, despite it remaining 'deeply divided' by the fact of reasonable pluralism (*PL*: xi).

As an intangible 'good', or at least the 'what' within an intergenerational setting, the liberty to choose cannot be distributed across generations *per se*. It is for this reason that the just institutions are to be regulated by the two principles of justice, and that together form the basic structure of a well-ordered society that is to be preserved from one generation to the next. Rawls's definition of the well-ordered society changed little throughout his career. Pre-*TJ*, Rawls noted: 'the problem of distributive justice . . . should be viewed as a problem of distributing and assigning rights in the design of the general system of rules defining and regulating economic activity.' Rawls continues that if 'one assumes that law and government effectively act to keep markets competitive, resources fully employed, property and wealth widely distributed over time, and maintain a reasonable social minimum, then, if there is equality of opportunity, the resulting distribution will be just or at least not unjust' (Rawls, 1963: 88). In *TJ*, Rawls states that 'thus it is in a society in which everyone accepts and knows that the others accept the same principles of justice, and the basic social institutions satisfy and are known to satisfy these principles' (397). By the time we reach Rawls's later, political liberalism, a society can be said to be 'well-ordered' when the good of liberty is realized and the fundamentals of justice are established; a point when 'everyone accepts, and knows that everyone else accepts, the very same principles of justice' (*PL*: 35). We find here a form of trust and a civic arrangement between free and equal citizens who each accept the priority of liberty within the well-ordered society: a recognition of the equal moral, political, and legal worth of all citizens in the modern period, regardless of their conception of the good. Citizens' *political* identities, and associated rights, remain fixed even if they choose to revise the comprehensive doctrine they hold. This particular interpretation, on the subject of intergenerational justice, supports Rawls's own view that justice between the generations is guaranteed only once the well-ordered society is secured, and so we must continually seek to build and maintain its just institutions. Here, we need not think of intertemporal comparisons or metrics for measuring distributed goods between individuals. Pertinent to our endeavour here is to consider the development of a well-ordered society, being bequeathed from one generation to the next, as a primary means of guaranteeing a continuous timeline of justice. These institutions, developed under fair conditions of deliberation, are to be the actual *what* of Rawls's scheme of intergenerational justice because they are the manifestation of the liberal values of liberty, equality, and fairness. Just institutions do not merely epitomize these principles – they also embody such liberal goods. Beyond the OP, they represent the societal conditions under which citizens can pursue their freely chosen conceptions of the good and their associated interests, green or otherwise. Liberty, equality, and fairness cannot in themselves be physically distributed across generations, but when embodied in just institutions they can be. As outlined above, once these just institutions

48 *Rawls and the Environmental Crisis*

are preserved, net saving can be reduced to zero, and so it is the well-ordered society that is to be bequeathed to future generations. Just institutions are thus to be the *what* of intergenerational justice, and are vital to the functioning of the well-ordered society. The well-ordered society, in turn, is not only instrumental as a means of allowing a plurality of citizens to pursue their self-authored visions of the good, but it is also the embodiment of the transpolitical good of a modern, intergenerational project of human cooperation.

What of the second stage of the process? What is to be the metric of this good within an intergenerational setting? How could we feasibly compare 'bundles' of a well-ordered society? There are two reasons why it is unnecessary to progress too far into the currencies debate and, thus, the second stage of the process. The first comes from Rawls himself in stating that his idea of primary goods – again, the most important of which are the basic liberties – are goods that are required by all citizens *qua* citizens. To be sure, they are stand-alone goods that are instrumental to the realization of a citizen's two moral powers (a capacity for a sense of justice and a conception of the good). Free and equal citizens will require these primary goods to exercise their two moral powers, and the only corrective mechanism is the difference principle that ensures that distribution is of benefit to the least advantaged. Any redistribution requires neither responsibility nor a notion of desert. For Rawls, this is an index of goods within the political sphere of society only, applicable to the basic structure. To go further would be to go beyond the scope of political justice.

The second reason for not delving too far into the currencies debate is to instead focus on the tension that arises from within Rawls's principle of just savings. With it comes a change of gear as we are forced to look beyond a language of rights and liberal justice and begin to explore the duties citizens now have in building and preserving a well-ordered society, the spirit of which future generations will come to inherit. It is about bequeathing something altogether more unquantifiable, and something almost immeasurable. The political in Rawls becomes more than just about the securing of liberties and opportunities across time, as it opens up the idea of citizens serving both as *stewards*, or *trustees*, of an intergenerational project of justice, and as the guardians of the just institutions that comprise the well-ordered society.

Finally, to whom are we to bequeath the just institutions of a Rawlsian well-ordered society? We now turn to the *scope* of intergenerational justice that presents us with two initial challenges. The first is to outline Rawls's overlapping generations model, and the second is to consider this paradigm within the context of his move from a comprehensive liberalism in *TJ*, through to his later works that argue for a freestanding political liberalism. It is important, however, to make a brief assumption regarding this topic. In *TJ*, Rawls's idea of justice between generations rests on the belief that contracting parties in the OP, placed behind a veil of ignorance, will naturally wish to secure a future for their potential offspring. For Rawls, those situated in the OP are to be heads of households. The significance of the veil of ignorance ensures that the parties will be ignorant as to whether or not they will produce children or grandchildren once the veil is lifted. Either way, the bargaining parties must rationally pre-empt this possibility, and thus negotiate a contract that guarantees that the successive generation and, at a push, the generation following our immediate successors, are to inherit the means of living a full and meaningful life. Justice between generations is secured, therefore, because citizens of all generations will save for their potential, immediate offspring. The scope of Rawls's liberalism is thus approximately two to three generations at a time, indefinitely, as each proceeding generation, in turn, cares for their immediate offspring, ensuring a continuous timeline of justice. Rawls's initial take on intergenerational justice unfortunately suffered from an internal defect, as pointed out by both Manning (1981) and Thero (1995). Rawls's OP is built on the assumption that bargaining parties are purely self-interested, and so he ran into a motivational lacuna: how can parties be both mutually disinterested owing to their acceptance of one another as free and equal whilst at the same time be expected to care altruistically for other persons through a love of their offspring?

In *PL*, Rawls reintroduces the 'constraint principle' as a means of dealing with this problem (244 and 273–4). On the one hand, he rejects as 'fantasy' the type of suggestion put forward by both Manning and Thero that the OP should include representatives from all generations. Yet despite this Rawls acknowledges the inadequacy of hoping that intergenerational justice will be secured by relying on flimsy notions of ties between different generations of the same family. In order to avoid the inevitable confusion that would follow in trying to secure justice between all generations, Rawls maintains a present-time of entry position; that is, parties are to remain as contemporaries. He now adopts a Kantian-inspired 'categorical imperative' in arguing that a contracting generation will adopt a principle (in this case the 'just savings' principle) that they would wish *all previous generations to have followed* (Beckman, 2008: 8). Beckman uses the term *Kantian* here to denote the fact that agreement on a principle of intergenerational justice becomes morally binding, akin to making a promise, and is therefore truly contractualist. The constraint principle is a prerequisite of intergenerational justice, as it provides the foundation of social trust between citizens and restores the mutual disinterest of the parties. It also adjusts the veil of ignorance to preclude the knowledge of the place a citizen's particular cohort holds *within the succession of generations*. Parties will therefore be motivated to agree on a savings principle fearing that they may find themselves, once the veil is lifted, belonging to a generation born into a time when previous generations had set aside little in the way of goods and resources. The overlapping generations model, which Rawls advocated for in *TJ*, is abandoned. Rawls now presents an OP that forces mutually disinterested contemporaries, ignorant of the position their generation holds within the timeline of humanity, to agree to a just savings principle that they would expect all previous generations to have followed.

Despite Rawls's own rejection of the overlapping model, recent scholarly work in this area has sought to reinvigorate elements of his initial stance

50 *Rawls and the Environmental Crisis*

outlined in *TJ* (Heyd, 2009; McCormick, 2009; Wissenburg, 1998, 1999). McCormick (2009) identifies a distinct strength of an overlapping model of intergenerational justice by arguing that although it may be morally objectionable to not care for remote or abstract generations (even if overlapping) it is certainly not unjust. Distributive justice requires both interaction and reciprocity between citizens. Without interaction, there can be no justice, and certainly no duties (McCormick, 2009: 456). In fact, McCormick goes so far as to label altruism as 'unhelpful' within an intergenerational setting. We cannot extend the justice we owe to our immediate descendants infinitely to *all* future human beings. The central premise of McCormick's idea is that 'we feel intuitively that acts or policies of ours that threaten the well-being of future, overlapping generations violate the requirements of justice' (457).

Following on from the above contradiction within *TJ*; namely, that although parties in the OP were to be representative of disinterested, unencumbered individuals but then were expected to care for any potential descendants, Wissenburg draws on the constraint principles as being the key motivational factor contained within Rawls's notion of intergenerational justice that rectifies this problem (Wissenburg, 1999: 175–6). Not only this, but Wissenburg highlights the strength of Rawls's initial overlapping model in asserting that intergenerational justice is not simply 'a system of transfers from one generation to the next' (177). Of course any Rawlsian-inspired savings principle relies on the assumption that a generation possesses an inherent sense of justice, capable of spanning beyond the here and now. Is this a realistic assumption, however, in the face of the possibility of generations freeloading on the back of the prudent saving of previous generations? Does reintroducing Rawls's early overlapping model again rely on an all too flimsy notion of trust? According to Wissenburg, the notion of rationality inherent to Rawls's model prevents the risk of generational defection. Wissenburg explains:

> It is true then that trust plays a crucial role in the new Rawls's justice between generations, but there is no altruism in it, no other-regarding attitude – just self-interest and mutual disinterest . . . Since generations exist as contemporaries, defecting generations impose a cost upon society of which they will have to pay a part: defection destroys the basis of trust on which society was built.
>
> (178)

It would therefore be irrational for a generation to defect from an intergenerational savings principle, as it would only harm itself in the not so distant future.

Wissenburg provides us with the following example to illustrate this point. Say there exists, at one time and in an overlapping fashion, three generations: the lost generation, the baby-boomers, and generation X. If the baby-boomer generation decided to break the contractual obligation by not setting aside goods for the benefit of the next generation (generation X), then the

baby-boomer generation will inevitably suffer when it replaces the lost generation as senior citizens in society. This is because generation X may not have
been bequeathed the adequate resources to look after the older generation it
takes over from, in this case, the baby-boomers. So by defecting from a principle of just savings, a generation not only breaks the bond of trust and the
subsequent capacity for a sense of justice that must exist between generations,
but they also jeopardize their own futures by acting without the necessary
foresight. The just savings principle thus becomes a 'necessary condition of the
just society' and allows us to circumvent the issue of attempting to cater for
both remote and abstract future generations (180). The generational overlap
ensures that *intergenerational* justice follows on from *intragenerational* justice.

The interpretation of Rawls offered so far, with the 'what' of intergenerational justice being the well-ordered society, means that the overlapping
model retains a prominent place in his political liberalism but for reasons that
differ to McCormick's and Wissenburg's analyses. Yet the 'what' increasingly
starts to resemble an outright transpolitical good of intergenerational justice.
Despite the constraint principle reasserting the primary motivation of citizens
projecting justice as fairness to future generations, out of mutual disinterest,
the preservation of the just institutions of a well-ordered society mean that
they are also to be motivated by a higher, transpolitical good that relies on the
motivational force of seeing one's self as part of a wider timeline of human
cooperation, and as having faith in agreement on basic principles of justice.

Remaining questions

So far, and looking back to the three key features of Rawls's OP, green concerns are seemingly relegated to the periphery within justice as fairness. The
limited scope of constitutional essentials and the basic structure of society; the
notion of a freestanding political agreement; and the idea that justice is to be
built on ideas implicit in the public political culture, limit Rawls's own hopes
for a 'natural' inclusion of green concerns within his theory, beyond only a
very light green, shallow instrumentalist theory of environmental justice. In
the process, however, it seems that this is not the end of the road for those
hoping to assign a significantly more enlightened green role to justice as fairness. There are two ways of viewing political liberalism as a theory that takes
green concerns seriously. First, the separation argument is seen to belie what
could only ever be a shallow instrumentalist attitude towards wider nature
or those groups at risk from deteriorating ecological conditions. By treating
green concerns as separate to the fundamentals of political justice, they are
demoted to the non-political public and private spheres. Alternatively, green
political theorists can become Rawlsian in stepping outside of this theory, and
invoking the spirit of political liberalism in domains beyond contemporaneous human justice. Although this still alludes to political liberalism inspiring
a theory of environmental justice that seeks to protect wider nature primarily
for the resources it provides in making human cooperation possible in the first

52 *Rawls and the Environmental Crisis*

place, it seems to be the avenue that Rawls himself hoped would be taken, and the one that he believes to be the most *natural*. Yet an examination of the *who, what,* and *how* of the principle of just savings starts to suggest a much more nuanced theory of intergenerational justice that demands virtues of citizenship more characteristic of stronger green concerns. Consequently, we can now start to trace the move from the shallow to the more enlightened shades of environmental justice present in political liberalism.

The point to make here is that within the green critique several theorists rightly draw upon the principle of just savings in order to flesh out a more coherent Rawlsian theory of environmental justice. A point often overlooked, however, is the tension raised between the *what* and the *who* of the just savings principle. Initially, it seems that the just institutions of a well-ordered society are merely instrumental to the realization of individual liberty, and thus they are the embodiment of liberal values. This picture becomes increasingly blurred, however, by the more conservative implications of the *who* aspect of the principle, and the suggestion that generations are bound by an agreement – and a transpolitical good – that transcends their individual lives. Ensuring that these institutions endure from one generation to the next would seem to commit citizens to acting as trustees, or *stewards*, for the sake of political liberalism's key aim: the ongoing project of political cooperation and agreement in the modern age. This tension means that it is difficult to see the just savings principle as purely an instrumental means to the individual good, as it starts to resemble something much more profound.

From our above overview we are left with the idea that, in *TJ*, Rawls places his own theory at the mercy of a metaphysical conception of the green common good, or at least a vision of how humans are to organize their relationship with wider nature. How we would go about discovering this truth – presumably akin to Platonic philosopher-kings – is another matter. This argument is, at first glance, left behind by the time we reach *PL*, as Rawls now accepts that citizens of a well-ordered society cannot hope to reach a meaningful, stable agreement at such a controversial level of thought. But the most natural means of extending his theory, he argues, retains the bold ambitions of *TJ*. Taking justice as fairness forwards, outwards, and inwards seems to represent an attitude of liberal triumph within the new frontiers of justice.

Developing a meaningful Rawlsian sense of environmental justice also complicates the central conceptual problem of political liberalism. How can it develop an approach thick enough to ensure consensus, and to motivate citizens to potentially sacrifice their own immediate interests, whilst remaining thin enough to be identifiably freestanding? How can holders of darker green concerns buy into such inherent shallow instrumentalism? In Rawls's words, again, it should 'gain free and reasoned agreement in judgment'. In navigating this challenge, a new question emerges, and it is one that is seized upon in the ensuing green critique. According to Rawls, the OP is limited to the basic structure of society and its constitutional essentials. Because the remit of justice as fairness is restricted by its scope, it is by no means disingenuous for

Rawls on green concerns   53

him to argue that it can remain separate from green concerns. The problem is, however, that we arrive at the issue of efficacy and influence, given that the basic structure of society is described as 'pervasive' in his main works. So if it is indeed as influential as Rawls states, then the impartiality – and even indifference – of the basic structure with regards to green concerns could also mean that citizens, within their non-political public and private aspects of associational life, would be encouraged to ignore the plight of non-humans and future generations and make no effort to take it forward, outward, or inward to those at risk from deteriorating ecological conditions. The political, on this reading, sanctions a societal indifference to wider nature, as it is valued only as a provider of resources for the enduring search for justice by humanity. These two questions – the feasibility of a freestanding political agreement and the influence of the basic structure – set the tone for our two-part analysis of the green critique.

Notes

1 A potential problem here, however, is that in attempting to engage only with the sources relating specifically to green concerns, it overlooks the fact that much of Rawls's move to a political liberalism formed a response to leading critics. How is it possible to understand this move without engaging with these sources? There are two responses to this. The first is that Rawls himself recognized the limitations of his earlier *TJ* and sought to reduce the scope of his theory of liberalism so as to make it truly freestanding. As such, Rawls's mature theory offers a rejoinder to these criticisms with little need to consider the catalyst for the changes made. A second response, perhaps more justifiable than the first, is that, as outlined in the previous chapter, Rawls's central aim remained broadly the same throughout his long academic career, and that was to argue for the possibility of political agreement on the fundamentals of justice within deeply diverse societies. So although Rawls altered – and indeed *limited* – the scope of his theory significantly during the 1980s, his main aim of establishing of a stable, well-ordered society built upon a shared consensus of political values endured.
2 Rawls states that his idea of justice as fairness is far from 'procedurally neutral', and it is rather the case that he seeks 'common, or neutral ground' that 'hopes to articulate a public basis of justification for the basic structure of a constitutional regime working from fundamental intuitive ideas implicit in the public political culture and abstracting from comprehensive religious, philosophical, and moral doctrines' (see Rawls, 2001: 154).
3 There is an increasingly diverse body of literature that explores the works of Rawls and the idea of *global justice*, with particular reference to environmental crises and climate change. The subject could soon be worthy of an entirely separate volume on Rawls and green concerns. See, for example, Simon Caney (2005); Stephen Gardiner (2011); Sarah Kenehan (2015); and Stephen Vanderheiden (2008). Again the focus of this particular monograph, however, is on the extension of justice to non-human species and future generations.
4 Having said that, Rawls does rewrite his idea of just savings in §44 of the revised edition of *TJ* (1999) in order to overcome the contradiction between mutual disinterest and a care for one's immediate offspring when considering what we owe to future generations.
5 Rawls is referring here to the basic structure of society that 'can be effectively regulated by relatively simple and clear public principles of justice so as to maintain background justice

over time' so that 'perhaps most things can be left to citizens and associations themselves, provided that they are put in a position to take charge of their own affairs and are able to make fair agreements with one another under social conditions ensuring a suitable degree of equality' (Rawls, 2001: 159). Essentially, Rawls's basic structure is a process of perpetual adjustment of a societal disposition that inevitably results in 'greater inequalities in social status and wealth, and in the ability to exert political influence and to take advantage of available opportunities'.

6 Rawls explains the relationship between the basic structure and background justice as thus: '[t]he basic structure is the background social framework within which the activities of associations and individuals take place. A just basic structure secures what we may call background justice' (Rawls, 2001: 10). For example, the accruing of mass wealth by a few individuals could jeopardize the political liberties of other citizens and prevent the equality of opportunity.

3 A green critique of Rawls

The green critique, as already stated, can be split into two relatively distinct parts. The first is distinguishable from the second by virtue of the fact that it seeks to modify, or update, Rawls's theory for a world now facing deteriorating ecological conditions. The second critique, offered in *Chapter 4*, avoids any such modification in order to make the case that political liberalism embodies a theory of stewardship in and of itself that moves us towards a more enlightened position on environmental justice. Rawls's separation argument; that is, his own reluctant dismissal of green concerns as too controversial for a political agreement by identifying them as existing separately from matters of 'strict justice' and 'constitutional essentials' has led several critics to accuse his theory of being, at best, indifferent to the plight of those at risk from deteriorating environmental conditions and, at worst, serving as an apologist for a more general anti-green attitude within a citizenry, beyond the political. Two weaknesses stand out when conducting an in-depth survey of the first part of the green critique. The first is that there is a lack of conceptual clarity regarding the notion of 'the environmental crisis'. Although widely employed as a summum malum capable of shaking the very foundations of Rawlsian liberalism, the literature examined in Chapters 3 and 4 reflects a plethora of competing and increasingly disjointed notions of environmental and ecological justice. The second is that those who have seized upon Rawls's abstraction of justice between contemporaneous rational humans remain unable to articulate the link between this separation, and the supposed theoretical encouragement of disregarding environmental attitudes amongst a citizenry, beyond the OP. As stated at the end of the previous chapter, the viability of the green critique is dependent upon an assessment of the influence the basic structure is said to have on citizens' attitudes in the non-political public and private spheres. This second weakness means that we are mostly left to infer the answers individual contributors would give if asked why they had sought to green Rawls in the first place. The first part of the critique, as presented here, is broken down into four specific themes: the idea of a third principle of justice; a challenge to the overlapping consensus; the question of non-humans; and finally, freestanding exploitation. The works covered in this chapter relate to Rawls's move (or retreat in the minds of several green political theorists) to a more

56 *Rawls and the Environmental Crisis*

limited political liberalism. Daniel Thero (1995) provided a thorough overview of the literature on *TJ* and emerging notions of the environmental crisis, hence there is little need to add to his impressive analysis of early extensionist efforts immediately after the publication of *TJ*.[1] Having said this, Thero's conclusions are worth revisiting so as to assess any developments in the green critique during the ensuing period. Our enquiry commences in the late 1980s, by which time it was clear that Rawls's political thought was changing. The salient feature of the green critique discussed in the sections that follow, is that, to date, a consensus emerges stipulating that Rawls's mature work can only take liberal theory so far in addressing the gravest environmental threats. The key aim is to get these individual pieces working together for the first time, and as a continuous dialogue, so as piece together a potentially self-contained critique built on an analysis of the separation argument and the influence of the basic structure.

A third principle of justice?

Could Rawls's theory of justice benefit from a *third* principle of justice? Given the rapidly changing environmental circumstances of justice, Wouter Achterberg (1993) argues that if a 'structural solution' to the supposed environmental crisis is to be found, how can the sanctity of 'neutrality', 'acquired rights', 'established interests', and 'deep-rooted lifestyles' that comprise the modern liberal democratic order be challenged (82)? Put slightly differently, how can we legitimize infringements of established liberal values, concomitant with the modern period, in the name of environmental crises? This, of course, is a highly generalized framing of a wider discord between a liberal notion of individual freedom and the limits imposed by green concerns on unrestricted consumption and growth. Theorists are engaged in what he calls the 'alteration' or 'supplementation' of Rawls's increasingly *political* liberalism (Achterberg incorporates Rawls's papers from the late 1980s) because the idea of an overlapping consensus represents 'a theoretical elaboration' of the aforementioned liberal norms that are to be curtailed (81). Drawing on his own earlier theories on the value of nature, Achterberg proposes that a structurally sound theory of environmental justice would not only 'preserve nature as a basis of our social activities for generations to come (sustainability of our use of the environment)', but would at the same time involve 'protecting, maintaining and developing nature for its own sake (sustainability of nature)' (see also Achterberg, 1990: 80–1). Achterberg is therefore keen to green Rawlsian liberalism internally via a 'modification', 'alteration', or 'supplementation' of justice as fairness in recognition of liberal societies having reached a 'turning' point (1993: 95). A prerequisite of Rawls's circumstances of justice is that parties in the OP deliberate against a backdrop of favourable material circumstances. The predominant circumstance is 'the fact of moderate scarcity', a fact that has had to undergo significant reappraisal. In Achterberg's words: '[i]f there were only one thing we could learn from the environmental crisis it is that it is doubtful whether scarcity is that moderate, particularly in the long run, and certainly, if, in spite of population growth, a fair international distribution of wealth or resources is pursued' (95). Simply put, deteriorating environmental conditions deplete the material resources available for distribution, and force a fundamental reconsideration of theories of justice.

The environmental crisis, then, is a human crisis, and so Achterberg's modification proceeds as thus: 'There is reason enough . . . from the perspective of Rawls's own conception, to consider how the overlapping consensus can be supplemented with new elements in order to enlarge the durability of this consensus itself *and thus of liberal democracy as well'* (ibid. emphasis added). Before exploring the implications of this statement (for liberal democracy, that is), it is worth noting Achterberg's proposal for a supplementary third principle of justice; namely, a 'transmission' principle drawn principally from the work of Richard Routley and Val Routley (1982).[2] This new principle acts as a final check on Rawls's first two principles of justice but, more important, it appears lexically prior to both a compatible scheme of liberties for all *and* the difference principle. Or, in Achterberg's words: 'the application of the two principles of justification depends on the condition that the third principle can be complied with' as it is 'an intergenerational principle of equal opportunities' (Achterberg, 1993: 96–97). Although thin on details, the main thrust of the principle is that contemporary generations are not to leave the world in a worse-off state to their successors. Equality of intergenerational opportunities is a seemingly natural extension of equality of opportunity between contemporaries but a crucial break is made in abandoning the need for reciprocity. Drawing on the Dutch Constitution, Achterberg reiterates an appreciation of wider nature due to its 'self-standingness', where wider nature 'deserves' the opportunity to be left to flourish (97). There is no reciprocity here, no mutual tradeoff: the scope of justice is expanded to include entities beyond those who are reasonable. Wider nature's intrinsic value therefore stems from its self-standingness, and its independence.

Based on the new circumstances of justice (the unsustainability of our liberal, 'deep-rooted lifestyles'), Achterberg embarks on three-stage 'controlled modification of Rawls's argumentation for his two principles' (99). The first is, again, that the criterion for reciprocity between parties within (and beyond) the OP is dropped in a move that leads him to question whether or not 'Rawls himself could agree with this modification' (97). This is a tricky argument, not least because the reasons for the change are to incorporate what could be an overtly doctrinal vision of darker green, ecological justice (the 'flourishing', 'self-standingness' of nature). By removing reciprocity and expanding the scope of justice, citizens are asked to agree upon a controversial doctrinal ecologism. This is incompatible with the central aim of political liberalism generally, Rawlsian or otherwise, and its search for a 'consensus through reduction' (Forst, 2004: ix). The second stage signifies Achterberg's own rebuttal of this particular criticism as he invokes the process of 'reflective equilibrium' and the popularity of sustainable development in the Netherlands. Not only is an overlapping consensus a foremost feature of liberal democracy in that

58 *Rawls and the Environmental Crisis*

particular country, but also there is consensus, too, on the need to allow wider nature to flourish (as set out in Dutch legislation) born out of what Achterberg describes as 'enlightened' anthropocentricism. Just as Rawls's mature political thought would seek consensus on principles latent in the public political culture, a third principle of 'transmission' would reflect beliefs already held in Western societies on the necessity of initiatives and legislation to promote greater sustainability. A principle of intergenerational equality of opportunities is a political manifestation of these reflective, considered judgements.

Yet if political justice is to be 'greened' in this way, then something quite different is asked of a liberal citizen of a well-ordered society, as they have to buy in to Achterberg's faith in a darker, 'thicker', green conception of the good. Looking at it slightly differently, they are led to discover an ecological truth, or dualism, whereby wider nature can exist both independently and indifferently, to human activity. Despite Achterberg's hope that the politicization of sustainable development is 'able to fulfill the function which Rawls ascribes to a political conception of justice: the enhancement of social unity and the stability of pluralistic society over generations' (99), it does start to move us further away from the key tenets of justice as fairness. The third principle does not follow the first two coherently. In fact, it disrupts the lexical ordering of the two principles of justice and 'corrects the effects of the other two in such a way that the basic possibility of sustainable development is secured' (96). So the principle of transmission appears to come first, outweighing the other two. If not first, then it is certainly a new layer of accountability more than capable of putting the breaks on the first two principles should they violate Achterberg's new theory of environmental, or rather, *ecological* justice. Ultimately, and due to the fact that Achterberg wrote this just before the publication of *PL*, Rawls would take a different route with his constraint principle, and avoid any direct appeal to darker green, more comprehensive concerns.

If the separation argument is to be overcome by acknowledging the new circumstances of justice, and modifying the OP by adding an intergenerational principle of equality reflecting intuitive, green concerns already accepted in the public political culture, then this has meant introducing a controversial ecological comprehensive doctrine via the back door. This could well compromise the freestanding nature of justice as fairness. Achterberg, therefore, applies an external test to justice as fairness in the form of a much darker green ethic, rooted in the idea of nature as freestanding. Recall from the last chapter the balance between the three key features of Rawls's political conception of justice: it is to be limited to the basic structure; it is freestanding; and it is built upon ideas implicit in the public political culture. Achterberg's attention on the latent ideas of a polity comes at the expense of the limited and freestanding nature of the OP. Yet his recognition of the changing circumstances of justice is the guiding principle of the green critique as a means of doing away with the separation argument. As demonstrated with Achterberg's critique, however, the changing circumstances of justice usually imply a very anthropocentric notion of a crisis, and one that is in tension with the move to a darker green ethic, even one which he himself believes to be implicit in the background culture. Rawls appears more hopeful that the issues raised by green concerns can be left to the 'vote', beyond the domain of an overlapping consensus.

Simon Hailwood (2004, 2005, 2006) adopts a similar attitude to Achterberg in looking to the idea of nature's 'self-standingness', but one that does *not* start from intuitive ideas already present in the public sphere. Hailwood refutes the idea that Rawls's political liberalism already embodies only a weak green, instrumentalist, and exploitive conception of environmental justice. The key to reconciling justice as fairness and green concerns, according to Hailwood, is to recognize the 'analogous' relationship between a freestanding conception of political liberalism and the 'independence' of wider nature, concluding that 'a certain continuity of reasonableness is there' (2004: 16). In doing so, however, Hailwood claims to avoid the more ambitious assertion in *TJ* (and *PL*) that human justice will be reflective of a wider theory of humanity's place in the world. Yet two questions are left unanswered by Hailwood: first, the problem of citizenship duties and, second, by describing the link between political liberalism and nature's 'otherness' as being 'analogous', the theory is in danger of remaining largely suggestive. On this last point this is not a problem *per se*, but it does mean that Hailwood's theory remains speculative and at risk of falling into a methodological impasse characteristic of the green critique; namely, that his 'test' for political liberalism is just as arbitrary as Achterberg's darker green theory of ecological justice. These two points are covered in more detail in Chapter 4 when the wider context of Hailwood's thought is discussed, but for now the focus will be on the claim that the separation argument can be overcome without resorting solely to the declaration in *TJ* that human justice 'cannot be too far wrong' regarding the metaphysical conception of 'broader relationships' between humanity and wider nature (*TJ*: 448–9).

Hailwood begins with the idea that nature should be valued as an external, reasonable, and liberal public commitment – or what we might think of as a third principle of justice – owing to an appreciation of nature's 'otherness'. Drawing on the work of John Passmore, Hailwood identifies wider nature's 'strangeness' and 'independence' as part of the reasons why it exists as something that 'we can't fully master' or 'humanize' (Hailwood, 2004: 16–18). In order to transcend 'anthropocentric narrowness' (and thus shallowness) and the idea of nature as a resource (instrumentalism), a liberal society must recognize the 'independence' of nature – an independence that is 'indifferent' to human interests (18). Although humans have always 'landscaped' nature by identifying it as part of the human landscape, natural features and entities must be respected as possessing some form of intrinsic value but by virtue of their otherness – and indifference to – the value humans place upon them (24). Acknowledging nature's otherness, he argues, amounts to neither an environmentalism nor an ecologism, and instead retains the spirit of a freestanding conception of justice. Hailwood is confident that such a view can

60 *Rawls and the Environmental Crisis*

accommodate both light and dark green concerns, as Rawls himself hoped would be the case for his political liberalism.

For Hailwood, naturalness can be defined as 'an origin and capacity for continued existence independent of humanity', yet it is 'not intended as *proof* that nature has non-instrumental value' (2006: 174, emphasis in original). By 'independent', Hailwood states that humans must respect 'the reality of nature as other . . . independent of landscape' (176) and move beyond the narrow confines of specifically human landscaping. He defines a landscape as 'the shape of local nature as modified by culture' (2004: 24), with nature, therefore, being entangled within human valuation: 'independent nature should not be identified with the significances attributed to it within local cultural landscape' (56). He thus claims that his theory of valuing nature's 'otherness confers extrinsic, non-instrumental value' and is thus not as dark green as Achterberg's notion of intrinsic value (47). Such a theory depends on a specific observation regarding the pure, subjective valuation of nature insomuch as humans only value certain species at certain times (for example, protecting individual animals during, say, a hunting season), and as a result the subjective value of nature is merely 'fragile' and 'contemporary' (48). It is temporal-spatial and exists only briefly, at a specific time, with humans fleetingly 'injecting' intrinsic value into elements of wider nature.

The idea of nature as autonomous, however, stipulates the possibility that a liberal society can focus less 'on cultural landscaping and instrumentalism', and instead view nature from a new position of 'appropriate objectivity' (51–3). This kind of objectivity is deemed appropriate by Hailwood because it states that a new 'outlook' – with the individual 'detaching from the contingencies of the self' – does not amount to an acceptance of a supernatural, metaphysical being. In summary, Hailwood presents the case that nature exists indifferently to – and independently of – both human valuation and action. Humans subjectively, and sporadically, value non-human species and natural processes but such a fleeting view does not account for the worth of their ongoing existence, independent of such intervention. Crucially, this approach does not rely on controversial, darker green theories of value.

Apropos the specifics of the separation argument, Hailwood is cautious not to exacerbate the exclusion of green concerns from strict justice: 'to assert that one should respect the otherness of nature, and so not simply identify the non-human with human values and purposes, is to preach alienation from nature, a listless disengagement from the wider world' (90). For Hailwood, 'the political cannot be completely isolated in every sense from the private', adding that the political also acts 'as a constraint on the pursuit of conceptions of the good' (ibid). Let us take stock here for a moment. Assuming 'the otherness view may be incorporated within liberal theory without undermining its self-understanding as politically reasonable', as Hailwood claims it can, then we arrive at the conclusion that there is nothing in Rawls's political liberalism that excludes, isolates, or perpetuates a disregarding attitude towards green concerns. But surely the argument here must go further than the 'analogous'

A green critique of Rawls 61

and the suggestive? The influence of the political sphere, and here Hailwood means the basic structure of society, is indeed pervasive by serving as a reasonable constraint on the preferences and aims of rational citizens. The fact that he argues the political will remain persuasive challenges the feasibility of Rawls's own separation, or 'exclusion' as Hailwood calls it, of human justice from a theory of environmental or ecological justice. The fact is that it is one view of otherness, and still external to Rawlsian political thought. The next chapter will see a return to Hailwood's ideas but will argue instead that if justice as fairness is to progress beyond a very weak green position, then a deeper examination of his account of wider nature as other is required.

For now, Hailwood's notion of nature as independent initially leads him to propose, like Achterberg, a third principle of justice. Although Hailwood avoids this term, as he prefers to see it as a 'liberal public commitment', the positioning of nature as other relative to justice as fairness seems to be one of separateness. Hailwood elaborates: 'The otherness view is available for incorporation; it is not excluded by the political liberal strategy with respect to the internal or subjective circumstances of justice – it is continuous with it' (2004: 117). There is a sense here that Hailwood, again like Achterberg, believes Rawls to have been mistaken in believing that his theory of justice could not be extended in a natural way. Indeed all of the thinkers covered in this chapter seek to develop justice as fairness in a continuous fashion, for better or worse, but both Achterberg and Hailwood argue that a third principle of environmental justice is to be found at the end of the extensionist process.

The problem we encounter here, though, is that Hailwood's primary aim of developing an approach to green concerns that is analogous to the freestandingness of political liberalism is at odds with Achterberg's claim that his third principle is to be found latent in the public–political sphere. Hailwood's focus on the freestanding element of the OP comes at the expense of a need to develop a third principle of Rawlsian justice that is built on ideas implicit in the public culture of a democratic society. Hailwood's valuation of nature as independent is perhaps too philosophical – too abstract, even – to be considered as an idea widely shared amongst a citizenry, not least because it serves as a darker green theory of environmental justice that is non-hostile to ecological justice. Hailwood departs from Rawls's idea than an instrumentalist theory of environmental justice would be the most reasonable within a citizenry, even by those holding darker green theories of ecological justice. Hailwood therefore seemingly seeks a modification of justice as fairness. Not only this, but Hailwood's explicit unease that the basic structure of society is much more pervasive than Rawls himself admits, insinuates that he is seeking to correct political liberalism rather than present a theory of environmental or ecological justice that complements – or at least supplements – justice as fairness. Casting nature as 'other' as a liberal public commitment, despite promising first impressions, still serves as an external test for political liberalism. What is clear, however, is that the concept of a third principle of justice involves a series of tradeoffs rendering a significant departure from Rawls's own stated aims as inevitable.

62 *Rawls and the Environmental Crisis*

A light green, interim ethic?

Daniel Thero (1995) expresses no interest in developing a third principle of justice, suggesting instead that there is 'something fundamentally misguided about Rawls's entire project' (105). He continues that: 'it seems not only confusing, but also inconsistent and contrived to claim that our duties to animals and to nature in general are based on some metaphysical conception of the world' yet the demands of strict justice are free of 'such metaphysical considerations', relying instead 'on original position psychology' (103). What Thero does point out is that the inherent anthropocentrism of disinterested parties in the OP prevents extensionism as there are simply no checks and balances on humans, paving the way for them to commit environmental injustices in cases of conflicting human and non-human interests. We see in Thero's work the indictment that the remoteness and abstraction of strict justice from a wider concern for the plight of non-humans, and non-contemporaries, emulates a much shallower instrumentalist disposition towards the vulnerable at risk from environmental degradation than Rawls admits. The separation argument is seen as tantamount to the tacit political consent of tangible environmental injustices, and so the light green theory espoused is seen by Thero to be wholly unsuited for the task at hand.

Thero adopts a doctrinal standpoint based not only on the view that the political is secondary to the search for a wider theory of sustainability, but also on a predetermined concept of environmental *injustice* – a concept that leads him to conclude that Rawls's theory 'lacks the potential to serve as a grounding for a fully developed and *comprehensive* environmental ethic' (106, emphasis added). Although Thero believes his early account of contractarianism can serve as a short-term, 'aid to decision making', it is but a sideshow to a 'philosophical discourse (that) proceeds in its nascent quest to piece together a more encompassing theoretical framework for environmental philosophy'. It is then, for Thero, akin to Dobson's characterization of a 'second-division' political theory. His analysis ends with a non-rhetorical question: 'if contractarianism is unsuitable as the basis for a long-term environmental ethic, is it, in fact, legitimate to employ it as the basis for a short-term interim ethic?' The suggestion is non-rhetorical here because it engages directly with the final moments of *TJ*. Recall that Rawls stated if justice as fairness were on the right philosophical track, so to speak, it would mirror an appropriate metaphysical ordering of humans within wider nature. Thero's response is that a theory of justice constructed on a principle of psychological, mutual disinterest lacks the human virtues necessary for the inculcation of environmentally sensitive attitudes within a given citizenry.

Thero's criticism of the lack of virtue present in Rawlsian liberalism will be reviewed in the concluding chapter. For now, however, the most striking feature of his account is that the proclamation that the 'nascent quest' for an environmental philosophy suggests a doctrinal faith in a revelation, or a discovery, of a true configuration of humanity's relationship to wider nature. Thus, Thero argues, 'further theoretical inquiry concerning the metaphysics of nature may pay off down the road a bit'. If the criticism that Rawls separates the metaphysical search for a true conception of human and non-human relations from the purely psychological OP is to hold firm, then Thero must propose at least a potential means of discovering a true environmental philosophy that proves Rawls's own notion that 'it seems reasonable that if it is sound as an account of justice among persons, it cannot be too far wrong' (*TJ*: 449). Thero, then, takes on Rawls at his own metaphysical game by arguing that contractarianism founded on mutual disinterest will *not* reflect the true, and discoverable, ordering of humanity within wider nature. Thero's implied holism is just that: implied. A much more substantive 'nascent quest' must be outlined if it is to discredit justice as fairness – and contemporaneous contractarianism more generally – as being unrepresentative of a correct metaphysical configuration of associations between humans and wider nature. This, of course, applies also to Rawls if he is to place his theory at the mercy of metaphysics. Even an initial framework for discovery is missing. Having said this, Thero does claim that a social contract theory could serve as an interim guide, or as a means of mediating between conflicts of interests between human and non-humans, whilst we move towards a deeper understanding of the world. This in itself is both a timely and accurate conclusion that captures the essence of the first part of the green critique; namely, that Rawls can take us only so far towards a more robust theory of environmental or ecological justice. Not only this, but neither Thero and Rawls, who arrive at the same methodological point, seem unwilling to offer how such a 'nascent quest' is to proceed.

This second challenge becomes more pronounced once we look to Rawls's later works if we focus on Thero's search for a 'comprehensive environmental ethic'. In testing Rawls's political thought against such comprehensive and doctrinal environmental truths, then the game is again fixed. The freestanding nature of political liberalism meant that its very aim was to avoid establishing principles of justice premised on comprehensive ideals. To then pitch his theory against the search for a said ethic, if taken as true or correct, is to naturally set him up to fail. Not only this, but the OP is primarily philosophical and not psychological. In conclusion, Thero's piece is perhaps too ambitious in scope. Not only is it unable to establish a framework directing the 'nascent quest' for a metaphysical conception of humanity's place within wider nature, especially for when environmental injustices are committed, but it also assumes that the link between the separation argument and a neglect of environmental injustice is watertight. Thero's argument is intuitive only in arguing that a discovery of the 'truth' will one day render Rawls's mutual disinterest as irrelevant.

Beyond Thero's acceptance of the short-term usefulness of Rawlsian liberalism, even the more optimistic contributors to the green critique envisage only a limited role for *PL* within the discourse of green concerns. Yet such contributions offer a noteworthy defence of Rawls against accusations that justice as fairness is representative of an environmentally destructive attitude towards green concerns, masked by only a shallow instrumentalist theory of environmental justice.

64   *Rawls and the Environmental Crisis*

Derek Bell (2002, 2004a, 2004b, 2006) believes Rawls's theory is incorrectly implicated as the source of an ecological, or environmental, crisis, but – as we have already seen – is one of the few green political theorists to provide a more systematic approach to the extension of Rawlsian liberalism to the new frontiers of justice and the plight of those at risk from deteriorating environmental conditions. Rather than engaging with a meta-narrative of modernity, Bell identifies Rawls as offering a mainstream and coherent system of liberal justice that is perfectly placed for 'greening' (2006: 207). In fact, Bell offers more of an open-ended theoretical exploration of Rawls's work maintaining: 'political liberalism is *prima facie* a plausible political theory for contemporary democratic societies to see what we can learn about both political liberalism and environmental education' so that we 'may develop interesting insights' (37–8). Extensionist scholarship, then, can be seen as an arena for teasing out how green liberals can justify the widespread incorporation of green concerns into modern societies. Rawls's theory, on this reading, becomes a philosophical playground – a testing ground for understanding how these debates play out in abstraction. Bell is also sensitive to the competing versions of environmental or ecological justice at work in this field of research.

Bell's overall approach to the extension of justice as fairness is to examine any *indirect* benefits the idea of justice as fairness may have to wider nature so as to mount a defence of the separation argument. Bell considers the implications for non-humans, future generations, and environmental refugees that would come about from a deeper, more ecological, understanding of justice as fairness. There is little in the way of modification, and Bell adopts the method Rawls himself adheres to when extending political liberalism to the areas of health care and international law. Bell's environmental political thought, it could be argued, does not actually involve extensionism in that it is more interested in inferring the indirect green credentials of political liberalism. His ideas could be criticized, although unfairly, for treating any green outcomes of Rawls's theory as a mere bonus or as a fortuitous side effect of contemporaneous human justice.

It is again the very timing of the application of Rawls's theory in incorporating green concerns that is crucial to understanding Bell's method. In effect, he is exploring the implications of Rawls's own hopes for post-OP deliberation. Insofar as he rejects Rawlsian liberalism as a form of 'intrinsically green liberalism', he does conclude that it can reveal itself to be a 'contingently green liberalism' (Bell, 2002: 721). His central argument is that justice as fairness can accommodate both light green versions of environmental justice (and theories that we would identify as belonging to the environmental justice movement) *and* theories of ecological justice within democratic deliberations. Bell, like Rawls, places green concerns within the realm of the non-political public, and the private, and not the *political*. First principles are not modified and, unlike Achterberg and Hailwood, no new principles are added. If comprehensive views, including darker green theories of ecological justice, can win out at a policy or legislative stage of deliberation, then there is no requirement, according to Bell, to reconstruct the OP. From this, Bell now has to make a serious case for the exoneration of political liberalism from the accusation that it perpetuates unsustainable lifestyles. He therefore has to defend the view that if Rawls's theory was adopted as a normative guide for society – if Rawls was done 'properly', so to speak – then green concerns are not excluded from the post-OP setting and, consequently, the separation argument need not imply a blatant disregard for such views.

To assess this indirect influence, and as outlined in the previous chapter, Bell argues that any substantive theory of environmental justice, Rawlsian or otherwise, can be divided into three straightforward sections: *who*, *what*, and *how* (2004a: 290–3). To elaborate, Bell stipulates that a given society, taking into consideration the needs of future generations, must deliberate on which persons or groups are to be the subject of justice; which goods (or 'bads') are to be distributed; and, finally, upon which principle(s) of justice such distribution is to adhere. As will become clear, the application of this framework to Rawls's principle of just savings, as it was presented in the previous chapter, differs considerably from Bell's own interpretation.

Armed with this framework, Bell sets to work on the key theoretical impasse, in much the same way as Achterberg does, in asking the general question as to how a liberal state can enact policies or initiatives based on eco-centric principles (Bell, 2006: 2) whilst remaining mindful of the 'fact of oppression'. As ever, Rawls's claim that his political liberalism is to be freestanding means that it cannot justify imposing a moral or metaphysical doctrine upon individuals via the just institutions. At an individual level, the reasonable citizen will also appreciate 'the burdens of judgement' in that they will respect the fact that no matter how impartial they may consider themselves to be, their self-authorship of the good life results in a purely personal preference (*PL*: 54). Rawlsian political liberalism cannot endorse a green 'common good' via a concept of ecological justice. This is because, in Rawls's own words, a 'well-ordered constitutional democracy' is to be 'understood also as a deliberative democracy' and so 'when citizens deliberate, they exchange views and debate their supporting reasons concerning public political questions' (1999c: 139).[3] The engine needed to drive green concerns to the forefront of the political, above the level of individual preference, is the idea of an all-encompassing, value-neutral environmental crisis.

Yet rather than having to modify Rawls's theory, there are, Bell believes, two aspects of political liberalism that suggest an accommodation – or an *absorption* – of stronger visions of ecological justice, and accompanying notions of a much more profound ecological crisis. The first is that, because it is freestanding, Rawls's political liberalism allows for a range of comprehensive doctrines to support an OC for reasons specific to each doctrine (*PL*: 10–12). There is no reason for Rawls's political liberalism to deny environmentalisms and ecologisms equal status within an overlapping consensus. Indeed Rawls

66 *Rawls and the Environmental Crisis*

comes to the conclusion that although fundamental justice must be achieved within the basic structure of society first, he points out that:

> political liberalism with its idea of public reason does not rule out as a reason the beauty of nature as such or the good of wildlife achieved by protecting its habitat. With the constitutional essentials in place, these matters may appropriately be put to a vote.
>
> (2001: 152 fn.26)

Environmental and ecological arguments can therefore *be put to a vote* and achieve ascendancy as a result of the democratic, deliberative process within a post-OP liberal polity. Here Bell fundamentally disagrees with the automatic dismissal of the separation argument formulated on the idea that is necessarily hostile to green concerns, and the insinuation that the setup of the OP dictates the terms of debate beyond the political sphere. Also, if Rawls's political liberalism is to be seen as a cover for a very shallow instrumentalist light green system of environmental justice, it is no more anthropocentric than most mainstream versions of ecologism, in Bell's view. Even ecologists themselves, in a Rawlsian sense, would reject moderate dark green theories of ecological justice that deem it unreasonable to allow *all* forms of life to flourish equally, for example, to allow deadly viruses to spread at the expense of human health.

Returning to the first avenue of thought, that a freestanding political liberalism can accommodate both environmentalisms and ecologisms, we start to see the elucidation of a central conceptual problem within the green critique, especially by those more sympathetic to justice as fairness. Is Bell being too optimistic when it comes to placing faith in citizens' post-OP deliberations, beyond the reach of strict justice? This approach is in danger of leaving little more than a 'get-out-clause' for liberalism; that is, if members of a liberal society fail to embrace a view of environmental or ecological justice, it is the fault of the citizens themselves, and not of the liberal theory underpinning such a polity. Bell, however, makes an important point: the onus lies with citizens themselves to change unsustainable patterns of behaviour. Yet what he seems to be suggesting here is that what citizens decide to do beyond establishing first principles of justice is firmly beyond the workings of the basic structure of a well-ordered society.

Again, we soon arrive at the challenge outlined at the end of the previous chapter, and one much overlooked by the green critique: just how pervasive would the basic structure be in post-OP, public-political; non-political public, and private deliberations surrounding environmental or ecological justice? The abstraction of human justice from wider environmental or ecological justice, and considering only the indirect effects of such separation, does not quite tie in with Rawls's own views. He himself states that the basic structure is targeted in the first place because of the influence it has on the direction of citizens' lives. To further defend the separation argument, however, Bell explains what makes a green concern, or a theory of environmental justice, reasonable, and thus able to form part of the overlapping consensus alongside other doctrines. Put another way, how can an eco-centric view be *politicized* so as to conform to

Rawls's idea of 'public reason', and thus form part of an overlapping consensus, when considering the fourth problem of extension outlined by Rawls – the 'claims of animals and the rest of nature' (*PL*: 245)? Rawls, when using the example of how a citizen might make the case for what he calls a 'traditional Christian ages' doctrinal view of green concerns – or what we may recognize as a traditional ethic of religious stewardship denoting humanity's duties to God in line with a great chain of being – states:

> There are numerous political values here to invoke: to further the good of ourselves and future generations by preserving the natural order and its life-sustaining properties; to foster species of animals and plants for the sake of biological and medical knowledge with its potential application to human health; to protect the beauties of nature for purposes of public recreation and the pleasures of a deeper understanding of the world. The appeal to values of this kind gives what many have found a reasonable answer to the status of animals and the rest of nature.
>
> (*PL*: 245–6)

Initially, it appears that the politicization of comprehensive green views is an exercise in sanitization, and strengthens the idea that am overlapping consensus embodies the key tenets of a light green, shallow instrumentalist view of environmental justice. Controversial, doctrinal views are toned down to suit an audience of reasonable and *political* persons, thus making them acceptable to most positions within the continuum of green concerns. 'The reasonable', then, is synonymous with 'the reductivist-instrumental'. The first *political* value, 'preserving the natural order and its life-sustaining properties' for the sake of human flourishing, relates to the argument that any society must live sustainability within its surrounding ecosystems in order to preserve human life whether that society is liberal, socialist, theocratic, or otherwise. Implementing basic green policies that preserve earth's 'life-sustaining properties' in the interests of human health is a logical and necessary action to take for any state, regardless of the political principles (or lack thereof) that govern its main institutions. The second point in the above text is again, a straightforwardly instrumentalist position: 'to foster species of animals and plants for the sake of . . . human health' again values non-human species in terms of their use-value to humans only. Such values are both acceptable to most citizens and can be supported by holders of reasonable comprehensive doctrines as it would be hard to reject the fact that a community of justice must implement light green concerns as a minimal commitment to preserving nature. The first half of the third point: 'to protect the beauties of nature for purposes of public recreation' is again, a straightforwardly instrumentalist position to take.

At this point, we run into a contradiction within Rawls's example of the politicization of green concerns. Bell highlights the controversial nature of the second half of the third point made by Rawls that we are 'to protect the beauties of nature for the purposes . . . of a deeper understanding of the world' (2002: 705). Bell states that free and equal citizens within Rawls's fair system

68 *Rawls and the Environmental Crisis*

of cooperation are not required to be so 'philosophical', and, consequently, this is *not* a political value acceptable to all reasonable citizens.[4] To clarify his argument, a citizen can justifiably maintain a light green public–political instrumentalist position as well as hold both a non-political public and private comprehensive doctrine that promotes what Rawls labels as a 'natural religion' ecologism. Yet such citizens cannot reasonably be expected to use nature as some form of 'blueprint', or rather an ideal guide as to how they and their societies should correctly function. Rather than seeing this as the 'sneaking in' of darker green concerns, there is the argument that free and equal citizens must be informed and educated as to the political values of society in order to become fully cooperating, free and equal citizens of a well-ordered society (Rawls, 2001: 156). Having said this, it remains unclear as to why Rawls states that this is a political value when he does not mention it elsewhere, including in his discussion of the two types of political values, with the first kind being the values of 'political justice' (including the principles of freedom and equality and the equality of opportunity etc.) and the second kind being that of 'the values of public reason' ('the guidelines for public inquiry' ensuring fair deliberation': 91). So it could be the case that Rawls is simply wrong and Bell is right: that to 'protect the beauty of nature for the purposes . . . of a deeper understanding of the world' is too controversial to be deemed a political value. Further, Rawls himself informs us that: 'it is unreasonable that any citizens, or citizens as members of an association . . . to insist on using the public's (coercive) political power – the power of citizens as equals – to impose what they view as the implications of that doctrine upon other citizens' (184).

One response to this is to state Rawls is only wrong in the ordering of the values he invokes in this passage. The third political value relating to the fostering of a 'deeper understanding of the world' could be a prerequisite to the previous two political values (furthering the good of ourselves and future generations and improving human health, respectively). This is in line with darker green concerns: humanity must learn to develop a more symbiotic attitude towards wider nature so as to fully understand how best to live sustainably within wider ecosystems. This would be akin to the aims of *TJ*, and what Thero would call the 'nascent quest' for a metaphysical conception of relations between humans and wider nature. A somewhat tenuous link, but a connection nonetheless missed by Bell with regards to the search for a correct configuration of humanity's place in the world, mentioned elsewhere in Rawls's thought. It may, of course, be that this is just a clumsily stated instrumentalist argument. If this is indeed the case, then a 'deeper understanding' of Rawls would mean appreciating the uncontroversial capacity of ecosystems to support life on this planet. Again, does this add to the idea that political liberalism embodies a light green, shallow instrumentalist doctrine whereby a 'deeper understanding' of the workings of wider nature materially benefits humanity, and carries no metaphysical connotations? If so, then Bell may struggle to substantiate the claim that the political is inclusive of darker green theories of ecological justice.

The second element of Bell's work looks to the work of Palmer and Neal (1994), who argue for a 'radical transformation of the attitudes, preferences and lifestyles of the citizens of contemporary liberal societies' (Bell, 2004c: 38). Through the sub-discipline of environmental citizenship education, Bell then explores the compatibility of freestanding liberal views on citizenship with a 'justice-based', 'universal', and 'compulsory' curriculum of environmental, or ecological, citizenship. Does citizenship education offer a site of reconciliation between theories of darker green, ecological justice and the notion of a freestanding political sphere? Rawls's idea is that both state and non-state education should prepare citizens 'to be fully co-operating members of society' and further, 'should also encourage the political virtues so that they want to honor the fair terms of social co-operation' (Rawls, 2001: 39). In this much less abstract area of contemporary political philosophy, can environmental, or ecological, citizenship education remain non-comprehensive, yet at the same time commit justice as fairness to a stronger theory of environmental justice? What does this tell us about the influence of the basic structure on non-political (but political–public, public, and private) institutions that will be responsible for the implementation this education?

First, Bell must distinguish a non-comprehensive theory of environmental citizenship from a more eco-centric position. Bell himself is resigned to the fact that 'accounts of environmental education tend to be ambiguous between "environmentalism" and "ecologism" – although, the underlying idea may be closer to environmentalism' (2004c: 51). Yet the commitment to a very limited, impartial, and universal environmental citizenship remains difficult, and will no doubt struggle to avoid charges of doctrinal ecologism. Take, for example, Bell's thoughts on the need for an element of 'critical thought' within such a curriculum – an element that sees citizens 'motivated to play their part . . . by participating in discussions and decisions about the limits that should be placed on what the current generation does to the environment' (47). This returns us not only to the pervasiveness, and influence, of Rawls's basic structure on the background culture of society and post-OP political, public, and private deliberations, but also to the much broader question as to the ability of liberal polities to implement green policies. But green education, with its commitment to the inculcation of 'critical' environmental citizens is liable to being hijacked. Environmental citizenship, despite Bell's conclusion that it leans more to environmental than to ecological theories of justice, it could be argued, cannot be anything other than eco-centric. Not only are such citizens expected to be critical of the global order that perpetuates perceived environmental crises, but they are also to be pioneers of a new transformational, ethical, and thus *comprehensive* process leading partly to the creation of new individuals. In the name of citizenship education, the basic structure could become something much more persuasive in impressing a darker green ecological conscience upon unsuspecting citizens. So although Bell sees no need for citizens to be so philosophical in adhering to the overlapping consensus, he does suggest that they will need to be critical.

70 *Rawls and the Environmental Crisis*

Encompassing both of Bell's ideas is his idea in the inherent intergenerational qualities of a theory that looks to posterity regardless of a notion of impending ecological ruin. Justice is transgenerational for Rawls, so Bell argues, in that it takes seriously 'sustainability' rather than more contentious ideas of 'sustainable development' (46). The commitment to equality and fairness within Rawls's political liberalism could again indirectly incorporate a concern for non-human species. Just as the non-rational are protected by the rational, so, too, are the 'least advantaged' (who are 'not identifiable apart from, or independently of, their income and wealth') in society via the difference principle. The difference principle, in Rawls's own words, 'expresses, as any principle of political justice must, a concern for all members of society' (2001: 71). Bell believes that the difference principle, in taking justice as fairness 'inwards', by its own definition provides a 'theoretical framework for assessing environmental justice claims' and thus, no extension of political liberalism to non-humans is required (2004a: 288). The principle states that inequalities in society are justified so long as they are to the 'greatest benefit of the least advantaged' and, as such, 'we are to compare schemes of cooperation by seeing how well off the least advantaged are under each scheme' (Rawls, 2001: 59). A system of justice then has to select the most appropriate scheme in the interests of the least advantaged. The 'advantage' is measured in terms of the primary goods (again, the all-purpose means of developing the two moral powers) a citizen possesses which are secured by the principles of justice. Of course the difference principle provides a 'natural focal point' for the competing notions of 'efficiency' and 'equality' (Bell, 2004a: 296). To clarify, efficiency can be adversely affected if equality means that there is a disincentive to work harder for greater reward.

So equality of reward is unacceptable under Rawls's difference principle as the equality of outcome may discourage those who wish to contribute more to society. Consider though the argument, first raised by Thero, that environmental goods could be considered as primary goods. Primary goods are the means of allowing citizens (that is, human, moral agents) to develop their two moral powers (a capacity for a sense of the good and a capacity for a sense of justice). According to Bell, basic environmental goods must be included within an index of primary goods or rather 'bundles' of goods that are to be identified as being of the greatest benefit to the least advantaged. A lack of regulation with regards to pollution and ecological degradation will directly infringe on citizens' abilities to pursue their freely chosen conception of the good life. Consequently, and as already discussed, minimal instrumentalist green concerns must be implemented, according to the dictates of justice, into the basic structure. Not only this, but the difference principle dictates that such light green concerns, including clean air, clean water, and low pollution, must become part of the 'social minimum' in the best interests of the least advantaged (Bell, 2004a: 302–3). Although not committed to zero pollution or even equality of exposure to pollution, Bell argues that the difference principle strengthens the need for a robust social minimum that would surely encompass green concerns. Put another way, Rawls's circumstances of justice (that is, the fact of moderate scarcity) were overly optimistic, and the absorption of reasonable green doctrines requires only a slight modification of the index of primary goods. In fact, the only modification is the application (*or* the taking 'inward') of the difference principle to a new set of external circumstances of justice that place limits on individual citizens' pursuit of the good. In effect, Bell implements a Rawlsian-inspired inward extension of justice as fairness to the plight of the redefined 'least advantaged'. Bell preserves the shallow instrumentalist makeup of Rawls's theory of environmental justice but argues that such a view will *indirectly* benefit wider nature.

In conclusion, the theory of environmental justice that Bell attributes to justice as fairness is constructed in accordance with his own *who*, *what*, and *how* framework. The *least advantaged* (now including future generations at risk from the changing circumstances of justice) are to be recipients of *environmental primary goods* (a social minimum incorporating environmental factors that will affect the ability of citizens to act as self-authors of the good life), in line with the *difference principle* potentially complemented by a form of environmental citizenship education. This, then, represents the *who*, *what*, and *how*, respectively. Bell's description of extensionist green political thought opens up two intriguing, and as yet unanswered, questions. The first is that we are now faced with a choice as to how optimistic we could be in hoping for a final victory of green concerns during post-OP democratic deliberations. Modification involves only updating the circumstances of justice, and the move from moderate scarcity ostensibly to scarcity *per se*. Bell states that the onus remains in the hands of citizens themselves to abandon their ecologically damaging preferences. Taken together, this idea propounds the greening of Rawls by refusing to shift the blame for unsustainable behaviour onto political liberalism. Liberal theory itself cannot be held accountable for the materialistic preferences of individual citizens. Yet if the citizenship education individuals receive is overtly eco-centric, this view is difficult to maintain, as they would be steered towards a radical transformation of their ideas about humanity's place in the world. Is the creation of 'critical' citizens bordering on the doctrinal?

Secondly, if the separation between the first principles of justice applicable to the basic structure of society and the wider scope of environmental or ecological justice is to be preserved, then the question of the influence of the basic structure is left unresolved. Bell stumbles upon a contradiction within Rawls's makeup of the basic structure that comes to prominence when discussing the taking inward of justice as fairness to the 'least advantaged': if Rawls hopes to distinguish 'strict' justice from the broader ethical questions of humanity's role in nature, then the permanency of our unchanging political identities as citizens must take priority over these more controversial questions. In fact, unlike Achterberg who proposes a new ecological principle of justice that supersedes Rawls's original two principles, the basic structure of political liberalism cannot remain impartial. What Bell's discussion of political liberalism and environmental citizenship education shows (and this is his *direct* intention) is that the separation of political justice from environmental or ecological justice has

72 *Rawls and the Environmental Crisis*

to demonstrate both that the primacy of Rawls's first principles will not limit the inclusion of green concerns beyond the political sphere, and also that there is enough substance to the principles just savings to embody an inherent sense of environmental justice.

The question of non-human species

A fair amount of the green critique deals specifically with the taking outward of justice as fairness to the plight of non-human species. This particular facet of the green critique focusses not only on the separation argument, but also on the idea that a political agreement need not be as limited as Rawls makes out, *if* it is to be built on ideas latent in the public–political culture. So far, we have seen that Achterberg is notably sanguine that the OP would actually lead to the uncovering of deep green attitudes that would then be reflected in new principles of justice, despite Rawls himself choosing to avoid this line of argument. Contrary to this, Bell is hopeful that it is beyond the OP, at later legislative stages of justice, that politicized green concerns are welcomed by political liberalism – and even Thero argues that it could serve as an interim ethic. It is worth considering Mark Rowlands's (1997) work in this area, as he, too, sees cause for optimism and, despite limiting his enquiry to a question of whether or not Rawlsian liberalism pre-*PL* is capable of assigning greater moral significance to non-human individual animals, he offers some useful insights into the difficulties faced when dealing with the separation argument. To be sure, Rowlands explores the congruence between a theory of justice concentrated on the basic structure of society, and the wider ethical and moral concerns beyond these fundamentals. As Rowlands puts it: 'the sort of arguments developed by Rawls will be conceived of as, in principle, capable of deriving general principles of morality, and not simply principles relating to individuals to basic societal structures' and that the 'scope' and 'application of the contract idea is . . . by no means idiosyncratic' (1997: 236). Or, returning to Rawls's own views, human justice 'cannot be too far wrong' when it comes to a theory of environmental justice and humanity's correct relationship with wider nature.

Rowlands's extensionist efforts work from within the OP. His begins by stressing that the OP is embedded within the rationality of the parties entering into the social contract situation. The principles of justice selected are *by* the rational and *for* the rational (237). For Rowlands, the OP is not based on a metaphysical view of the self, and it unnecessary to imagine ourselves as radically unencumbered. Rather, we should appreciate it as a heuristic 'intuitive test of fairness' (239). Rowlands's interpretation is that it is not independent of the idea of intuitive equality held by liberalism, and instead the two are mutually reinforcing. Principles chosen are in fact yielded as we 'work from both ends' (240) in the spirit of the reflective equilibrium. Rowlands's focus on the 'dialectical' composition of the OP rejects an 'ultra conservative interpretation of Rawls' that states it 'is wholly at the mercy of our intuitive judgements of equality, themselves seen as *not subject to this kind of review or modification*'

(241, emphasis added). An 'unreflective equilibrium' would rely solely on 'commonsense views', for example, giving individuals their due based on merit or ability. It is fair to say that this belief is both intuitive and widely held in Western societies but holds no favour within *TJ*. A principal motivation for Rawls was the notion that individuals simply do not deserve their abilities, or their faculties that would make them seemingly more entitled to distributive honours and rewards.

But what does intuitive equality have to do with the extension of Rawlsian liberalism to accommodate green concerns? If we are to extend justice to non-contemporaneous rational beings, it must be truly reflective as well as 'consistent with the application of the intuitive equality argument' (242). For this to happen the OP must be turned in on itself and brought into line with Rawls's own view that, for the sake of consistency, intuitive equality must be applied to rationality itself. So even knowledge of whether the individual represented in the OP is in possession of rationality is therefore to be bracketed off from deliberations. The circumstances – or conditions – of justice are modified when it is determined, intuitively and through the use of reflective equilibrium reasoning, that the individual ownership of rationality is morally undeserved. Including rationality as a prerequisite for consideration within the OP means that those who possess an arbitrary trait bestowed upon them by nature would benefit unfairly from what amounts to sheer good fortune. In Rowlands's words: 'our possession of rationality is not something over which we have any control'. Rational persons therefore benefit from first principles of justice that guarantee their pursuit of rational life plans. Contrary arguments, according to Rowlands, would not survive the process of reflective equilibrium as we work back and forth devising the OP and reflecting upon our intuitive beliefs.

Rowlands argues that his revisionist account of the OP 'coheres much better with one of Rawls's ways of characterizing it as a situation whereby the participants have knowledge of all general principles of psychology, sociology, economics and the like, but *no* particular knowledge about themselves' (243, emphasis in original). The OP requires updating so as to account for Rawls's mistake in denying the role of intuitive equality in his account of fairness built on non-arbitrary characteristics. Rowlands extends justice as fairness *backwards*, resulting in a form of green political theory that is not so much *Rawlsian* but somewhat *Rawls revised*. This is a difficult position to defend because it alludes to the question as to the degree to which justice as fairness can be modified before becoming unrecognizable. To what extent can we modify, extract, adapt, or expand his ideas before they can no longer be considered Rawlsian? The limit that seems reasonable to place on extending political liberalism is to maintain the freestanding nature of an overlapping consensus, and the fact that justice as a discourse is a modern, rational, and reasonable human endeavour. This does not infer a blind acceptance of Rawls, nor does it present an image of him as a prophet, but rather it leaves his key ideas largely intact. It is also more attuned to the idea of extensionism as the taking forward, inward, or outward of justice as fairness.

74 *Rawls and the Environmental Crisis*

In summary, Rowlands draws on the work of Peter Carruthers (1992) to conclude that the exclusion on non-humans from anthropocentric considerations is *non sequitur*. 'Even if', Rowlands argues, 'morality were constructed by human beings in order to facilitate interactions between human beings, it does not follow that this sort of origin exhausts the present content of morality nor that it delimits its current scope' (1997: 245). Morality, despite being a largely human affair, does not necessarily have to limit its own scope of influence. Or, to repeat Rawls's adage, justice is but one part of the moral view. Unfortunately, much of Rowlands's piece is rendered obsolete by the time we reach *PL* as Rawls's mature thought brings to the fore the need for a greater sense of political justice, beyond mere rationality. A straightforward capacity *for* (rather than actual exercise *of*) a sense of justice is all that is required in *TJ*, but in *PL* the scope of justice seems more strenuous: it demands that citizens adhere to the great political virtues. So if rationality is underserved, why would the human faculty of being imbued with an intuitive sense of right and wrong be in any way different?

Rowlands steers the OP away from philosophy to the psychological makeup of persons. Rawls himself, as stated in the previous chapter, had argued that being just is part of the human condition: it is naturally embedded within us, and so on this reasoning we do not deserve the benefits of being human. The question arises, however, of at what point we stop. If we do not deserve to be free and equal citizens just because we are human, then the whole premise of Rawls's view of modernity is called into question. The modern condition, and the inherent liberty and equality of the individual that it prizes, is an essential component of justice as fairness. These are ideas implicit in democratic societies according to Rawls. Thickening the veil of ignorance to include knowledge of rationality means that the interests of non-human species would then affect the outcome of the OP and the principles of justice chosen. Any such modification, however, would undermine the spirit of Rawls's later *PL* in challenging the centrality – and sanctity – of the individual self-authorship of the good life, freed from doctrinal and Salvationist religious creeds. Rowlands's idea nevertheless does indirectly echo the important link between Rawls and modernity, and the wider connotations of the green critique to political thought. The separation argument is targeted because it represents the inviolability of the free and equal individual to use their rationality and reason to devise, pursue, or revise their own beliefs on their place in the world. When the separation argument as outlined in the OP is challenged, as it is here by a vision of environmental or ecological justice (a vision that Rowlands does not explicitly outline), then the project of modernity is also threatened.

Also utilizing the plight of non-humans at risk form environmental degradation, and the arbitrariness of excluding the non-rational from the OP, is Robert Garner's (2003) account of the greening of Rawls that is particularly scathing of a limited, political conception of justice on two counts. The first resembles Rowlands's argument about the sidelining of intuitive beliefs widely held in society that express sincere concern for the fate of individual non-humans – as well as entire species – at risk from cruel and unsustainable human practices. Again, if Rawls hopes to build a consensus around reasonable first principles that are for 'moral persons' only, then his theory rests on an 'artificial' and 'discriminate' exclusion of non-human species. Like Achterberg, Garner argues that many green concerns are far from hidden within democratic societies and are manifested within the 'existence of animal protection statutes in the vast majority of developed democratic countries' (10–11). The second front on which Garner focusses his critique of Rawls strengthens the first: the fact that the OP is designed to lead to a certain outcome, namely, justice as fairness, renders 'the contractarian approach redundant' (10). Rawls's defence that we are to uncover shared, intuitive principles of justice latent in the public political culture is attacked by Garner who, like Rowlands and not unlike Achterberg, argues that it would only uncover much darker green intuitive notions of environmental justice, including a concern for the plight of non-human species. A political conception of justice cannot be freestanding as it is dependent upon (ideally) beliefs nascent in the public political culture, or (non-ideally) on 'pre-existing values' and the 'ideological baggage' consistent with a high liberal view of the self (10).

Garner's critique of Rawls commences with what he sees as the deficiencies of the OP. As a deliberative process *for* the reasonable *by* the reasonable, he concludes that 'Rawls's liberal approach to the moral status of animals is so incomplete and, in some places, flawed' (3). 'Incomplete', perhaps, is more accurate than 'flawed', not least because Rawls himself recognized that his theory could potentially be extended to adapt to changing circumstances. It is the centrality of moral pluralism to Rawls's account of justice that forbids the state, and the political sphere, from 'interfering with individual moral codes or conceptions of the good life . . . The way in which we treat animals, therefore, becomes a moral preference rather than an obligation insisted upon by the state' (4). Curiously, Garner himself admits that this interpretation of political liberalism is one that is '[t]aken to its logical extreme'.

In echoing Dobson's claim that 'any theory of justice which did not incorporate animals would be regarded as a second division theory', Garner continues to explore the implications of the separation argument, and the supposed neutrality of excluding non-humans species from the language of 'strict' justice between humans. Justice as fairness, on Garner's *ad extremum* reading, soon progresses from mere political indifference towards the plight of non-humans (and presumably, all groups, human or otherwise, at risk from ecological degradation) to a nefarious *apologia* for the 'ceaseless exploitation' of non-humans (14). The alleged jump from indifference/neutrality to 'ceaseless exploitation' is made on the basis that Garner, too, believes that political liberalism already endorses an inadequate shallowly instrumentalist, light green theory of environmental justice. In much the same way as the thinkers we have covered so far, Garner believes that political liberalism reflects – and indeed implements – a specific conception of environmental justice that encourages the arrogant instrumental utilization of non-humans for human benefit (even

76 *Rawls and the Environmental Crisis*

if there is indirect benefit to non-human species). There is a fine line between *separation* and *indifference* in Garner's view, and he seems to be again focussing on the inability of Rawls to produce a truly freestanding political conception of justice, independent of an exploitative instrumental comprehensive doctrine of environmental justice.

Garner adds two further considerations to his critique of the 'artificial' separation of justice from wider morality, and what he sees as the inevitable progression from indifference through to exploitation. The first is that justice is to be a primary feature of life in the well-ordered society, and that individual citizens will be expected to organize their public and private lives according to its dictates. Justice is not only the first virtue of public institutions: it is also the guiding principle for the daily, post-OP public and private lives of citizens (presumably due to their own innate humanistic sense of justice). The second point made by Garner is that the 'liberal article of faith that moral disapproval or disgust does not count as harm for the purposes of state or societal intervention' results in the treatment of non-humans becoming 'merely a preference rather than a fundamental principle of justice' (17). Again, though, he goes further than this in stating that such indifference is 'inimical' to an extension of moral concern to non-humans as it 'makes it much more difficult for *any* kind of restrictions on the way humans treat animals to be introduced' (19–20, emphasis in original). The political sphere, and its two principles of justice that preserve both unity and consensus, is too pervasive to remain separate from wider ethical concerns and will inevitably permeate wider society according to Garner.

Garner's argument that 'we probably should look elsewhere in a search for the most appropriate ideological location for animal protection' (20) is powerful yet not without fault. For one, Garner's own *ad extremum* reasoning can be turned in on itself when he states the case that the existence of a considerable amount of animal welfare legislation in Western Europe 'reflects our moral intuition that animals ought to be protected by the state' (19). Returning again to Bell's idea that it is not the normative responsibility of liberal political theory to transform an individual's conception of his or hers relationship to wider nature, including non-human species, and taking into account that there is a strong intuitive demand for the political protection of non-human species in the West, then would Garner not acknowledge that green concerns could come to the fore in post-OP deliberations despite the separation argument? Whilst important, there is also something slightly unsatisfactory about Garner's choice of target in the first place. His criticisms seek to undermine Rawls's 'elevated position in the profession' (3), suggesting that this is an attack on political liberalism *per se* rather than an impassioned defence of the plight of non-human species. The green critique, to which Garner successfully contributes, could be seen as no more than the hijacking of a line of attack designed purely to discredit political liberalism. Put simply, scoring political points against Rawlsian liberalism, a theory that represents a realistically utopian hope of a well-ordered society guided by principles of justice, will do little to improve the plight of non-human species. The argument would work better if taking Rawls's theory to its logical extreme highlighted how a shallow instrumentalist, very light green theory of environmental justice, with its language of maximizing gains and minimizing losses in the form of primary goods, could be shown to inculcate a disregarding non-political attitude towards wider nature, well beyond the workings of the OP. At present, several parallel approaches to Garner's, invoking any number of global and transnational problems (for example, flu pandemics or global terrorism), could proceed to reject Rawls based on the inability of his theory to take these pressing matters seriously. On this reading, notions of 'the environmental crisis' again seem superfluous.

Ruth Abbey (2007), too, like Garner, focusses on the 'Rawlsian resources' available to those concerned with the plight of non-human species, yet her work raises several questions regarding Rawls's wider engagement with environmental or ecological justice. Of particular note is Abbey's claim, in opposition to Garner's view, that the 'move' from *TJ* to *PL* oversees a 'depletion in the normative resources in Rawlsian thought for addressing these issues' (2). Abbey's alternative reading of justice as fairness covers two other topics. First, she seeks to break from both Rowlands's and Garner's positions by not detracting from Rawls's central ideas (think Garner's 'logical extreme', above), and secondly, with regards to the separation argument, she seeks to 'preserve rather than elide Rawls's distinction between justice and morality' (5).

Abbey seems to suggest that Rawls calls for a much stronger sense of duty towards non-humans species in *TJ*, especially in the sense that the 'capacity for feelings of pleasure and pain and for the forms of life which animals are clearly capable' (Rawls, in Abbey, 2007: 6). For Abbey, this hints at the Aristotelian undertones of Rawls's early work, but more important, in rejecting both Rowlands and Garner, the separation argument does not mean political society must eschew its duties towards non-human sentient beings. For Abbey, Rawls 'departs from the dominant trend within contemporary rights theory that the rights of others call forth our duties' (8).

There is also a sense that Abbey's piece in no way lends itself to Rawlsian-inspired extensionist theory; for example, she writes that not only does he stress the need for 'us to develop other ethical vocabularies for discussing relationships with non-humans', but also that it is 'intriguing that this salutary warning about the limits of rights discourse comes from one of its most successful and influential twentieth-century proponents' (9). Yet we are still left with the question as to whether or not Rawls's separation of green concerns from the subject of political justice can be maintained. For Abbey, this separation reinforces Rawls's own now oft-quoted remark that a conception of justice is but one part of the moral view. Rather than applying the rights-based discourse to every ethical problem we may encounter, Abbey strengthens Thero's thesis that we should look to other moral theories, and alternative ethical narratives, for answers to subjective notions of the environmental crisis. There is no need to extend justice as fairness – indeed, there is no need to become Rawlsian, as

Rawls himself did in his later works. Rather, the concept of justice as fairness permits those holding green concerns to freely develop their arguments politically, yet beyond the OP and the whole rights-based discourse. Abbey leaves it unclear as to why we are to look back to *TJ* for normative resources, but then simply drop Rawls's more ambitious view that his theory will reflect both a metaphysical and a holistic account of humanity's place in nature. In selecting elements of Rawls's theory that are to be retained, and dropping those that are seen as non-essential, then Abbey is in danger of engaging in the modification of his ideas whilst simultaneously denying any form of extensionism.

Abbey's work does offer a very valuable and enhanced appreciation of Rawls's contribution to green political thought insomuch as she alludes to the idea of Rawls representing a sort of paternal, public intellectual, able to offer guidance and critique on wider issues. This, however, is problematic for two reasons. First, it is difficult to overlook Rawls's own call for his theory to be limited to 'but one part of the moral view', a statement that demonstrates his shying away from wider ethical dilemmas and metaphysical views of humanity's place in wider nature. This self-regulation is even more pronounced in *PL*, and so in light of Abbey's own argument that there is a 'depletion' of normative resources, it confounds the notion of Rawls as public intellectual even further. Secondly, and this is testament to Rawls's own influence on contemporary political thought, if we are to interpret him as authorizing – or even blessing – citizens to develop a theory of environmental/ecological justice beyond the realms of a rights-based liberal justice, then we arrive at a point of contention. Abbey seems to be suggesting here that Rawlsian liberalism is again an accurate representation of, or apology for, current liberalism. By asking for Rawls's permission to proceed, it suggests a level of deference that is neither appropriate nor reflective of Rawls' own ambitions. Why look to him for guidance in the first place? Why would the development of a theory of environmental justice, outside of a liberal rights-based discourse, be dependent upon his sanctioning? Abbey does hint at why considering justice as fairness is central to any debates within green political thought. Regarding the dominance of liberalism (in theory and in practice), and the need to impose restrictions on free individuals, she states: '[i]f we stop trying to squeeze all ethical issues into rights language, we are more likely to be receptive to alternative ways of thinking about the well-being of animals' (16). Extensionism, then, could actually be a hindrance to the establishing of robust theories of environmental, or ecological, justice if we are obsessed with thinking it necessary to reconcile them with a rights-based liberalism. So rather than taking justice as fairness outwards to those at risk from deteriorating environmental conditions, it could be argued that there is no need to even bother with Rawls's ideas in the first place.

So far, then, we see a variety of competing conclusions reached by green political theorists, but large gaps remain. First, there is little in the way of an explicit link drawn between Rawls and environmental crises (that is, an answer to the *why Rawls?* question), and second, there is little agreement on the extent to which the separation argument can be said to inculcate a negative disposition towards wider nature within a citizenry. On this second point, it is again a question of timing – can we modify the circumstances of justice to ensure that a new principle of *environmental* justice is agreed upon as a guide for the basic structure of society? Or, can we leave Rawls's theory alone and accept that his ideas would allow for the inclusion (or at least the non-exclusion) of a plurality of reasonable light and dark green concerns within the post-OP legislative stages of democratic deliberation? The post-OP political and legislative stage is, after all, integral to the development of an overlapping consensus. Is it enough to hope that citizens can be trusted to act on their politically reasonable green concerns in protecting wider nature, when put to the vote? Further still, we could potentially develop a Rawlsian-inspired theory of environmental or ecological justice fit for the twenty-first century and the new circumstances of justice. This latter option, however, still struggles with a matter of timing. Are we to develop an analogous theory that complements his political liberalism, or do we extend his ideas – almost unrecognizably – to match a preconceived notion of environmental or ecological justice? That is, do we extend Rawls's theory forward, outwards, and inwards so as to absorb general green concerns, or do we work backwards from a subjective theory of environmental or ecological justice (our theoretical 'test') to then either condemn or condone political liberalism as part of a wider 'nascent' philosophical quest for a greater understanding of humanity's place in the world?

Freestanding exploitation

What should we make of the argument that even if Rawls's justice as fairness could be extended meaningfully to the new frontiers of justice, it will still only belie an arrogant theory of dominion? Before answering the previous section's concluding question as to which way round we should extend political liberalism, it is necessary to further explore Garner's anxieties regarding the *ad extremum* implications of a liberal theory that arguably preserves a traditional Christian Ages theme of dominion. Dorothee Horstkötter (2004) is one such proponent of this criticism, yet she starts her account of the greening of Rawls with an approach similar to Bell's earlier idea that there is an inherent sustainability to his political liberalism that presupposes a commitment to intergenerational justice. She argues that 'no serious notion of justice can *ever* be pursued by a society unless the interests of future generations and other societies (let alone nature) are taken into proper account' (Horstkötter, 2004: 160, emphasis in original). Horstkötter continues that: 'A theory of justice does not work without an environmentalist perspective of one kind or another.' As with other works discussed in this chapter, the premise of Horstkötter's extensionist project is that Rawls overlooked, or took for granted, the fact that sustainability is now a constitutional essential, and that the very circumstances of justice are in need of revision. Notions of an environmental crisis, as previously mentioned, are used to force a revision of the foundations upon which political liberalism proceeds. So at what point, then, does the inclusion of the

80   *Rawls and the Environmental Crisis*

new conditions of justice arise? In an argument similar to Achterberg, Horstkötter favours an internal modification of Rawls's theory but, as this section as a whole will demonstrate, theorists are as ever divided as to the point at which these modifications should take place.

Horstkötter sheds new light on the separation argument and whether or not the abstraction of the basic structure (the political) from the wider background public, and indeed ethical sphere of comprehensive ideas (environmental, ecological, or otherwise), can be sustained. The very nature of this challenge is both ideal and non-ideal (theoretically speaking) – a point Horstkötter is keen to stress. Horstkötter's conclusion that Rawls's circumstances of justice are in need of dire revision rests on three premises. First, that liberal neutrality is not only environmentally destructive, but also self-destructive; secondly, that a more pragmatic approach is preferable to what she identifies as theoretical 'endisms'; and thirdly, perhaps most strikingly, it is necessary to admit that Rawls's political liberalism is not freestanding at all. Although Horstkötter's green critique of political liberalism is both timely and penetrating, insomuch as it wrestles with the ecological implications of Rawls's move towards a limited, *political* theory of justice, the three points outlined are somewhat disjointed and at times contradictory.

The first of Horstkötter's arguments highlights the standard connection drawn by green political theorists working in this area, namely, that the liberal impartiality of Rawls's justice as fairness is 'an ambiguous ideal: as a principle fostering freedom and equality in pluralistic societies it is admirable, but it is at the same time a principle that is self-defeating and one that fosters injustice' (161). The position assumed here by Horstkötter only works if Rawls's theory is to be identified as an apologetic for an ecologically ruinous political system, a link that is never explicitly made. There seems to be an exaggeration of the freestanding nature of political liberalism, however, as Horstkötter states that such political 'neutrality' cannot exclude any comprehensive or doctrinal vision of the good life, nor can it 'forbid or hinder activities seeking to undermine the basic structures of liberal pluralism'. Ultimately, liberal neutrality cannot 'increase the likelihood of the chosen ways of life leaving enough material welfare and ecological integrity for others now and in the future' (ibid.). For Horstkötter, then, Rawlsian liberalism is both *intragenerationally* and *intergenerationally* unjust because it undermines the ability of some individuals to pursue their unique conceptions of the good life now and in the future. Yet it remains unclear as to why Rawls is the target here. He not only rejects the term neutrality, as we have seen, labelling it as 'unfortunate', but his hope remains that unreasonable and intolerant comprehensive doctrines will die out and fade into obscurity within the overlapping consensus of a well-ordered society. Rawls's basic structure is certainly not a state of licence: the 'great political virtues' of cooperation, reasonableness, and fair-mindedness commit citizens to a duty of civility. Justice as fairness cannot simply be categorized as neutral or indifferent to its own fate, as citizens will naturally seek to preserve a well-ordered society for the sake of future generations, a point that will further be explored in the remaining chapters.

Horstkötter's second conclusion, that a form of environmental pragmatism is more appropriate than the 'endism' of a reflective equilibrium, is in keeping with the collection of essays edited by Wissenburg and Levy (2004) that discussed *the end of environmentalism* within liberal democracies, of which her work forms a part. Horstkötter, however, is unable to justify how Rawls's theory, in her own words, could be used in the service of 'bridging the gap between plurality and sustainability' (165). If his theory is to represent the side of 'plurality', and an unclear notion of environmentalism as a rival form of 'sustainability', then his work is to be seen as a reflection or an apologetic for contemporary liberal democratic states. The argument cannot work, however, if her own conclusion is that environmental pragmatism is preferable to green first principles. What is needed, according to Horstkötter, are 'concrete situations and concrete social groups . . . that are neither merely abstract nor purely relativistic'. Further to this, 'real life and in real societies are the most appropriate courses of both ecological and social action differ from situation to situation . . . They cannot be prescribed in advance, nor explained *post factum* by any one particular theory.' Her vision of plurality within liberal societies is clearly not reflected by Rawls's 'realistically utopian' vision of the well-ordered society. She goes even further, however, in that she not only removes the normative value of establishing first principles of justice in addressing green concerns, but she also denies the explanatory, *post-hoc* use of Rawlsian political theory as reflective of a 'real' society divided by reasonable pluralism. For Horstkötter, Rawls's notion of reasonable pluralism provides neither a satisfactory analysis of the unsustainability of liberal societies, nor does it offer hope for a way out. The obvious question again is why should Rawlsian liberalism provide the focus of Horstkötter's account of extensionist green political thought, given she has a specific, predetermined notion of sustainability and environmental justice (opposed to what she sees as Rawls's own theory of environmental justice) that should be strived for in the first instance?

The third and final point of Horstkötter's work is the most interesting as it directly questions the freestanding and independent nature of Rawls's political account of justice. In her own words 'the greater the claim of politics to abstract rationality, neutrality and independence, the less scope there will be for democratic participation and the more static the political sphere will become: a reflective equilibrium needs reflecting humans . . . A political concept cannot stand free' (160). This point, that ' "public reason" nor any "overlapping consensus" are ever free-standing, but always depend on input from a diversity of comprehensive social doctrines' (161) challenges a key aim of political liberalism and will be covered in greater detail shortly. Yet Horstkötter's claim goes deeper if we recall Rawls's statement that the aim of a political conception of justice is to uncover ideas latent in the public–political culture. Now if Rawls hopes to maintain that the just basic structure and the political conception of justice can remain abstracted from wider doctrinal disputes, then Horstkötter's point must be taken seriously. She acknowledges Rawls's notion of public reason, and the 'inclusive view' (*PL*: 247), whereby citizens are entitled to 'politicize' their green concerns in a manner that makes their

82 *Rawls and the Environmental Crisis*

key arguments agreeable to most reasonable citizens and can thus form part of a post-OP, public–political overlapping consensus. This, according to Horstkötter, becomes a duty for citizens and further weakens Rawls's case that the basic structure of society remains separate from green concerns.

So if the basic structure of society and a public conception of justice cannot remain insulated from the realm of comprehensive doctrines and irreconcilable visions of the good, then we have to be clear what is being asked of citizens of a well-ordered society. Rawls argued that it is vital for the basic structure of society to be just because it is so prevalent in influencing citizens' opportunities to develop their two moral powers. He states, regarding citizens' complete lives, that it is 'the pervasive influences of the basic structure that shape their character and ends' (*PL*: 68). The qualities required of the citizens of a well-ordered society, and the virtues demanded in the preservation of the just liberal order, could prove incredibly useful to the 'greening' of Rawls. Not only this, but if the overlapping consensus is to be agreed to by holders of politicized green concerns, then it is perfectly possible that they form part of a freestanding, yet acceptable, conception of political justice. These virtues will be considered in greater detail in the concluding chapter. Of immediate concern is that Horstkötter raises the prospect of what it is exactly that will be uncovered within the public political culture, and the values nascent in the collective lives of Western citizens. Should we be optimistic that we will indeed uncover a strong sense of environmental or ecological justice, if we choose to develop such theories within the actual setup of the OP or, as Bell argues, in post-OP deliberations? It is not only the scope of the basic structure that is key here, but also its organization. Is it reflective of – or does it establish a prerequisite for the encouragement of – what Robert Garner has already identified as preexisting, liberal 'ideological baggage'?

Rupert Read's work on Rawls and green concerns is perhaps the most telling of all, and goes some of the way towards answering these questions. Read goes further than Horstkötter and drops any semblance of academic deference to Rawls. Despite at no point engaging with other theorists in this area, nor with Rawls's mature political liberalism, Read's bombastic style is particularly useful to our current enquiry. Read's principal aim is to expose the dependence of Rawls's theory on an exploitative modern relationship between humanity and wider nature. Like Bell, Read is explicit in the reasons he chooses Rawls as a target, but unlike Bell he sees him as a figurehead for something altogether more sinister. For Bell, employing Rawlsian liberalism is more of an ethical testing ground for green extensionist political thought, whereas for Read attempts to extend Rawls 'with some added bells and whistles' as a means of dealing with the 'ecological crisis', belie the inherent inegalitarianism of his theory (Read, 2011: 82). From the outset, Read intends 'to prepare and clear the way for *ecosocialism* by disposing of (Rawlsian, etc.) liberalism' (81, emphasis in the original). His strategy for rescuing ecosocialism from its current 'eccentric "outsider"' status, if it is to be successful, requires a fourfold methodology. First, he must define the ecological crisis; second, justify the targeting of

Rawls; third, reject previous attempts to 'green' Rawlsian liberalism; and four, demonstrate the superiority of his brand of 'egalitarian ecosocialist philosophy'. This would keep it in line with the analysis of the green critique covered so far, as opposed to reinforcing the idea that looking to green Rawls is simply a matter of deference.

This proves difficult not least because of Read's reluctance to engage with the established literature on this subject, or what he again describes as 'a growing cottage-industry'. Not only does the tone suggest a combative approach to the green critique, but also a bold prediction that once citizens have been shown the 'truth' about Rawlsian liberalism and, subsequently, the alternative pathway of ecosocialism, then we reach an 'endism': liberalism and its ecologically speaking internal contradictions will be banished forever. In Read's words: 'liberalism is at an end . . . [t]he exploitation of the Earth and by us of on another that is licensed by today's dominant political philosophy is literally unsustainable. The future must be ecosocialist' (94). Although he is keen not to take any part in this 'cottage-industry', Read does represent a central figure in the first part of the green critique.

In working through the four-point strategy, it should become clear that the actual target of Read's critique is the political and economic system Rawls is seen to uphold; chiefly, a 'property-owning democracy'. First, Read's definition of the ecological crisis is synonymous with Meadows et al.'s Limits to Growth Thesis (see Meadow et al., 2004). This is straightforward enough, but Read must make it explicit as to why Rawlsian liberalism is such an anathema to Meadows et al. How does challenging Rawls's political theory assist Read, or any green thinker for that matter, in promoting the Limits to Growth Thesis? Why, specifically, is 'the ecological' crisis chosen? It would seem (as with Garner, above) that any crisis would fit the bill if the attack is on global capitalism, and not liberalism as a theory of justice.

Next, Read offers a second, much more political notion of the crisis that falls under a Marxist ecological critique. Read explains that once the system of capitalism has become established, 'it reproduces itself, creating and then further reproducing the relations between the bourgeoisie and the proletariat, exploiter and the exploited, leading inevitably to the expansion of the market until it encompasses the globe and commodifies every facet of the world' (2011: 89). Read is explicit here: capitalism is 'driving ecological destruction, and liberals such as Rawls have been peculiarly blind to it'. Rawls's system of distributive justice, and the metric of his primary goods, is basically a *post-hoc* allocation of goods built on the unjust social relations created by capitalism. Rawls, then, 'treats this *outcome* of capitalist relations *as the very basis of social relations* themselves' (ibid., emphasis in original). Here we find the crux of Read's argument: with Rawls, 'as usual for apologists of capitalism, reality is thereby turned upside-down to justify (or even to make pseudo-natural) the unjustifiable'. Rawls's theory is concerned only with the aftereffects of unjust distribution, and the pursuit of an individually chosen good life, regardless of the inherent, and alienating, organization of the social relations that endure

84   *Rawls and the Environmental Crisis*

under capitalism. The goods we seek, the 'parts of the Earth' that Rawls helps to allocate under a flawed system of egalitarian distribution, especially as far as future generations are concerned, are in fact 'bads'.

It is the difference principle in particular that becomes embroiled with capitalism's fetish for the 'institution' of money – a fetish embraced by Rawls in his tacit acceptance of the ability of one individual to earn more from another's labour, than he or she is willing to pay the labourer for such work. The profit made then entitles the holder to more goods and more commodities, which represent the political and social bases necessary for the pursuit of a self-authored vision of the good life. The difference principle is designed only to make the worst off as best off as possible and in doing so, 'naturalizes' the acceptability of wealth inequality (87–8). This, in turn, further alienates humans from not only their own labour, but also from their fellow-beings. This, according to Read, is most recognizable in Rawls's OP when the only motivational attitude allowed is one of mutual disinterest. This all takes place against the *backdrop* of Read's vision of the ecological crisis whereby (a) the goods distributed are actually bads because they are based on non-renewable, unsustainable economic practices when future generations are involved, and (b) the difference principle is an '*engine* for growth' as the least advantaged are 'prepared to tolerate others being incentivized to be better off for the worst-off's alleged benefit is very largely only because the worst-off can see themselves eventually rising to the level of the better-off' (86).

For the first time within the green critique we start to see the implication of Rawls in the alleged eco-crimes of late capitalism. His analysis of the political arrangements necessary for pursuing a self-penned vision of the good life, including green concerns and theories of environmental/ecological justice, are built on an uncritical acceptance of exploitative economic relationships far removed from the true 'basis of life', and our species-being. Again, the mutual disinterest of parties behind the veil of ignorance comes under attack insomuch as, for Read, it undermines the original rejection of the means/ends relationships characteristic of utilitarian thought. Rawls assumes that citizens' 'harvests' of primary goods are allocated 'independently' of one another, but in reality such bundles are inherently linked to the subjection of the wage labourer to the capitalist. Read, like Abbey, argues that mutual disinterest becomes a much more corrosive form of motivation when it manifests itself as systemic indifference, legitimizing 'a certain kind of inhuman relation-as-to-a-thing' (91). Before Read descends too far into a solely Marxist refutation of Rawlsian liberalism, the notion of the ecological crisis makes a reappearance to justify the charge that justice as fairness functions 'as an apologia both for unsustainable takings of "income" from the Earth and for the ongoing justice of labor purchasing' (92). The difference principle, according to Read, is a form of false consciousness on the part of Rawls that is used in the service of legitimizing tokenistic and 'oxymoronic . . . "green growth"'. Labelling wealth and income and other primary goods as 'stuff', argues Read, means that Rawls's theory is anything but rational. For Read, more 'stuff' means more opportunity to gain more rights, and more power over others – an endless unsustainable acquisition 'that has damaged social solidarity over the past couple of generations by free-riding on the earth and future people, and by failing to treat workers as ends or true equals and concentrating only on the desired end-product of their work'.

Read's arguments set out a blanket rejection of previous extensionist efforts yet, willingly or unwillingly, he, too, stumbles across our separation argument. The ecosocialist alternative is left, presumably, for another day but it is curious that there is no mention of fellow green political theorists concerned with Rawls. More striking is the fact that Rawls's later political liberalism is overlooked. Of course Read does not need others' permission to join the green critique, but there is something rather hasty, and uncritical, in not doing so. Returning to Read's aim that if justice as fairness can be seen to fail, 'then the way may be comparatively open to replacing liberalism with another political philosophy, or at least forcing liberals . . . into dialogue on equal terms with rival philosophies' (80–1). Read continues, '[e]galitarian ecosocialist philosophy will at the very least then appear as a live option . . . and not as an eccentric "outsider" to "mainstream" debate' (81). The language here, of 'forcing' a meeting, and attempting to 'strangle the aforementioned cottage industry at birth' (82) seems unnecessarily antagonistic, and lacking in meaningful engagement. Had Read addressed the nuances and intrigues of the separation argument, it would have prevented his ideas from becoming self-defeating insomuch as it will continue to remain outside of the debate in its rush to claim that 'liberalism is at an end'. The notion of an ecological crisis appears superfluous in this context, as Read's goal is to provide a socialistic critique of the difference principle. His interpretation of the Limits to Growth Thesis is secondary to his critique of the difference principle. It is purely an add-on to mask a different kind of rejection of justice as fairness. With regards to the separation argument, Read's work is particularly striking. Rawls's OP and concept of the political is inherently built upon unsustainable, exploitative capitalist relations – the very relations that are to blame for the ecological crisis. The OP and ensuing overlapping consensus, therefore, are the epitome of an arrogant and shallow instrumentalist theory of environmental justice, framed around an exploitative theory of dominion over wider nature, for the sole benefit of certain classes of humanity.

Concluding remarks

There are good reasons, then, for thinking that the first part of the green critique serves as a coherent body of work offering important new insights into Rawls's political theory. There is a sense that justice as fairness represents an embedded shallow instrumentalist, light green theory of environmental justice that underpins modern liberal democracies and, in turn, the hyper-capitalist economic system that accompanies these states guaranteeing the liberty and equality of its citizens. This could, however, represent an opportunity to *green* liberal societies by investigating their ability to take seriously

86 *Rawls and the Environmental Crisis*

environmentalisms and ecologisms, beyond ranking them as mere comprehensive doctrines alongside similarly controversial theocratic, or metaphysical views of humanity's correct place in the world. Yet the problem remains that extensionist efforts only serve to express a positively anti-green, and exploitative, nature of liberal societies in practice that continually downgrade stronger notions of environmental or ecological justice to the periphery. For better or worse, then, Rawls's theory – with regards to first principles of justice and their immediate influence on the public–political culture of a society – are seen to remain firmly within the lighter shades of a spectrum of green concerns by valuing wider nature only for the most narrowly instrumentalist reasons.

The critique suffers from a major weakness, however, in that each theorist covered focusses on a particular element of justice as fairness to the detriment of another; for example, Achterberg and Horstkötter look to ideas implicit in the public culture whilst neglecting the notion of the freestandingness of an overlapping consensus, whilst Hailwood's development of an analogous theory of environmental justice that is indeed freestanding perhaps comes at the expense of a more realistic expectation on behalf of what Bell identifies as not-so-philosophical citizens. It is clearly the case that the motivations of each theorist appear markedly different, so much so that they each apply a unique test, or standard, to Rawls's theory based on subjective notions of environmental or ecological justice. These competing tests are motivated by a variety of ideas starting from the argument that Rawls's theory can be seen as an ethical playground for considering how liberal societies can enforce environmental legislation and take a plurality of green concerns seriously, through to a full frontal assault on liberal democracy as a perpetuator and apologist for unsustainable human development. Combined with the fact that these theorists only engage with one another infrequently, if at all, the efficacy of the criticisms leveled at the separation argument can be tenuous. No conclusive link is drawn between the abstraction of Rawls's notion of justice as fairness from green concerns and the inculcation of a wider societal disposition to neglecting the plight of those at risk from deteriorating ecological conditions. Yet it is this point that seems to form the frontispiece of the whole critique.

Notes

1 Thero draws principally on the work of Russ Manning (1981), Brent Singer (1988), and Peter Wenz (1988) and argues that a straightforward way of extending the OP to include non-human species would be to have the veil of ignorance 'thickened' or 'lowered' to encompass rational, but not necessarily reasonable, life forms. Thero acknowledges, however, that the OP will inevitably retain an element of exclusivity. Thero separates nature into three parts: plants, natural features, and species. Only sentience applies here, as he states that we cannot entertain the idea of representing a mountain behind the veil of ignorance. Also, parties within the OP, placed behind the veil of ignorance, cannot realistically imagine representing a tree, despite it being a living thing. Only species capable of some form of rational action or thought could potentially be included in the OP. Indeed Thero, Singer, and Wenz all argue that some individual members of a particular species

may be more rational than some of their human counterparts. Unfortunately, however true this may be, the problem is that we must consider this in the light of Rawls's *political* liberalism. Rationality is no longer enough: citizens must be reasonable also in possessing a capacity for a sense of justice. So the argument is a non-starter when we introduce Rawls's restricted sphere of concern, chiefly the basic structure and constitutional essentials of a liberal state (the domain of the political). Justice as fairness is now a restricted, political conception designed to develop citizens' two moral powers, and so non-human species can neither be agents of justice nor adhere to the principle of reciprocity.

2 Interestingly, Rawls's earlier articles alluded to a different – but not entirely irrelevant – third principle of justice rewarding contribution to the 'common good'. This was quietly dropped, however, prior to the publication of *TJ* (see, for example, Rawls, 1963: 73–7).

3 Rawls adds to this point: 'public reason is a way of reasoning about political values shared by free and equal citizens that does not trespass on citizens' comprehensive doctrines so long as those doctrines are consistent with a democratic polity' (Rawls, 1999c: 179). For Rawls, the ideal of 'public reason' is a moral 'duty of civility', achieved when citizens 'think of themselves as legislators' (135).

4 Hence why Hailwood's (2004) theory could be deemed too 'philosophical' as a foundation for reasonable agreement within a citizenry.

4 A second green critique

There is, however, an alternative means of developing a green critique of Rawls that involves considering the just institutions of a well-ordered society (the good, or 'what', of intergenerational justice) as representative of a more enlightened theory of light green environmental justice that is closer to a modern theory of 'liberalized stewardship'. This chapter differs from the previous insomuch as the literature covered (with perhaps the exception of Hailwood) neither attempts to dismiss, nor even modify, Rawls's theory, in an attempt to green political liberalism. So far, the consensus again appears to be that only a minimalistic, light green theory of environmental justice can be extracted from justice as fairness. Some theorists, however, allude to the idea that his theory could well be analogous to a darker green notion of environmental justice that although does not go as far as a embodying the key tenets of 'ecological justice', it would indeed be representative of something altogether more enlightened. Greening Rawls in this way, however, must be understood as forming part of a wider process of attempting to liberalize the concept of environmental stewardship itself. The key challenge faced by contemporary proponents of the concept is to offer a transpolitical, or 'higher', good of intergenerational justice, that will compel individuals to make sacrifices to their freedoms, at various levels, in order to elevate the protection of wider nature on a par with Rawls's two principles of justice. The main aim of this chapter will be to demonstrate how recent developments in the literature on environmental stewardship have stumbled, unwittingly, upon similarities between a liberalized version of the concept and the key tenets of Rawls's political liberalism. What we are left with in following this alternative method, however, is a marked tension between the separation argument that leaves citizens free to decide for themselves why they should protect wider nature in post-OP deliberations (the liberal OP) and a much more conservative reading of Rawls's notion of a well-ordered society that endures from one generation to the next (the conservative principle of just savings). The focus of this chapter is therefore to trace recent developments in the literature on environmental stewardship, and the ability of the concept to overcome its inherent belief in the human dominion of wider nature (that is, what we now recognize as a shallowly instrumentalist attitude).

Beyond mutual disinterest

Even if there is broad agreement that the circumstances of justice outlined by Rawls need updating, we have seen how disagreement remains regarding the point at which these revisions are to be made. Aside from these matters of timing, most argue that Rawls's political liberalism, for better or worse, is committed only to preserving the material conditions necessary for future citizens to pursue their unique visions of the good life. Crucially, according to Bell, this is potentially inclusive – or certainly not *exclusive* – of darker, but politicized, post-OP green concerns. Regarding the 'fundamentals of justice', however, the 'mutual disinterest' of the parties in Rawls's OP precludes the inclusion of any other-regarding attitudes contributing to the agreement on principles that will come to govern the basic structure of society. It is possible to piece together a series of works by eminent theorists on the subject of environmental stewardship, and the concept of humanity as engaged in an intergenerational project of political cooperation that reveal a hitherto unexamined means of greening justice as fairness, and which begin to look beyond the primary motivational force of mutual disinterest. Drawing the links between this disparate collection of writings alludes to an inherent notion of darker green, environmental stewardship within Rawls's political liberalism. The prerequisites for this occurring, however, are not only to return to his enduring aim that reasonable political agreement remains entirely possible in a world lacking outside support, but also that we must take seriously the more conservative implications of his principle of just savings.

The reason for acknowledging the more conservative aspects of justice as fairness is not just that it exposes a fault line within his mature political philosophy; it is also due to the fact that any hope of addressing environmental degradation will involve acts of sacrifice and self-denial on the part of individual citizens, beyond the motivations necessary for establishing a political consensus on mutual disinterest alone. The immediate needs of the individual's own material and moral wants, and his or her disinterest towards his or her fellow citizens' preferences save for recognizing their status as both free and equal individuals, must sometimes be foregone for a transpolitical good that goes beyond these rational, contemporaneous interests. If not sacrifice, then there must at least be a recognition of the existence of such transpolitical goods beyond the fleeting life of the individual. Karen Litfin (2010) has argued that individual sacrifice need not necessarily imply a 'painful exercise in self-abnegation' or 'a superstitious act of futility or a heroic act of altruism' (117). Instead, she claims, sacrifice can 'articulate a life-affirming perspective' if 'understood as a fundamental law of the cosmos'. For Litfin, 'the' environmental crisis is a 'crisis of meaning' whereby 'the mass extinction of species, unprecedented climate change, unsustainable resource depletion, and myriad pollution dangers' conspire to impose the need for sacrifice and self-denial within a citizenry (118). Our behaviour (green or anti-green) is therefore built on theories of meaning, and so crises that affect 'human action, relationships,

90 *Rawls and the Environmental Crisis*

and their material effects are a reflection of human consciousness' (118). Much like Pier Stephens (2001a), 'the' environmental crisis can be seen as a 'metaphysical crisis', and one that compels individuals to reconsider humanity's role in the cosmos.[1]

So how can Rawls's theory maintain a just savings principle, which demands sacrifice beyond the mutual disinterest of citizens, whilst avoiding an appeal to similar metaphysical notions of the environmental crisis? Surely this requires a stronger notion of motivation built on the willingness of citizens to sacrifice their own immediate interests or preferences for a transpolitical good that is in keeping with broader liberal aims. *Stewardship* – a concept that was once an integral part of a supposed tripartite relationship between God, humanity, and nature, with humanity seen to bear special responsibility for carrying out God's work on earth – is a theory that once compelled individuals to appreciate just such a higher entity, or concept. A defining feature of modernity is the fact that this traditional tripartite relationship (God–humanity–nature) has broken down following the removal of God from many individuals' sense of their place in the world. Again, humanity has lost its 'outside support'. What, then, are the transpolitical goods that could replace the notion of a deity in this tripartite relationship, so as to bring it up to date with a liberal appreciation of the free and equal citizen? In the modern period, this has involved focussing more on the relationship between humanity and wider nature, as opposed to invoking a 'higher' being that determines such relations. If we were to again utilize Bell's framework for assessing a proposed theory of environmental or ecological justice, a modern notion of stewardship confronts three important challenges: *what* are we to sustain from one generation to the next; *for whom* should it be sustained; and *by what* principle should this come about? Yet an overarching meta-question hangs over such a framework: how can we avoid, should we wish to, embarking upon doctrinal and comprehensive reappraisals of humanity's relationship with wider nature (as Litfin does, above) in a modern secularized world that has removed God from the tripartite relationship? One means of reinvigorating stewardship, so as to make it fit for a world now lacking in divine outside support, has been to *liberalize* the concept by replacing the God aspect with an idea of wider humanity as cooperatively engaged in a perennial search for justice.

Rawls's political liberalism, as we have seen, ruled out controversial searches for meaning in the political sphere and the establishing of principles of justice upon a notion of a *summum bonum*. Yet it will be argued in this chapter and the conclusion that there remains an inherent commitment to stewardship within justice as fairness as it proposes answers to at least two important questions thrown up by green concerns; namely, what we are to bequeath to future generations (or, in other words, of what we are to be stewards) and the relationship between humanity and wider nature. *Prima facie*, the idea of a freestanding consensus around political principles, in addition to the principle of just savings, means that surely Rawls envisages contemporary rational agents acting as *stewards of a liberal order* that is to endure from one generation to the next.

A second green critique 91

Modernity is seen to represent a complete break from the Christian ethics of the medieval age. Yet this assertion is problematic, not least because of the self-evident fact that as a process, it is still unfolding. If Rawlsian liberalism can be said to offer a substantive vision of stewardship, we may find a direct riposte to the idea that justice as fairness represents a mere *apologia* of modernity and its ecological woes as expressed by the first part of the green critique in the previous chapter. Under its most recent guises, a theory of environmental stewardship attempts to recapture a lost form of accountability and sense of duty to an entity, or concept, beyond the inviolable rights of the individual. The main challenge for extensionist green political thought is that the inherent intergenerationalism of Rawls's later work leads to the disjuncture from liberal individualism and potentially subordinates a language of rights and mutual disinterest to a wider theory of stewardship, in a manner similar to the overt aspirations of *TJ*. This tension demands recognition of the fact that once future generations and non-human species are involved, his mature theory starts to depart from the light green conclusions reached in the previous chapter and, in doing so, represents a hopeful means of subtly 'darkening' what is so far only a minimally light green theory of environmental justice.

So if a liberalized theory of environmental stewardship is to address a perceived crisis of modernity – a crisis mirrored by the separation argument inherent to Rawlsian liberalism – it has to replace the higher authority of a deity with a worship of humanity itself, *sans* outside support. Interestingly, the liberalization and concurrent secularization of the term claims to delegate not only the self-authorship of the good life to the rational individual, but also the decision as to the makeup of the individual's relationship with wider nature. In layman's terms, it is solely up to the individual to decide *for whom* or *for what* he or she wishes to preserve wider nature, if at all. Whilst still concerned with the meaning of humanity's place as *a part of* or *apart from* nature, the secularization of the term removes the notion of God, or any deity for that matter, from the once tripartite God–humanity–nature relationship. In abandoning the theological origins of the term, however, the process of secularization must wrestle with a key motivational feature of political life; namely, the idea that there exists a sacred duty to protect wider nature, *and* an enduring political agreement, for the sake of something more important than only the mutual disinterest of citizens and their recognition of one another as free and equal citizens above all else.

The aim here is not so much to provide a genealogy of stewardship, from its Biblical origins through to the most recent scholarship on environmental political thought, but rather to specifically consider a modern (or late-modern) corpus of scholarship that deals with a secularized version of the idea, and one that relates to Rawls's own brand of liberal thought in the modern period. Limiting the discussion further still is the fact that it is only the Judeo-Christian concept of stewardship under consideration. To be sure, the focus of the ensuing argument centres on the interpretation of a liberalized theory of stewardship and the extent to which its religious roots belie an attitude of arrogant human

92   *Rawls and the Environmental Crisis*

dominion over nature. This, in turn, reinforces the conclusion of the previous chapter that, even if justice as fairness could be said to possess an inbuilt theory of environmental stewardship, it merely reflects a shallow instrumentalist light green notion of environmental justice framed around a traditional Christian ages' view of the human dominion and exploitation of wider nature.

In the context of Rawls, it becomes apparent that an intergenerational commitment to preserving just institutions cannot straightforwardly be reconciled with a recognition of the liberal belief in the inviolability of the rights and liberties of the contemporaneous individual. There are, however, promising signs that the intergenerational credentials of Rawls's political liberalism lend themselves to a modern theory of stewardship and its concomitant requirements of citizenship. This, as with any post-Reformation theory of political liberalism, however, repeats the notion that justice as fairness must again face the perennial problem of having to remain thick enough to inspire loyalty and sacrifice yet thin enough to gather a viable number of reasonable adherents. It must, therefore, be simultaneously both meaningful *and* freestanding. In this instance, Rawlsian stewardship finds itself treading carefully between Hailwood's 'otherness' or Jennifer Welchman's (2012) 'catch-all' thesis on the one hand, and the Christian, doctrinal idea of humanity's duties towards God on the other. The former denote neutrality, and the latter invokes creedal dogma. As will now be demonstrated, there is a danger that if we follow Hailwood and Welchman then we merely hollow out what is an important theory of environmental or ecological citizenship. Unadulterated secularization could simply represent neutrality personified, and may do little more than justify the freedom of the individual to pursue a relationship with wider nature that is indeed marked by dominion and exploitation.

A break from Christian stewardship

If able to abandon all vestiges of human dominion over wider nature (and therefore the charge of shallow instrumentalism), could stewardship endure as a meaningful concept for the modern period? What is lost during this process of liberalization if the theological underpinnings of the concept are taken away? It has been asserted by some that Judeo-Christian ethics provided the very foundations of modernity, and thus our current ecological problems, and so there is little use to be had from invoking similar religious principles as a means of dealing with such challenges. The bottom line for those taking this position is that stewardship can never be anything other than a theory of narrow dominion. The supposed Christian roots of environmental crises are laid bare in the well-known argument put forward by Lynn White who argued 'that Christianity bears a huge burden of guilt' for the belief that 'we are superior to nature, contemptuous of it, willing to use it for our slightest whim' (1967: 1206). Rawls's own position on environmental justice can be seen as a continuation of this ethic. The history of the idea of environmental stewardship often follows a set narrative regarding the meaning of God's instruction to humanity in Genesis 1:28: "Be fruitful and multiply; fill the earth and subdue it; have dominion over the fish of the sea, over the birds of the air, and over every living thing that moves on the earth". White concludes that 'modern technology is at least partly to be explained as an Occidental, voluntarist realization of the Christian dogma of man's transcendence of, and rightful mastery over nature . . . over a century ago science and technology . . . joined to give mankind powers which, to judge by many of the ecologic effects, are out of control'. Modernity, according to White, is merely a product of centuries of Christian theology.

Several theorists have claimed that White's article misunderstands the central themes of Genesis. In Peter Harrison's (2006) words, White's analysis is 'historical rather than hermeneutical' and offers, instead, an alternative interpretation of Genesis, claiming that God's instructions for humans to 'be fruitful and multiply, and fill the earth, and subdue it; and have dominion' refers to a desire for humanity to have control over the base instincts (19–22). 'Dominion' becomes self-discipline: a Platonic belief in the virtue of overcoming our passions – our 'mad-masters'. Ernest Fortin (1995) picks up on a similar confusion regarding the term 'dominion', stating that in instances when the Bible 'uses the word, it is always in its primary sense, the *dominus* or "master" being the one who rules his subordinates for the good of the whole rather than for his own private good' (216). Wider nature is not merely instrumental to individual human preferences: it is to be managed for a higher good. Similarly, for Jeanne Kay (1989), a more realistic interpretation of the 'dominion commandment' from God invokes a ' "good shepherd" stewardship model of kingship as normative, rather than a kingship model of tyrannical oriental despot' (221). It is not only the phrase 'dominion' that has divided theologians but also, according to Desmond Gillmor (1996), the word 'subdue; which is translated from the Hebrew *rada* meaning "to trample" ' (261). The 'dominion commandment', therefore, points to a 'divine mandate' (262) for a trashing of environments by humanity. Gillmor goes on to highlight numerous passages from the Bible, however, that challenge such narrow instrumentalism, including how Adam was sent forth as a conserver of the Garden of Eden; the simple lifestyle of Jesus Christ treading lightly on the earth; and natural disasters such as famine and pestilence as proof of a providential check on human arrogance. Coming full circle, it could be argued that if it was indeed Christian ethics that got us to this point, it is in fact only the scriptures that will bring about an end to these crises. White again: 'since the roots of our (ecological) trouble are so largely religious, the remedy must also be essentially religious, whether we call it that or not' (1967: 1207). The contentious nature of stewardship – as either a hope or a folly – is clear to see.

There is, however, a dearth of scholarly output on this subject. One explanation for this is inferred by R.J. Berry, who states that a belief in stewardship is a central pillar of the Christian faith: 'it is a default word, not a considered concept' (2006). When subjected to closer scrutiny, the term can be reduced to an exploration of the troublesome tripartite relationship between God, humanity,

94 *Rawls and the Environmental Crisis*

and nature. The Fall indicates a break with humanity's relationship from God, nature, his fellow-beings, and his or her self. Medieval interpretations of the Bible, the Enlightenment, and the rise of modern consumerism have done nothing to remedy the dualism of humanity and wider nature, and so Christian environmental stewardship continues to seek reconciliation between God and humanity, and a restoration of the broken relationship between the two. If the relationship is to be repaired, then humans must fulfil their duties to God. Scholars working on the subject of Christianity are inevitably faced, when considering what humanity's duties to God are, *to whom* does wider nature belong, or, *for whom* is it to be preserved? The question of ownership becomes central to this endeavour, and if humanity is to act on God's behalf, what are their duties, and over which goods are they to act as custodians?

Much of the work done in this area has involved tracing stewardship back to its theological roots so as to determine whether or not it has always represented a hubristic environmental ethic. In doing so it addresses the issue raised by White, above, regarding the perceived mistake made, or the wrong path taken, by humanity in the modern period. Is it the case that the increasing secularization of environmental stewardship inevitably follows a permanent disjuncture between humanity and wider nature (a *second Fall*), or is it rather the case that the arrogance of seeing ourselves as the workmanship of God – as 'little gods' on Earth – was merely a rebranding of a traditional Christian attitude of dominion?[2]

With White as the catalyst for the dispute over the Biblical meaning of 'dominion', the view that Christian ethics reinforce a mentality of 'God rules over humanity; humanity rules over non-human nature' (Berry, 2006: 5) is further contested. Gillmor (1996), again, claims that to blame the Judeo-Christian tradition 'as being guilty of causing the world ecological crisis is a somewhat partisan and simplistic view' (268) in promulgating a 'divine mandate for resource exploitation' (62). Yet Gillmor's faith reinforces White's thesis that dehumanized modern science is indeed the offspring of Christian stewardship: '[m]odern science, including the study of evolution and ecology, has helped to narrow the perceived gap between the two worlds, reinstating the unity of creation' (267). Gillmor assigns four overlapping roles to Christians within the tripartite relationship between God, humanity, and nature: stewards, trustees, companions, and priests. This also ties in with Bell's earlier framework for theories of intergenerational justice. We are to be *stewards* holding the earth 'under tenure' accountable to God; *companions* in the sense that we honour God by entering into inter-relational companionship with wider nature; and *priests* insomuch as humans represent God on earth with the aim of 'striving to save nature with the restoration of order and harmony' thus immersing 'creation into a relationship with God, sanctifying it and giving to humanity a huge responsibility for the survival of all creation' (268). The tripartite relationship outlined by Gillmor highlights the interdependency of the three elements as part of a singular act of creation by God. It is Gillmor's role of human as *trustee* that highlights the alleged contradiction between traditional Christian stewardship and its modern, secular counterpart. As 'custodians' of the earth, 'trusteeship involves the proper conservation of the Earth's commodity and amenity resources, in the interests of the future welfare of humanity and of the continuation of the inherent beauty of nature as an expression of its creator' (267–8). The creeping influence of secularization is plain to see here, as Gillmor's analysis of the preservation of earth for 'the future welfare of humanity' *and* 'the inherent beauty of nature as an expression of its creator' could appear at odds with one another.

It is evident, then, that within more recent Christian interpretations of environmental stewardship, there are traces of the move towards the idea of *humanity* (albeit in the service of God) serving as a higher, transpolitical good for which individuals may be required to sacrifice their own self-interests. Before exploring this point further in the next section, the central criticism that any version of stewardship must defend itself from is the danger that humanity's position of steward, custodian, or guardian of wider nature – whether God-given or otherwise – descends quickly into that of capricious tyrant. If God entrusts humans to take care of the world, then it is left to subjective scriptural interpretation as how best to act towards wider nature. Such arguments are not restricted to theological visions of humanity's place in the natural world. Secular debates also inevitably run into similar questions, especially if the roots of impending environmental crises are considered. This, in turn, takes us back to the question of whether or not a liberalized theory of stewardship can break free of its Judeo-Christian roots, and thus its inherent notion of human dominion over wider nature.

Palmer (2006) argues that, at best, God was only ever an 'absentee landlord', and that this inevitably promotes an unhelpful ethic of mastery (68). God is lord of humanity, and humanity, in turn, is granted the freedom to exploit wider nature and the resources it provides. Simply put, environmental stewardship as inspired by Christianity will find it difficult to shake off this particular yoke. James Lovelock (2006) has identified environmental stewardship as an 'imperial concept' that again reinforces a hubristic attitude towards wider nature (108). Modernity's dualism, then, and its arrogant anthropocentrism inherited from its Christian predecessor, offers us little hope for a more enlightened (yet still instrumentalist) attitude to wider nature. Even if positive duties from God were discernible in the Bible (a point which Palmer rejects) the concept would be too paradoxical to work in practice. All that such a theory provides, according to Reichenbach and Anderson (2006), is a contradictory message involving the need to both preserve *and* change (113). To be sure, there is a simultaneous need to conserve the resources provided by wider nature, whilst at the same time taking risks with precious, non-renewable resources for the good of humanity. The Fall is supposedly testament to this particular anxiety, as humanity cannot be trusted to act justly when there is too much temptation to act despotically. Just as with Christian stewardship, where God has delegated humanity a large degree of freedom to carry out their earthly duties, so, too, do modern theories of stewardship appoint humanity as trustee of wider nature. There is, then, a much more profound and existential question of the role humanity assigns itself in a period of modernity – the period of their separation from wider nature. This, as we have seen, can be said to be the true crisis of modernity. Rawls's defence of the separation argument, with his idea that human justice is put one part of the moral view, leads us neatly to Levy's (2004) 'curse of humanism' as it is only humans, alone in the world cooperating together in an anthropogenic endeavour, who can decide what role they are to play. Crucially, as soon as theories of politics decide to incorporate future generations and non-human species into their deliberations, they inevitably require a theory of stewardship.

The main issue here is that modern theories of environmental stewardship must work with a seemingly inherent – and endemic – ruler–subject form of dualism given humanity's unique position in the world. Returning to White, our modern ecological crisis is a crisis of 'an emerging, entirely novel, democratic culture', and so the question becomes whether or not 'a democratized world can survive its own implications' (1967: 1204). This perhaps *late*-modern crisis seems, however, to be a natural outgrowth of Christianity, and ever since the European Reformations, humanity has once again had to continually assess and critique its relationship to wider nature and future generations. Modernity can, again, be seen to resemble a second Fall of humanity, as it abstracted itself from wider nature in assuming the role of 'little Gods' on earth. So critics of White maintain that modernity, and the subsequent break from the Christian teachings of stewardship is the exact point at which humanity took another wrong turn in history, as it did in the Garden of Eden. Can a modern, secularized theory of environmental stewardship address the question of dominion and, specifically, the separation argument so as to green our 'entirely novel, democratic culture' now steeped in liberal values? More importantly, can Rawls's political liberalism be said to embody a theory of liberalized stewardship, free from an excessive notion of dominion, or shallow instrumentalism?

Stewardship liberalized

If it is to compel individuals to make sacrifices, or to practice restraint and self-denial, a modern liberalized account of environmental stewardship must address the two key challenges outlined in the previous section. First, it has to replace the God aspect of the once tripartite relationship between God–humanity–wider nature model with an entity, or concept, that can hypothetically be of greater moral concern than the individual; that is, they require something or someone *for which* to make sacrifices – or *to which* they can be held accountable for their actions. Second, it has to take seriously the problem of dominion, and it must somehow make sense of humanity's unique capacity to simultaneously both protect and destroy entire ecosystems. Rawls's principle of just savings also faces these two challenges. If his political liberalism can be said to embrace (or at least incorporate) a theory of modern liberalized environmental stewardship, it must then address the overarching, perennial problem of political liberalism as stated in the first chapter. To reiterate, it must tread carefully between thin, and meaningless, notions of impartiality when it comes to apportioning political resources to both green and non-green concerns, as well as remain substantive enough to attract the allegiance of citizens in providing reasons for limiting their destructive impulses.

It is possible to trace a line of scholarship from the 1970s onwards that looks to just these problems. As something of an unrecognized pioneer in this field, John Black (1970) attributed the idea of an ecological crisis to three key factors: 'man's belief in his absolute right to dominate the rest of nature'; 'the propriety of an ever-increasing human population'; and 'a failure to elaborate a conception of responsibility' (125). Black believed that environmental stewardship, or in his words 'man's dominion', could be reinvigorated, and updated for our current age, through a commitment to the higher glory that is humanity. Black's own genealogy of stewardship is very much of its time insomuch as for him, it was the modern liberal democratic state that had replaced Christendom: 'we have come to accept the position of the state as the ultimate authority to which the individual owes a duty for the management of the natural resources 'entrusted' to his care' (75). So the transpolitical good of society, in the absence of God during the latter half of the twentieth century, would be the state with its short-term interest in increasing the material welfare of its members. The state is therefore to be seen as the embodiment of a cooperative venture undertaken by humanity. Looking back to the once eschatological nature of stewardship whereby humans are accountable to God through fear of his final judgement, Black argues that in the modern period the state becomes the only comparative restraint on individual behaviour (108). It is the notion of progress, according to Black, that is the key to discerning the break from Christian stewardship to modern, secular, and liberalized notions of human perfectibility. The former places faith in the unravelling of God's grace, with the latter looking to human society's move away from mystery and superstition to the practical conquering of wider nature. Yet the two positions both represent 'onward-looking movement towards the future' as they 'both acknowledge that there *is* a future for the human race which is better than the present, and much better than the past' (emphasis in original).

Black arrives at the meta-ideal of humanity as he looks to the question of motivation and duty within a theory of stewardship. Put slightly differently, what exactly is the transpolitical good that will place external limits on individual and societal actions? Where is the accountability that will lead to a 'present sacrifice' by a 'majority, who are both spatially and intellectually removed from the resources on which their survival depends?' (88). Again, it is inadequate to present an environmental or ecological crisis as a *summum malum* and expect an instant recognition of the changed circumstances of justice, in the hope of a motivational shift in society. This, as already stated, would be the simplest way to modify Rawls's political liberalism given that the circumstances of justice are changing dramatically from conditions of moderate scarcity to merely plain scarcity.

98 *Rawls and the Environmental Crisis*

Black was clear that the concept of an 'indissoluble unity of mankind' (124), which could bring together the Western intellectual heritage of 'dominion, stewardship and progress' (111), would be a new ethic requiring a 're-examination of our timescales' (124). Yet by describing the 'recrudescence' of stewardship in the modern period as being able to both fill a 'vacuum' (118–19) and force a reconciliation of progress and a duty to posterity, critically speaking it remains no less a 'myth' than a duty to God. Again, at the time of writing Black identified stewardship as being compatible with the workings of the Western social democratic and welfarist state, and no doubt had he been writing in today's academic climate the myth may well have been identified as a hyper-globalized or transnationalist one-planet image.

The most intriguing aspect of Black's work is the difficulty he faces in the method of developing an appropriate ethic for a secular society (hence the need for reconciliation between dominion and progress). His starting point is the failure of the modern period to leave behind the Christian teachings of dominion and the subsequent separation argument. Black seems torn here, methodologically-speaking, in recognizing that 'to replace 'dominion over nature' by 'harmony with nature' is to remove from western civilization its most significant attribute, and would involve its replacement by another, albeit a better, civilization' (123). Although he argues that this is the 'only course open' to us as individuals, we are nevertheless asked to make sacrifices for the 'whole of humanity, dead, living or as yet unborn . . . regardless of the position of the individual along the time axis of the world', in order to, again, 're-examine our timescales'. Yet, again, Black acknowledges that such a transformation of values is 'foreign to our accepted concepts of time and history' (124). He goes on to claim that historically, stewardship has been able to adapt to whatever the myth of that particular age happens to be but the relationship between a flexible concept of stewardship and such myths is left unexplained. Black fails to offer an account of the conceptual makeup of the term that has endured for centuries, despite changing political, economic, social, and technological conditions. He misses a trick here by not highlighting the fact that stewardship's ongoing appeal is firmly rooted in accepted attitudes and modes of behaviour, insomuch as humans throughout history have indeed always looked to transpolitical goods. This point shall be returned to in due course.

Within Black's 'concern for posterity' there is a discernible sense of enlightened instrumentalism, but instrumentalism nonetheless. If there were to be a 'unity of mankind' whereby individuals are prepared to sacrifice their own contemporary interests 'by stretching the present rather than as contracting past and future to a single point in time', the problem would be that such a process would 'probably involves too radical a change in traditional attitudes to gain general acceptance'. This 'expansion of the present' comes from a position of 'privilege' (139), and we 'should be careful not to judge the future with the eyes of the present, but these are the only eyes we have, and we have only our emotional response to our environment to depend on' (144). Touching on what Derek Parfit (1984) would come to call the 'philosophical puzzle' of intergenerational justice, it is only possible to project our own contemporary needs and attitudes onto the future as we conserve only what we believe our projected future selves would need. Black thus hints at the fact that stewardship and a unity of mankind will inevitably hinge on the unchanging motivational force of self-interest. The adaptability of stewardship presumably also owes much to the idea that it works as more of a conceptual framework for assessing the role of humanity in the world. This is without doubt an unchanging, and perennial, anxiety for human societies. Black concludes that a crisis is coming and so seems to acknowledge the limits imposed upon him by his own theory – that he himself has to buy into the myth of statism. 'Revolutionary changes' are forcing a reconfiguration of our 'fundamental approach to the world' (145). This impending cataclysm will 'allow for a more stable relationship between man and nature'. Crucially, if this will happen 'within the framework of our existing society or whether western civilization itself will have to be replaced', remains to be seen.

The very fact that it is only humans that seek to conserve certain environments in an organized and meaningful way is a symptom of our inbuilt sense of dominion. Dominion without responsibility, however, is *the* myth of our time, as Black explains:

> the idea that man's mastery over nature is so complete that he can create for himself the very environment he wants is a dangerous illusion and a pathetic myth, designed to conceal the discomforting reality that while man can undoubtedly change the environment beyond recognition, it may well turn out not to measure up to his expectations.
>
> (144)

Black's is a gloomy, but important, contribution to the literature on this subject, despite displaying an ambiguity between the progress of the modern democratic state and its accompanying notion of inherent mastery. His main message is that we are trapped within the particular myths of our age. The problem is that his account looks to stewardship and the 'unity of mankind' (or, *humanity*) both as a new ethic capable of transforming our relationship with the natural world, and also one that is also unable to shake of its predecessor's belief in dominion. This leaves us with the question of whether or not stewardship is an extreme, highly ideal theory *or* a realistic concept that adapts to, and is shaped by, whatever is the all-pervasive myth of the age happens to be, for example, the state, the individual, the nation, etc. This latter point suggests that humans have always looked to stewardship in order to serve goods and causes beyond their own immediate interests, yet Black continually asserts that stewardship may offer only a projection of our self-interest. There is a dichotomy here, as stewardship is simultaneously both a new theory *and* a timeless theory of human dominion that adapts to the political language of the age.

Beyond Black's generalized account of how stewardship would involve a replacement of a deity with the radical idea of humanity itself, through the

100 *Rawls and the Environmental Crisis*

vehicle of the state, Marcello Di Paola (2013) presents a much more individualistic and egalitarian account of modern environmental stewardship. He argues that as a virtue ethic, it assigns a 'role of guardianship characterised by self-restraint and the exercise of a variety of moral and intellectual virtues (like loyalty and prudence) . . . to be performed by every human being who is or will ever inhabit the earth' (504). Di Paola's efforts directly address the question of dominion, arguing that not only is the concept 'unacceptably anthropocentric and inescapably instrumentalist', but also that the term *guardianship* is merely a euphemism for an 'irrational', 'impossible', and 'preposterous' notion of the 'management' (that is, dominion) of wider nature. Although his work is not linked directly to Black's, it effectively transforms the notion of stewardship into something altogether quite different, and 'not as the management of nature but, rather, of humanity' (505). To perform our 'humble and accessible task', and it is one that *all* humans as cogs in the machine of humanity are to undertake, it must come about 'through the management of our own behaviour, not of nature itself . . . [t]his captures stewardship's focus on self-restraint and virtue, but excludes any gesture at arrogant domination and preposterous administration of nature'.

Di Paola's brand of stewardship is an unashamedly 'anthropocentric enterprise' in that he argues: 'we must ensure the conservation and preservation of all natural entities and systems that are necessary to the fulfilment of present and future human needs and to the cultivation of present and future human aspirations' (506). Not only this, but the concept is inherently liberal–egalitarian in that it is to 'be impartial about all axiological perspectives on nature, as part of that is precisely to ensure that humans can form and entertain whichever of these perspectives they like . . . including those that recognize non-human-centred values to natural entities and systems'. Regarding the egalitarian implications of Di Paola's argument, and the idea that this is a bottom–up obligation, 'it is also more desirable from a moral point of view [that] individuals should fulfill them for reasons internal to these obligations, and primarily out of morally justified personal resolve rather than out of obedience to regulations and fear of sanctions.' Unlike Black's faith in the regulatory power of the modern liberal–democratic state, Di Paola's interpretation of the concept of stewardship as one of virtue is given a decidedly liberal twist. The virtue aspect is almost theological, or Platonic, because as already suggested above, by Harrison, it advocates a self-mastery of our environmentally destructive impulses, but crucially – and this is where the similarities with Black end – because it is for *the good of humanity across time*. The use of the term 'axiological impartiality' leads us further towards a concept that is comparable to Rawlsian political liberalism, insomuch as it is freestanding between competing reasons for valuing wider nature. Combined with the egalitarian elements of her approach, and a respect for others' green concerns, it is clear that a modern secularized theory of environmental stewardship employs a firmly individualist language moving it ever closer towards liberal political thought. All pretensions of Christian guardianship over tangible features of wider nature, no matter how well meaning, are abandoned in favour of the idea that we are to be stewards of our own environmentally destructive selves, and thus capable of reining in our ecological vices for the good of humanity across the generations.

The indifference of wider nature

Returning now to Simon Hailwood's (2004) contribution to green political thought, his attempt to circumvent the separation argument led him to search for complementary liberal – yet impartial – freestanding environmental ethic (although he himself does not use the term *stewardship*). To be sure, Hailwood states that the 'independence' and 'otherness' of wider nature mirrors the key tenets of political liberalism. Not only this, but the above supposition sees a reappearance of Rawls's much bolder assertion in *TJ* (and the more tentative, yet equally ambitious, approach of *PL*) in that a theory of liberal justice could not but fail to exemplify a correct relationship between humanity and wider nature. Hailwood stresses that the separation argument is not necessarily a case of shallow instrumentalism, or outright speciesism, insomuch as 'the political cannot be completely isolated in every sense from the private', adding that in fact the political acts 'as a constraint on the pursuit of conceptions of the good life' (90). So is it the case that the political pervades the private, in the arena of green concerns and beyond, or is rather the case that political justice and environmental justice will represent two sides of the same coin? Maintaining these two positions – that the separation argument is bad for green concerns yet at the same time liberal principles of justice reflect a truth about humanity's relationship to wider nature – is the real test faced by Hailwood.

In defending such a position, he asks: 'how can the political culture of a liberal landscape be more than instrumentally respectful of external nature?' (89). Alluding to the aforementioned thin/thick perennial problem of political liberalism, Hailwood believes that a respect for nature's otherness, its independence, and its mysteriousness, is synonymous with the key aims of political liberalism in a manner that avoids a descent into a meaningless, and 'thin', conception. Taking a step back, and on the subject of why Rawls is selected as appropriate for greening, he offers only the briefest of reasons. He simply states that because it is representative of an inherent liberal attitude of instrumentalism reflected in its defence of the separation argument, and given that the aim of much green political thought is to shift liberal-democratic societies away from myopic dominion towards darker green theories of ecological justice, Rawls's political liberalism provides an appropriate site of reconciliation between these seemingly incompatible ideas.

Hailwood calls the separation argument 'the exclusion point', and proceeds to describe how the circumstances of justice – the prerequisite for any theory of distributive justice – cover two key features of human society, both in an internal and external sense. The internal circumstances are the fact of reasonable pluralism and the historical conditions established after the Reformations. Again, a liberal society encourages individuals to view themselves and

102 *Rawls and the Environmental Crisis*

others as both free and equal citizens, and, generally speaking, this is a widely accepted precept in modern liberal–democratic states, according to Rawls. The external circumstances of justice, that is, the basic competition within which humans find themselves locked given resources are limited and finite, are what Rawls identifies as the conditions of 'moderate scarcity'. This is a key problem for Hailwood as it adds another facet to the separation argument and fuels the claim that Rawls's political liberalism amounts to little more than a narrowly instrumentalist, and hubristic, form of environmental justice. Hailwood thus argues that within *PL*, 'non-human nature enters in only as a moderately unreliable provider of material instrumentally necessary for human survival and flourishing', adding that '[n]ature is niggardly enough to neglect guaranteeing everybody's wants and needs . . . but not so niggardly, at least not usually, as to make natural necessities so hard to come by that talk of distributive justice is pointless' (92–3). Wider nature is simply a collection of impersonal resources there for the sole benefit of liberal citizens and their 'landscaping' practices – citizens who, in turn, are to use it as a means to an end. The embedded narrative of environmental justice within Rawls's ideas, then, appears not to take us very far beyond a traditional theory of dominion.

Hailwood proceeds by exploring a view of nature as 'other' that does not compromise political liberalism's freestanding status via an 'unreasonable' colonization of the political conception by green concerns (94). This, he hopes, can then pave the way for the drawing of *analogous* comparisons between a freestanding political conception and the otherness view of wider nature in order to (a) prove that it is not a thick, substantive vision of the green good, akin to Rawls's notion of a 'natural-style religion' and (b) that it represents a reasonable political principle alongside liberty and equality. Hailwood explores the following three points of congruence between the idea of nature as other and political liberalism: neutrality; 'anti-expressivism'; and 'the extension of the virtues of "the reasonable citizen" ' (98–9).

Before taking these three points of congruence in turn, it is worth noting that viewing nature as other not only means that it is to be seen as independent of human landscaping (that is, 'nature-culture hybrids: the shape of local nature as moulded and interpreted by human culture . . . cultures generally need landscapes in which to locate themselves, as well as to develop as their physically necessary "raw material" for consumption'), but also as being neutral among 'many landscapes' (99). Although it provides natural constraints as to what can physically be achieved within a particular environment, wider nature does not provide a blueprint for what should happen, at either a moral or political level. In Hailwood's words: '[n]ature as other does not tell us how to live' (100). In addition to this, nature as other does not require an 'absolute' neutrality between landscaping, just as Rawls's political liberalism is not perfectly neutral between comprehensive doctrines. Some environments are limited in how they can be landscaped, with some allowing for a more harmonious, or sustainable, form of cultural shaping in a similar way political liberalism only allows for a consensus between reasonable comprehensive doctrines.[3]

There are limits to both but Hailwood acknowledges that his idea runs up against a logical inconsistency here as nature as other is specifically *indifferent* and functions on 'causes, not reasons', whereas a liberal conception of neutrality is to compel the reasonable into agreement. Nature is actually more neutral in this respect, and Hailwood returns to his idea that, although not comprehensive, nature as other acts as a '"reasonable idea of the good" (as opposed to a comprehensive doctrine, or conception for the good life)' (102). Rather than stating that nature as other directly corresponds to a freestanding political liberalism, Hailwood's aims remain more modest as he seeks only to establish an 'affinity' between the two. He also argues that nature's indifference need not necessarily imply an instrumentalist view whereby nature as other merely serves as a blank canvas for human society to landscape, because it is valuable in and of itself, and not just as a resource. Again, the two concepts are analogous: a notion of justice as fairness is not one comprehensive view of the good among others, just as nature as other is not merely another green comprehensive view, or theory of environmental or ecological justice.

The inconsistency between criticizing the separation argument whilst advocating the distinctiveness of the political from the natural order means that Hailwood has to prove nature as other does not necessarily serve as a moral or political blueprint. Put slightly differently, the political order of a liberal society governed by first principles of justice would not 'be validated as authentically natural by the external, non-human world', as it is rather the case that liberal citizens 'should see a kindred spirit in the otherness view's recognition that nature does not morally or physically dictate particular cultural landscapes' (110). So not only would citizens of a well-ordered society come to support a political overlapping consensus for reasons specific to their own doctrinal beliefs, they would also reject the instrumentalism of a political conception as being somehow a means to their ends. They should, therefore, 'take seriously the analogous neutrality that is part of the otherness view' and consequently 'incorporate the otherness view of nature within their political conception' (110–11). The otherness view, on this reading, resembles an additional and even, as previously argued, a third principle of justice within Rawls's political liberalism. Hailwood contends that liberal thought can be extended to green concerns in the spirit of tolerance and reasonableness in the sense that liberal values are applied to controversial disputes over the nature of the green good, as he modifies the internal circumstances of justice to include a reasonable pluralism of green concerns.

The second area Hailwood utilizes to strengthen his view is the historical liberal/conservative divide. He writes: 'to incorporate the otherness view within the political liberal conception is not based on an insistence that what is relevant in another (say political philosophy), lest each domain suffer a crippling alienation and the fracturing of the seamless whole of which they should be parts' (117). The shared 'anti-expressivism' means that again, the 'otherness view is available for incorporation; it is not excluded by the political liberal strategy . . . it is continuous with it', thanks to a 'deep-congruence'. Here

Hailwood argues that a principle of justice (added on, or as a stand-alone third principle, or at least a third *political virtue*) based on nature as other is not transcendent of both political and green arrangements, even though the affinity between a neutral political order and a conception of the bonds between humanity and wider nature is a matter of 'deep congruence'. Here, there is a rejection of a more conservative, organic, or holistic account of the relationship between a freestanding political liberalism and nature as other. For Hailwood it is a negative conception: 'it should be a question of "my enemy's enemy is my friend", where the enemy is the "cult of wholeness" '.[4] The analogous relationship between nature as other and political liberalism is not so much that they are two sides of the same coin, *sub specie aeternitatis*, but that it is more so the case that addressing green concerns does not mean we need to abandon liberalism for the sake of a holistic blueprint that leads humans to discover a higher truth from the teachings of wider nature.

Hailwood's third and final affinity between political liberalism and nature as other relates directly to the concept of toleration. Hailwood explains: 'respect for (involving toleration of) otherness looks continuous over the realms of people, state and external nature' (118). Highlighting Rawls's discussion of the 'political capital' of society, and the public virtues of reasonableness, fair-mindedness, the sense of justice, and the duty of civility, he argues that an appreciation of nature's otherness follows in the spirit of these qualities. Put slightly differently, it would seem disingenuous for a citizen of a well-ordered liberal society to be both reasonable and fair in his or her political life, but then to adopt an exploitative, and myopic attitude when it comes to determining his or her relationship with wider nature. For Hailwood, a 'disposition towards reasonable landscaping appears the order of the day here' (119). Again, he stresses the *affinity* between a liberal citizenship and an environmental citizenship that avoids any appeal to comprehensive, or thick, visions of the green good.

Nature as other, devoid of religious, spiritual, activist, teleological, or natural law implications, seems to act as a supplement to a politically liberal well-ordered society. Hailwood argues that 'respecting nature's otherness involves a general unwillingness to destroy natural eco-systems . . . and a heeding of ecological laws so as to understand the consequences for independent nature of various possible human courses of action' (122). Nature as other only excludes the ecologically unreasonable, so to speak, just as a politically liberal conception alienates intolerant, and unreasonable, political doctrines. A plethora of green views, Hailwood hopes, would come to support the otherness view for reasons specific to those particular doctrines. He is, therefore, much more optimistic than Rawls who hopes for agreement on explicitly instrumentalist grounds. Hailwood seems more ambitious in developing a Rawlsian-inspired theory of value and, although he does not state it directly himself, he clearly thinks that the recognition of nature's independence is a politically liberal *e pluribus unum* that overlaps irreconcilable green views.

To reiterate, Hailwood is not discussing stewardship *per se*, but his ideas are particularly pertinent to both parts of the green critique. What is most interesting about his substantial contribution to the greening of Rawlsian liberalism is the fact that it represents a significant development with respect to the question of how liberal thought intends to replace a deity in the modern period when it asks citizens to exercise self-denial and restraint in protecting wider nature. Impartiality is the primary point of affinity between nature as other and political liberalism, and this is then projected onto a focus on nature's independence. The selection of an environmental ethic – or point of agreement such as nature as other – has to reflect, complement, or embody the key tenets of liberal thought. As Hailwood points out, political liberalism is a more limited, realistic form of the idea as it eschews universal pretensions and is committed to principles latent in the public political culture. The very title of Hailwood's key work in this area is *How to be a Green Liberal* (as opposed to a *liberal green*) and so, like Wissenburg and Levy (2004), the focus for Hailwood is on how we go about preserving the gains of liberalism. So although he does not discuss stewardship directly, Hailwood's method of extensionism builds on the idea that liberal societies are to remain impartial between human differences regarding the reasons as to why wider nature should be protected. The question left unanswered by Hailwood is the issue of motivation because of his unequivocal rejection of the conservative implications of Rawls's well-ordered society. That is, how will citizens adhere to a much more philosophical conception of 'nature as other', over and above Rawls's belief in a much more straightforward form of instrumentalism, without an appeal to the more conservative values of duty when defending the gains of liberalism? Hailwood's extensionism is methodologically torn. On the one hand, he concludes that were a society to respect a plurality of green concerns, it will inevitably (but only indirectly) protect elements of wider nature, as they are central to individual citizens' views of the good. On the other hand, we see a full-scale modification of the principles of justice, as well as a belief that an application of these principles reveals an analogous 'truth' regarding the correct configuration of human and non-human relations, in a manner much closer to Rawls's own method of the taking outward of justice as fairness.

Although focussed on liberal thought more generally, Jennifer Welchman (2013) develops the individual arguments outlined so far in this chapter – from the idea of humanity as a transcendent good, to the need for an appropriately liberal and impartial approach, to a reasonable pluralism of green concerns capable of motivating citizens – and in doing so addresses the question of whether or not the secularization of stewardship, and the need to drop its traditional image as a theory of dominion, has rendered it meaningless. Black's work can be contextualized, not just in the sense that he alludes to the dominance of statism in theories of politics at this time, but also in the now archaic language used. Talk of *man's* dominion of nature and *man's* place in the world is precisely the kind of language that is representative of the more patriarchal and elitist roots of stewardship. Again, why look to an ethic that emboldens a sense of dominion over several oppressed groups – human or otherwise? Welchman's key aim is to defend a modern, secular environmental

106 *Rawls and the Environmental Crisis*

stewardship from the criticism, as already made by Lovelock (2006), that the steward's 'self-appointed' role carries no obligation unless, of course, one is a devout Christian.[5] The objection Welchman wishes to address, then, is the criticism that it would be *irrational* for citizens to adhere to the key tenets of a stewardship ethic and that beyond '[g]eneral duties of beneficence, non-maleficence and inter-generational justice' there is no 'morally obligatory role to undertake' (306). Not only this, but given that if they 'fail to fulfill these obligations in ways that affect only distant future generations, how can they be held to account?' Of particular note is the fact that she does not advocate a new, or what Black called a 'foreign', ethic, and instead seeks to develop principles of stewardship, like Hailwood, by working 'within the limits our prior and more encompassing moral principles, agreements and values allow' (310). Although Welchman herself admits that her work on the subject is incomplete, the liberalized account of environmental stewardship she provides is illuminating.

Welchman asserts that stewardship appears to be an attractive 'solution to the question of how to characterize morally appropriate interactions with nature' (299); that is, humanity's relationship to wider nature. She argues that there are 'four traditional associations' to stewardship, certainly in English-speaking countries, 'that seem to capture key aspects of emerging norms about humanity's relation to the natural world' (299). These norms have seen the term spread to a multitude of social and economic spheres, from household management to finance through to farming and the care of the commons. First, 'guardianship' (limiting personal interests); second, 'landholdings' (that portions of the commons are held albeit fleetingly by certain individuals); third, 'ongoing relationship' (goods are maintained over time by the same stewards); and fourth, 'moral virtues' (the possession of which include loyalty, temperance, prudence, and technical knowledge). Much like Di Paola's narrative, her characterization of the concept is that it has traditionally represented a virtue ethic, involving a degree of accountability to a higher authority, and so modern interpretations of liberalized environmental stewardship must stress that it forms part of the universal makeup of individuals, as opposed to selective appointments to the chosen few, who are worthy enough of the title of steward. Not only this, but the secularization of the concept removes the personal gains (financial or otherwise) awarded to stewards in favour of a more democratic language of the common good. Welchman explains: 'Individuals were called to serve the public interest, the interests of members of threatened species, or the interests of future generations, rather than their creator' (301). In addition to being voluntary rather than by 'formal appointment and/or remuneration for services rendered', citizens 'were called upon to appoint themselves stewards, rather than await appointment by others'. Combined with a more recent penchant for grass roots, 'peoples' movements' for the willing and the able to act as environmental stewards, Welchman presents recent policy developments under the banner of stewardship as the epitome of the democratic process. Whereas Black was interested in the statist implications of stewardship, both Di Paulo and Welchman concentrate on the more voluntary and localized aspects of its practical application in addition to any state-sponsored initiatives.

Key to Welchman's analysis of a newly secularized environmental stewardship, which she identifies as embodied in policies initiated from the 1980s onwards, is the liberal and pluralistic nature of its appeal to both 'instrumentally-valuable environmental services' and also 'non-use or "end" values' (302). Crucially, Welchman's 'common themes' of the concept, although not consciously articulated in the policies, include 'the management of one's own and other's exploitation of the natural environment constrained by active concern for present and future generations'. This balancing act – that is, the weighing up of the interests of contemporaries and the as yet unknown preferences of future persons – 'includes the management of any and all forms of production and consumption . . . by an appeal to beneficence and non-maleficence'. There is a deliberate mix of conservative and liberal thought here as Welchman again seeks to articulate the concept within embedded liberal norms, prevalent in societies, including a 'just, tolerant and equitable account of the interests of all concerned' (303). Not only this, but such a compromise takes place against a backdrop of religious pluralism 'where there is no publicly accepted procedure for settling debates about the points on which different faiths disagree'. This argument follows in a similar vein to Lercher's idea of an ecological conscience insomuch as Welchman argues that key values of secularized environmental stewardship include 'mutual tolerance' and 'equitable accommodation' not only on religious values but also on the value one ascribes to wider nature. Green concerns are, again, but one part of the fact of reasonable pluralism found in liberal societies, much like Hailwood's idea of the greening of the internal circumstances of justice. This objectivity – almost neutral in its application – is extended to green concerns so as to ensure that wider nature with its resources and life-sustaining ecosystems are sustained for future generations' potential instrumental and non-instrumental interests. Here Welchman also adds that this must be combined with 'the acceptance of significant answerability for one's conduct *to society*' (emphasis added), but the question remains as *to whom* exactly one is accountable. A preliminary answer, inferred from the discussion so far, would be a mixture of both an appreciation of an entrenched liberal order steeped in the language of rights, tolerance, and pluralism *and* out of the self-respect and integrity of our own individual faculties that allow us to act as stewards in the first instance. This concept of liberalized stewardship is lacking, however, given that it still requires a firm commitment to a transpolitical good capable of motivating citizens to curb their more environmentally destructive human traits.

Welchman attempts to strengthen the now liberalized concept by addressing key objections, new and old, to stewardship in all its forms. For Welchman the first main criticism is the anthropocentric, speciesist, elitist, etc. line of attack, and a heightened sense of the separation argument. Further, there arises here the suggestion that in trying to now tailor stewardship to fit in with modernity, pluralism, and secularism, it has 'rendered the conception effectively

108   *Rawls and the Environmental Crisis*

meaningless' (305). Presumably, like Hailwood, Welchman, too, seeks to avoid any appeal to conservative forms of holism and unity. Welchman's response to this particular criticism – that removing the deity leaves the term too thin or weak – is to draw an analogy with the development of democracy. Just as the birthplace of democracy, Athens, was elitist, anthropocentric, and sexist (as well as racist and xenophobic for that matter) it does not mean that we have abandoned a central pillar of Western civilization branding it instead as archaic. Stewardship, owing to its supposed adaptability, seems perfectly capable of freeing itself from the historical and genealogical roots that have led to its dismissal as anachronistic and fundamentally illiberal.[6]

In embracing the liberal language of rights, toleration, and justice, the concept inevitably accrues a new set of criticisms from those who believe that such 'salutary revisions' are either tokenistic or ineffectual (307). Simply put, the inherent sense of dominion remains as the concept perpetuates the separation argument. Welchman has two responses to this line of attack that form the crux of her defence of stewardship. The first is that although it is inescapably anthropocentric, environmental stewardship cannot be said to be 'uniformly' instrumentalist given that the 'values it promotes are human values rather than the value of nature independent of its role in human life'. Individuals will value nature for a host of incompatible reasons, yet these alone are not moral reasons. Environmental stewardship is thus modernized because it extends liberal rights to *human disagreements regarding wider nature*. For Welchman, then, this is simply another frontier of justice to be given the liberalization treatment. Rejecting the idea that environmental stewardship serves as a rival ethic to any other normative theory, Kantian, utilitarian, or otherwise, Welchman instead claims that it is a 'role', the performance of which is dictated by one's own wider normative belief system. Not only this, but 'individuals taking up the stewardship role must endeavour to show equitable concern for all values in play, instrumental and non-instrumental, anthropocentric and non-anthropocentric' (308). Welchman, much like Di Paola, adds that '*in practice of the role*, equity demands that they operate as pragmatic pluralists about the values and interest to be promoted' (emphasis in original). The key virtue of being an environmental steward, it would seem, is again to be tolerant and impartial with regards to other contemporaneous beings, as we should be with say, different religious or spiritual faiths. If anything, Welchman's ideas are comparable to Rawls's own position on taking justice as fairness truly *inward*, in that what is important is the stewardship on one's self, and our attitudes to our fellow humans. It is, therefore, about 'the management of human *behaviour* that degrades natural resources or values, not management of nature itself' (309, emphasis in the original). Again, much like Di Paulo and Hailwood, the argument is that modern environmental stewardship can only break free from its past by turning away from the idea of the oppressive management of nature, and by promoting a less divine and instead, a much more human virtue-based theory of self-management. Failure to act appropriately as an environmental steward means acting illiberally in harming one's contemporaries and their interests.

A second green critique 109

Welchman summarizes that in a similar way a 'murderer may rightfully be censured by persons other than the victim . . . those who refuse to exercise environmental stewardship may rightfully be censured by their contemporaries even for acts whose full effects will not be felt for several generations'. So to act as an environmental steward is to adhere to our already existing values of 'benevolence, justice . . . and compassion' so as not to harm other sentient beings regardless of one's own moral or doctrinal beliefs. The transpolitical good here is a stronger faith in a transgenerational commitment to liberalism.

Welchman's views differ significantly from Hailwood's sense of independent nature, which is much darker green in makeup, as according to her own understanding the very concept of wider nature seems of little relevance. In some respects, her work is an impassioned defence of Platonic self-mastery, but with relentless consumption serving as one of our present-day *mad masters*. Her ideas could just as well be about our attitudes to drugs, or alcohol, or any number of compulsive drivers that lurk within us. Her concern is with our responsibility to liberal justice, and citizens are to be stewards, it would seem, of an established liberal *attitude*, embodied in a tolerant society, set against a background of reasonable pluralism.

Two weaknesses to Welchman's argument do, however, prevent her model of liberal environmental stewardship from achieving its stated aim of overcoming the criticism that the secularization of the concept renders it meaningless, and thus unable to compel citizens to limit their own interests. The first is that the background of pluralism is perhaps not the most appropriate setting for a discussion regarding the valuing of nature. On the one hand, the subject matter is not as controversial as religious disputes, when different communities who cannot agree on principles of justice may find themselves in open conflict. Alternatively, it could be argued that humanity's relationship with wider nature is far too serious a business for the liberal language of rights and duties (a point not ruled out by Rawls), and so a much stronger vision of stewardship is needed to highlight the seriousness of such debates. This leads to the second problem with Welchman's view insomuch as her account is not recognizably one of environmental stewardship, but rather a stronger account of classical liberal thought extended to a new frontier. Accountability for individual actions lies with a transcendent notion of triumphant liberal values, but – and this is where there is a much greater affinity with Rawls – taking forward our individual sense of justice and reasonableness to future generations is neither as neutral nor impartial as Welchman hopes. This also returns us to the tension within justice as fairness that paints a picture of a conservatively liberal (or liberally conservative) attitude to intergenerational justice. Although we are moving towards a stronger theory of environmental stewardship that emphasizes the inculcation of liberal values designed to compel citizens to act as custodians of wider nature, the focus remains on a respect for a plurality of green values, and not wider nature itself. So far, this second version of the green critique, as a theory of environmental justice, eschews any positive engagement with wider nature other than restraining human

110 *Rawls and the Environmental Crisis*

arrogance, for the good of humanity, or in the case of Hailwood, nature's independent existence.

Thompson's 'lifetime-transcending interests'

If we are to consider how political liberalism in general could be extended to offer a transpolitical good, worthy of self-denial and sacrifice for the sake of wider nature, then doing so requires a more substantive account of how liberal values are tied into an intergenerational vision of humanity as enduring beyond individual human lives. Hailwood's recognition of nature as other proposes a supplementary, freestanding means of remaining impartial between competing green concerns. Welchman, too, proposes a view of environmental justice that promotes the liberal virtues of toleration, now seen as the stewardship of the self, to a plurality of green concerns. Perhaps the most detailed and comprehensive study of a similar line of argument comes from Janna Thompson (2013) who, like Hailwood, does not directly address the concept of stewardship, and instead outlines a much clearer distinction between *synchronic* and *diachronic* justice, with the latter (justice between contemporaries and members of future generations) serving as an 'addendum' to the former (justice between contemporaneous, rational agents). In remaining *synchronic*, traditional principles of justice fail to appreciate the fact that contemporary 'individuals are essentially second persons' insomuch as their very makeup is tied to their history, and should adherents wish to 'extend their theories to encompass diachronic relationships' then they will face a series of difficulties 'created by concepts and approaches that were not designed for these tasks' (4). Individuals have what Thompson calls 'lifetime-transcending interests'. Her argument is that the seemingly ahistorical approach taken by contemporary political theorists, including Rawls, overlooks how individuals 'locate and identify themselves in relation' to a past that existed before their birth' (5). Not only this, but individuals will 'also have desires and interests concerning a future that will, or could, exist after their lifetimes'. Given that these interests transcend one's own brief existence in the world, 'they are the basis of practices that enable citizens and members of communities to make moral demands of their successors and which, in turn, give these individuals obligations in respect to their predecessors'. Justice, according to Thompson, is not unidirectional, and so her key aim is to provide an 'account of what binds the generations together in relationships of entitlement and obligation' if we are to believe a polity is an intergenerational entity, or agent, in itself.

What is most interesting about Thompson's account is that she contextualizes the synchronic/diachronic debate within a much older discourse of late-eighteenth-century political thought and, specifically, the liberal/conservative divide. Outlining the more liberal position of Thomas Paine and Thomas Jefferson who 'thought it wrong that the freedom of democratic citizens to govern themselves should be limited by decisions over which they could exercise no control – whether made in another country or by people of the past' (6),

Thompson argues that this represents a purely synchronic view. In other words, citizens of a political society owe duties and obligations to their contemporaries and are free to shape the future direction of such a polity, regardless of the wishes of their predecessors. Juxtaposed to this position is the traditional and reactionary conservative outlook, with its roots in the works of Edmund Burke, that calls for a recognition of the fact that citizens are 'born into the obligations and entitlements that the partnership entails, and a morally sound person values his role in the partnership and accepts . . . the associated duties and the limitations that they impose on his freedom' (7).

Thompson's central objective is to locate Rawls's political liberalism where there is 'ample room for alternative conceptions' between these two extremes. Although it leans towards the liberal, diachronic side, as a contract theory it 'does not limit the freedom of present people to determine the nature of their political institutions, but it gives them a duty to provide for future citizens what they believe their forbearers ought to have provided for them' (8). In keeping with Bell's methodology, it is again helpful to focus on the *who*, *what*, and *how* of Thompson's assessment of the green credentials of Rawls. Throughout her account, Thompson stresses the centrality of *lifetime-transcending interests* as being the key motivation in her analysis of Rawls's political liberalism and relations between generations. As she herself puts it: '(a) polity that answers to the lifetime-transcending interests of its citizens is an intergenerational polity that acts as a responsible agent through time by keeping its long-term commitments' (12). Crucially, Thompson argues that 'we are predisposed to see ourselves as participants in relationships of cooperation that extend through time and unite members of past and future generations' (13). These 'relationships of cooperation' form the crux of a liberalized vision of humanity as engaged in a perennial, intergenerational, and arguably a transpolitical search for justice in the modern period.

On the subject of motivating citizens to agree upon a wider commitment to this vision of humanity as engaged in an intergenerational project of cooperation, and in line with the 'constraint principle' in *PL*, Thompson finds herself questioning the efficacy of Rawls's later work. Her contention here is that agreeing to a principle that we would expect previous generations to have followed does not in any way prevent a generation from weakening 'our institutions so that younger people of our society, though able to maintain institutions of justice during their lifetimes, will not have the means to save or provide the institutions as a heritage to those who are younger still' (26). Due to the fact that the contract situation only works if parties are physically able to maintain the just institutions inherited from their predecessors, 'there is no point in contractors supposing that they might belong to a deprived generation'. They are, then, within the limits of reason to choose a principle of intergenerational justice that gives citizens licence to exploit nature if it is of benefit for the generation as a whole. Thompson concludes that a return to the motivational assumptions of *TJ*, of heads of households caring for their immediate offspring, may be 'the best strategy' in order to include these 'non-contractual

112   *Rawls and the Environmental Crisis*

relationships that predispose or require them to accept obligations to each other' within a theory of intergenerational justice (27).

This is a routine problem for extensionist political theorists, and again we are faced with the difficulty as to whether or not it is acceptable to internally modify Rawls's theory to suit a given end. Is it possible to pick and choose the best bits of *TJ* and *PL* and present a 'corrected' theory of justice as fairness? On the other hand, green theorists are fully within their rights to view Rawls's work as one resource among many, much as Peter Wenz (1988) does, and establish new ethics from its remnants given the new circumstances of justice.[7] Yet for Thompson, the above contradiction means that two opposing forces are at play within Rawls's thought that inhibits any extension. We then arrive back at the fact that his later work reestablished a commitment to contracting parties remaining 'mutually disinterested', but for Thompson, this discourages the traits that would make citizens more inclined to support principles of intergenerational justice and goes against the real spirit of Rawls's faith in citizens' ability to cooperate meaningfully within a political society.

To overcome this contradiction Thompson sees lifetime-transcending interests as a key part of what gives a citizen's life meaning and identity, and that these can act as 'a legitimate basis for making *moral demands* on our successors' (38, emphasis in original). These interests, largely overlooked in liberal political thought, can either be an extension of one's own self-interest; they can be about the fate of other persons and their interests; or they can also be about 'things' that will continue to exist, as with the first two types of interest, long after that person has passed away (42). So how do intergenerational obligations arise from this? Thompson first imagines a single-issue OP, 'like the one described by Rawls in *Political Liberalism*' when there is a need to 'perpetuate social relationships which give their successors the opportunity to fulfill these desires' (51). Parties will need successors who are in a position not only to want to further these interests, but ones who are also able to do so. Although seemingly complemented by the constraint principle, and thanks to the ignorance of one's membership to a particular generation, citizens would not agree to a principle that severely limits successors in pursuing their own interests. Thompson, however, identifies two weaknesses to this method. First, the collection of lifetime-transcending interests would be too diffuse; second, there is no account of the institutional and political practices that would need to be established to provide the conditions for successors to continue their work. It is on this second point that Thompson bases her interpretation of political liberalism as representing a compromise between synchronic and diachronic positions. Not only this, but in making demands upon future generations, citizens will also simultaneously and 'tacitly' agree to respect duties towards their predecessors. Again, the true spirit of Rawls from Thompson's point of view is the idea of cooperation, as it is this that will generate intergenerational responsibilities. Mutual disinterest alone will not suffice.

The idea of justice as fairness becomes a reflection of human needs as opposed to something more profound because representatives in the OP are 'predisposed' to accepting such a principle (72). Justice as fairness, then, is to be modified so as to incorporate lifetime-transcending interests or, in Thompson's words, a 'just society ought to protect the intergenerational concerns of its members' as well as offering them 'opportunities to develop and pursue lifetime-transcending interests' (73) by reference to a Rawlsian-inspired, single-issue OP that deals solely with the subject of intergenerational justice.

Thompson's *what* of intergenerational justice is indeed the polity itself, but again, Rawls's just institutions are to be seen as a compromise between the two extremes of liberalism and conservatism, and two very different versions of history. For this liberal, Jeffersonian view of history and intergenerational justice, contemporary citizens are encouraged to remain positively sceptical of their inherited institutions and practices in order to meet the far more important demands of the present and the immediate future. Universal standards of justice are to act as principles by which we can critique the efficacy of institutions, and this view is juxtaposed to the conservative tradition that aims to celebrate the endeavours and sacrifices of our ancestors. Anything short of this is to dishonour the noble intentions of those who built the institutions we are now charged with conserving.

So far, then, we have the 'who' and 'what' of Thompson's Rawlsian-inspired theory of intergenerational justice. Just institutions, which provide the *means* of individual pursuits of the good life (whether lifetime-transcending or not), represent an ongoing, and almost timeless, project encompassing all citizens, past, present, and future. In addition, such a polity must maintain the environmental prerequisites necessary for the maintenance of these institutions, as well as the political practices necessary for intergenerational cooperation. These environmental conditions also embody 'things' that a citizen may wish to see preserved as part of a particular lifetime-transcending interest they happen to hold. An intergenerational polity, guided by the enduring human desire to build fair conditions of justice in the modern period, makes certain demands of its citizens, and so Thompson sets about answering the *how* of intergenerational justice.

Thompson picks up on the fact that contemporary injustices damage the descendants of the individuals on the receiving end of this unfair treatment, a point largely overlooked by Rawls. Again, the principle of just savings declares that once just institutions are established and able to distribute primary goods fairly, the dictates of justice no longer require a generation to save any more than is necessary to maintain said institutions. Thompson's theory relies on a lifetime-transcending ideal of intergenerational cooperation or, in Thompson's words: 'citizens who are committed to establishing a just polity are predisposed to conceive of themselves as participating in an intergenerational project of making, unmaking and reforming institutions of justice' (89). What is being inherited then is more than an embodiment of liberty in just institutions: it is a distinctly anthropocentric project of searching for what could ultimately be a 'true' or 'pure' conception of justice, and of humanity's place in the world.

114   *Rawls and the Environmental Crisis*

Thompson adds that her model of intergenerational justice not only favours the universalist approach, but is one that also 'keeps faith with our predecessors' (100). Her vision of an intergenerational polity, therefore, is one of adaptability, especially given her discussion of the ever-changing 'prerequisites' of justice. Each generation will have to contend with the inevitability of deteriorating external circumstances of justice, and so to continue in the eternal human search for justice '[i]nstitutions have to be reformed, injustices have to be corrected, reparations have to be made, threats to the perpetuation of just institutions have to met' (97). Modernity demands that the intergenerational polity will have to be flexible as well as self-critical. Thompson reiterates that individuals are naturally predisposed to this fact of modern life, and of the need to question the past for the sake of the future.

Thompson's theory also seeks a return to early Rawlsian liberalism in the form of his overlapping generations model and familial ties. As we have already seen, *PL* dropped this idea, but Thompson revives it in order to reach a similar conclusion to Wissenburg (1999). As already discussed in Chapter 2, Wissenburg believed that intergenerational justice can be secured through intragenerational, overlapping justice, because if a generation fails to maintain the institutions and practices that ensure that their predecessors receive adequate health and social care in their old age, then they will suffer a similar fate in the coming decades. In addition to educating younger generations so that they, too, will be able to maintain the just institutions needed to look after the generation currently engaged in securing their offspring's political inheritance, the linking of our familial co-temporal generational responsibilities with the idea of justice between the generations aims at bolstering the motivational force of her theory. The family, as a potential just institution, cannot be separated from the political, as it is the motivational ties that individuals have with their family that can feed into a political conception. The idea of family as an institution will come under more scrutiny in the conclusion.

This leads us to her 'fair shares principle' (114) as to the *how* of her theory of intergenerational justice; that is, 'what counts as just savings is determined by a judgement about what each generation should be prepared to sacrifice for the sake of establishing just institutions'. Here, Thompson links this to the aforementioned flexibility of an intergenerational polity in meeting ever-changing circumstances of justice, as well as appealing to the freestanding nature of Rawlsian liberalism (despite not using that exact term). The sacrifices made – and Thompson has in mind here those made by the least advantaged – can be for intrinsic and/or instrumental reasons (115). Ultimately it is history that will determine just how much citizens are required to save, as they will be predisposed to do more to ensure that future generations can benefit from the just institutions they have inherited from their predecessors. Crucially, according to Thompson, this occurs outside of the workings of the difference principle as the ongoing project of intergenerational justice, to which we are all committed, outweighs concerns for equality between the generations. For example, if a generation decides to 'level-down' and reduce their standard of living to either honour the past struggles of previous generations who were less well off, they may well end up carrying out less than their fair share as they leave future generations worse off by passing on weakened institutions. Likewise, if they were to try and reduce their standard of living to benefit future generations by providing a more sustainable, and frugal way of life, they would similarly compromise their successors' ability to pursue their lifetime-transcending interests given that they would inevitably inherit a poorer society. The *what* of intergenerational justice, or the good, remains the ability to engage in the project of justice as a perennial endeavour. Equality between generations is lexically ordered, like the difference principle, to the principal aim of liberty. So Thompson's interpretation of Rawls, faced with the new frontier of a concern for future generations, remains focussed on the spirit of cooperation and the liberty to pursue lifetime-transcending interests. This spirit of cooperation, the central feature of Rawls's liberalism, is contextualized as forming part of a wider project of humanity collectively engaged in an eternal search for justice, a project facilitated by just institutions and common political practices. Key to this is not equality, but more that we 'act to ensure that the members of succeeding generations will bear no greater burdens than members of present generations' (127).[8]

Thompson leaves us with the following definition for the ethos of her increasingly conclusive theory of intergenerational justice:

> Citizens of a polity ought to sustain just institutions, the ability to pursue historical projects and opportunities to appreciate and enjoy things that they and their predecessors regard as worthy of appreciation, along with resources and environmental systems to maintain these institutions, projects and things of value.
>
> (145)

Thompson addresses four criticisms of her final account: that it values nature only instrumentally; that it is unable to incorporate remote future generations; that it is ill-equipped for dealing with long-term environmental problems ('environmental time bombs'); and that it is inadequate as a theory of global justice beyond a single polity. It is, however, the first of these criticisms that is of immediate priority, especially given that a key aim of the extensionist political literature under review is to assess the extent to which Rawls's political thought can cope with darker green concerns, or put slightly differently, the extent to which citizens who hold darker green concerns, and theories of ecological justice, could form part of an overlapping consensus.

If the core duty of an intergenerational polity is to preserve its just institutions from one generation to the next, so as to fulfil its obligation of securing the conditions necessary for the continual project of justice, then wider nature is little more than a vehicle for human justice. This does little but add evidence to the charge that Rawlsian liberalism is little more than a light green, shallow instrumentalist theory of justice that pays no heed to the wider world of non-human life. Thompson's response to this particular criticism is limited

116 *Rawls and the Environmental Crisis*

and does not take us much further from the arguments already covered. Of course, Thompson has other aims, and so this is not a weakness *per se*. As previously discussed, she is hoping to locate Rawls's thought as existing somewhere between classically liberal and conservative visions of history. Thompson leads us back to the idea of an overlapping *green* consensus, whereby a liberal polity cannot expect to please all green views due to the inherent diversity (or spectrum) of environmentalisms and ecologisms present. For Thompson, 'a mass conversion or a departure from liberal neutrality is not necessary in order to hold that a polity ought to protect natural values' (147). There are, then, a variety of reasons for valuing nature, and Thompson's theory accepts that not 'all citizens are going to be persuaded that nature is worthy of respect, but the preservation of a plurality of valued objects is not only compatible with liberal neutrality, but required by intergenerational justice'. Thompson adds this is the 'the best that they can expect in the context of a liberal polity, and for political purposes it will suffice'. Like Hailwood, Thompson argues that preserving 'valued objects' in nature will have to remain 'human-centred' in respect of different lifetime-transcending values. Further, wider nature benefits only indirectly as a collection of 'things' that, together, is merely instrumental to a citizen's lifetime-transcending interests.

The extension of liberal rights

Despite the concept of humanity, as a transpolitical good, promoting a stronger theory of environmental justice, we have yet to witness the leap from a shallow to a more enlightened theory of environmental justice. Although it is to remain on the lighter shades of our spectrum, or continuum, of green concerns, it does represent the start of a significant development. Further, piecing together this quite diverse array of works, and *in lieu* of the divine element to the tripartite God–humanity–nature relationship central to a Christian concept, environmental stewardship in the modern period could look to Rawls's central idea of humanity as engaged in an intergenerational pursuit of justice, with only the power of reason to guide them in age devoid of eternal, outside support. This provides a starting point to the answer as *to whom*, or *for what*, environmental stewards could be called upon to sacrifice and limit their own self-interests. The second aspect pertinent to the greening of Rawls's mature work is that there appears to a belief that the intergenerational project of justice must be inherently liberal, and for that reason much of the green critique concerns itself with highlighting the reasonable plurality of green concerns. If we are to protect the lifetime-transcending interests of individuals, or respect their liberty of an ecological conscience, as well as the ongoing need for political cooperation within liberal societies, then wider nature, as Hailwood reminds us, remains merely instrumental and 'niggardly' with regards to this enduring endeavour. Within the discussion so far, there is a curious mix of virtue ethics and normative liberal theory. The point of convergence seems to be that tolerance is the key virtue needed for the liberal intergenerational project, particularly of one another's green concerns. This, in turn, is extended to an intergenerational setting to encompass the green concerns future individuals within a liberal society may possess. This is clearly different from the mutual disinterest of the OP. Yet the view from darker green concerns and those who hold a much stronger theory of ecological justice may still struggle to support a stable consensus around what they would surely see as the political epitome of the ecologically ruinous separation argument.

What seems to stand out in both parts of the green critique of Rawls is that neither actually require an environmental crisis, or in fact any in-depth discussion of environmental science, or ecologism, beyond an elementary understanding of the ecosystems that support life on Earth. As previously mentioned, this whole critique could, for example, function just as well by an appeal to the problem of drug addiction or a global flu pandemic. Any crisis that threatens an individual's interests now and in the future, or his or her ability to engage in mutually cooperative social and political endeavours that guarantee a fair system of rights and opportunities, becomes a target for liberal thought. Any concern for wider nature, even within Hailwood's much greener view of nature's 'otherness', remains secondary. The motivation of mutual disinterest endures, and though this means that the second green critique does little to modify Rawlsian liberalism, it does mean that the separation argument continues to alienate the view from darker green concerns. Perhaps Read's dismissal of Rawls no longer appears quite so radical.

If we are to talk of an intergenerational search for justice and enduring political cooperation characteristic of the modern period, then the concept of humanity has to be recognized as a transpolitical good. This, in turn, requires a liberalized account of environmental stewardship to make the point that citizens are to act as virtuous temporary custodians and stewards of this ongoing project. Rawls asks us to observe political liberalism as an enduring endeavour of human cooperation, the quintessence of which is the just institutions that comprise the well-ordered society. Once the question of what we are to bequeath to future generations is taken seriously, as we are forced to do so with Rawls's principle of justice savings, it is no longer the case that the idea of justice as fairness has only to be extended, or taken forward, to the guaranteeing the liberty of citizens to pursue *lifetime-transcending interests*, as there is also a much stronger sense of duty required. A commitment to the stewardship of 'things', and of wider nature, is needed, even if they are only to be seen as the material conditions of intergenerational interests or the goods with intrinsic value that those holding darker green concerns wish to preserve. As we have seen, Rawls held that views from ecological justice would deem this politically reasonable. Even if the majority of citizens do not recognize the intrinsic, or at least non-instrumental, value of these goods, it is out of a liberal virtue of tolerance that they should respect the stronger green concerns of their fellow citizens with whom they wish to cooperate for the wider good of humanity.

118 *Rawls and the Environmental Crisis*

These citizenship requirements are egalitarian in nature according to a modern, liberalized theory of environmental stewardship so as to make them the duty of *all* citizens, and not just the leadership, or 'dominion', of the infallible few. So this secularized account of stewardship is more about self-restraint, and the trusteeship of our inherent, and thoroughly modern, virtue of being a reasonable citizen in not harming the environments that are central to the flourishing of human cooperation.

The distinct impression so far, then, is that a liberalized theory of environmental stewardship could serve as a more favourable, but slightly disingenuous, green critique of Rawls. Its true aim seems to be to secure the political toleration of competing green concerns via an appeal to the mutual disinterest of citizens who view one another as free and equal. What is interesting about the theorists covered in this chapter is the fact that although they seek to invoke a transpolitical good of humanity, it is in danger of representing little more than a euphemism for what is still a shallowly instrumentalist, light green theory of dominion, under the auspices of a liberal intergenerational project of human cooperation. In addition to this, these theorists are explicitly keen to avoid any trace of conservative thought, or appeal to organicism, in the search for an appropriate configuration of human/non-human relations. The fear, presumably, is that if we were to stray too far from liberal thought in addressing green concerns, there would be a gradual slide into some form of illiberal organicism, and thus a regime that values the whole rather than the individual parts. Under a system of political liberalism, the freestanding political agreement develops into a consensus because it is built on a model of cooperation that secures the political liberty and equality of individuals regardless of their competing visions of the good life. What is most intriguing about Rawls's works, and this is a point rejected by both Hailwood and Thompson, is that the principle of just savings and the reliance on mutual disinterest of parties in the OP (and self-interest beyond the OP) raises a tension within his work between liberalism and conservatism, a tension that cannot straightforwardly be resolved by Thompson's indirect approach to the valuing of wider nature. To do so means taking seriously the much wider aim of Rawls's theory, and his hopes for addressing a perennial problem of modernity; namely, the idea of political of unity in a world devoid of outside support. The conclusion, therefore, will now address the indirectness of the second part of the green critique and reject the notion that the preservation of wider nature is merely a fortuitous by-product of the ongoing project of political cooperation in the name of humanity. In the process of offering an enlightened theory of environmental justice that has moved on from shallow instrumentalism, it refutes the claim made by Thompson, above, that Rawls's work steers a middle ground between liberalism and conservatism. Instead, it argues that the intergenerational aspirations of justice as fairness and the principle of just savings, in conjunction with the wider project of political liberalism, invites a much more conservative interpretation of his work that is fully compatible with a general liberal appeal to mutual disinterest.

Notes

1 In only looking to one aspect of the so-called crisis of modernity, namely, the separation argument, this does assume a set narrative. Joel Kassiola (2015) states that the Hobbesian theory of modernity, that individuals are driven by a constant fear of death and the desire to satisfy insatiable material wants (as a means of security), a drive that disappears only when we die and literally may rest in peace, renders modernity a flawed project. 'This flaw of modernity is highlighted by the environmental crisis, including various challenges to human health and the modern way of life caused by the environmental crisis, fomented by ecological limits' (28). Further, 'the single most important aspect of the environmental crisis may be its normative basis and unique demonstration of the unsustainability and undesirability of modernity, in a manner that no previous challenge to this seemingly invincible social order has faced in its history' (29–30). The environmental crisis is thus something external, yet at the same time internally produced that undermines the normative individualist and secular ambitions of modernity. Once unconnected environmental challenges now have a common root: modernity. The notion of an all-encompassing environmental crisis is symptomatic, and *post-hoc*, leading to a diagnosis that modernity is doomed. Compare with Marshall Berman (1983) whose identification of the crisis is the lack of internal coherency to the very project that we can call modernity. Berman argues that 'as the modern public expands, it shatters into a multitude of fragments, speaking incommensurable private languages' and in doing so renders null and void its 'capacity to organize and give meaning to people's lives' (17). Berman concludes that because of this fragmentation, the modern period is something of a betrayal: 'we find ourselves today in the midst of a modern age that has lost touch with the roots of its own modernity'.

2 See O'Sullivan (1976) for a further explanation of the term 'little Gods'.

3 Hailwood gives the following example: 'one might say that a seafaring culture, at home in coastal features, sea, tide and "natural harbor", could not develop in the Sahara' (2004: 100).

4 'The cult of wholeness' is a term used by Charles Larmore (1990: 351) to describe the key aim of the German Romantic backlash against the Enlightenment.

5 Even then, Welchman argues, believers would be waiting for divine assistance based on their own devotion (2013: 306). Ultimately, faith is placed in God to the extent that an earthly citizen has little dominion, or at least that seems to be Welchman's argument.

6 There is another point of clarification needed here, however, regarding the idea of 'concepts' and 'conceptions'. This is a distinction made by Beetham (1993) and Holden (1988), amongst others, in describing how the term 'democracy' is a concept that is accompanied by various 'conceptions' of democratic theory. Put another way, 'democracy' confers core principles, or at least an embodiment of unifying features, whereas rival democratic theories represent an application or even misapplication of such principles. For example, the *concept* of democracy refers to established ideas of rule by the people, the need for accountability, and the principle of equality. *Conceptions* of democracy can refer to theoretical or empirical applications of the term (Holden, 1988).

7 One of the more sustained, earlier explorations into extensionist Rawlsian political thought is Wenz's *Environmental Justice* (1988). Although not focused solely on Rawls, it presents an illuminating analysis of the challenges posed by the notion of an environmental crisis to the Rawlsian project. Unfortunately, and despite the year of publication, *Environmental Justice* does not address the changes that were under way in Rawls's move from a comprehensive to a political liberalism, and deals only with *TJ*. Wenz rejects *TJ* on the grounds that no singular, established theory of justice or ethics – Rawlsian, utilitarian, right-based, or otherwise – can resolve problems questions of environmental justice. His central thesis,

120 *Rawls and the Environmental Crisis*

a thesis that Rawls himself would also set out to refine, is that impartiality – or 'unbiased', 'good judgement' – are the order of the day in societies characterized by a plurality of theories of justice and ethical beliefs.

8 A preoccupation of Thompson's account of intergenerational justice is the population question (2009: 132–4). If we are to leave future generations with the conditions necessary to pursue their unique conception of the good, within a well-ordered society, then a growing population will mean contemporary generations have to set aside even more resources to ensure that their predecessors are left no worse off. The philosophical intricacies of the population question are beyond the scope of our current enquiry.

Conclusion

Towards a Rawlsian stewardship ethic

The previous chapter has outlined the potential stewardship credentials of Rawls's theory based on the need for individuals to be called upon to sacrifice self-interest for the good of a cooperative, universal, and intergenerational project of justice in the name of humanity. The problem is, however, that we are still only able to extrapolate a shallow instrumentalist theory of environmental justice built on human dominion, as any incentive to protect wider nature within justice as fairness is both indirect and merely a means to this higher intergenerational project. Here a stronger claim will be made that goes beyond Hailwood's idea of nature as 'other' and Thompson's 'lifetime-transcending interests'. Simply put, do the conservative undertones of Rawls's well-ordered society, and the virtues of citizenship necessary for its preservation, offer an outright theory of stewardship that can form an integral – as opposed to a complementary – aspect of political liberalism? The key aim here is to push beyond the suggestive and move more towards a recognition of the inherent tension within Rawls's mature idea of justice as fairness; namely, that it is liberal with regards to intragenerational justice, but conservative in its approach to intergenerational justice. This, in turn, will propose an answer to the question of 'Why Rawls?' Ultimately, the most convincing response to this question rests on the belief that his theory of justice is preoccupied with the preservation of a well-ordered society, upheld by principles of justice, and the inculcation of liberal 'stewards' capable of looking beyond their immediate, contemporaneous interests. It may seem that even after forty years of research scholars have not progressed very far beyond only the lightest shades of green concerns on our continuum, and that it is difficult to look further than the idea of a Rawlsian-inspired, post-OP, and speculative application of justice as fairness to the new frontiers of political thought. The recognition of the conservatively liberal approach of Rawls, however, does outline a more substantive theory of environmental justice that moves it from a shallow to a more enlightened instrumentalist view. This, it will be argued, is certainly not insignificant.

An indirect, 'Rawlsian-inspired' OP

It is the *indirectness* of the second green critique that is problematic to the greening of Rawls, as it still regards wider nature and associated green concerns as peripheral. If humanity is engaged in a perennial search for justice,

122 *Rawls and the Environmental Crisis*

then such an endeavour will require stable *external* circumstances of justice (that is, the ecological systems upon which human life depends), first because they make human cooperation possible, and secondly because such a view encompasses an increasing plurality of lifetime-transcending interests held by citizens, many of which will involve either light green or dark green reasons for preserving wider nature. This second reason is owing to what Hailwood has identified as the *internal* circumstances of justice, and these are the result of the modern view of the citizen as inherently both free and equal. Should citizens be called upon to sacrifice their own immediate self-interest for the sake of wider nature it would be out of respect for this ongoing, and enduring, liberal search for principles of justice built on the post-Reformation human condition. Again, any concern for the fate of those elements of wider nature at risk from deteriorating ecological conditions is because the inviolable rights of the free and equal individual, prized by a politically liberal society now viewed as an ongoing intergenerational project, are under threat. We call this *the liberalized theory of environmental stewardship*.

As noted in the previous chapter, Thompson looks at the feasibility of establishing a separate, single-issue OP specifically designed to tease out citizens' considered judgements on matters of intergenerational justice (2009: 51). This is an exercise in applying Rawls's own idea of taking justice as fairness forward to future generations, quite separate from the principle of just savings. The problem is, however, that any forward, inward, or outward extension of Rawls's theory to a new frontier of justice (for example, atmospheric justice, the wilderness, non-human species, etc.) will only be able to indirectly incorporate the view from darker green concerns as it will, again, treat such problems as peripheral. If humanity is to declare itself as 'master' of certain goods or concepts, then every capable individual member of the species is charged with looking after such goods so as to maintain the stable external and internal conditions required for the ongoing project of intergenerational justice. In doing so, humanity still assumes dominion over wider nature. Take, for example, the moral status of non-humans in such a theory, as they represent a key group previously excluded from political justice, and one at risk from what liberals can only see as the deteriorating, *external* circumstances of justice. The ongoing existence of non-human species, and in particular individual members of such species, will represent mere 'things' according to Thompson that are to be valued as component parts of citizens' views of the good. Non-humans species cies are, therefore, key to the *internal* circumstances of justice because of the existence of a plurality of green concerns a liberal polity is to respect.

Rawls's own account of political constructivism, as ever, seemingly affords only shallow instrumentalist reasons for the protection of non-human life, for example, 'to foster species of animals and plants for the sake of biological and medical knowledge with its potential application to human health'. He defends this view by stating that this is a political – as opposed to a metaphysical – reason for valuing non-human species that appreciates them only for their use-value, as a resource, to humans. They are thus at the mercy of dominant human interests because in cases of conflicting human and non-human interests, non-human species – at either an individual or at a species-level – are placed at a disadvantage. The best they can hope for is to be valued by a citizen, preferably as part of their lifetime-transcending interests. This way, a politically liberal society is obliged to protect them out of respect for the now sacred interests of the individual. Can Rawls's notion of justice as fairness extend its reach further than this politically narrow valuation of non-human life on earth?

In taking justice as fairness outward in this manner, Rawls rules out the potential for non-humans to be considered as moral *agents*, but the argument seems to be that political liberalism is able to consider such species as moral *patients* (see Regan, 1983; Singer, 1993). In appealing to sentientism (as Rawls himself does in *TJ*) to highlight that moral *agents*, in possessing rationality and the capacity to apply morality to the decision-making process, have a duty to include moral *patients*, who themselves experience pain and suffering similar to moral *agents*, within such processes.[1] If bestowed the status of moral patients, non-human species can represent a marginalized group – an excluded or minority body in need of protection (the taking outward of justice as fairness). Schuppert (2011) states that similarly, the inclusion of future generations into a system of justice represents a natural extension of liberal-egalitarian justice (the taking *forward* of justice as fairness). Excluding living entities on the grounds of race, sex, ethnicity, and, as Schuppert argues, generational identity, is wholly arbitrary. Just as egalitarian liberalism has sought to apply basic principles of justice including liberty and equality to previously excluded individuals, so, too, should it endeavour to overcome forms of oppression based on species-membership. A system of *political justice* is thus to be complemented by a corresponding scheme of *environmental justice* that allocates goods, resources, and, above all, moral concern to excluded groups.

Taking justice as fairness forward, outward, or inward will remain incomplete, however, if we wish to pursue Rawls's own idea that we should appeal to an ethical discourse beyond the sacred liberal language of rights and equal opportunities. It simply leaves us to infer the indirect benefits conferred to non-human species. It remains the case that principles of justice are capable only of an indirect concern for non-human species, future generations, and wider nature. In justifying the separation argument, any commitment to protecting wider nature, or those at risk from deteriorating ecological conditions, is the result of the political representation of the inviolable intergenerational interests of contemporaneous individuals, and not wider nature *per se*. A firmer commitment to taking theories of ecological justice seriously, beyond the language of the use-value of wider nature to humanity, is still missing from the greening of Rawls, and this, in turn, prevents a political consensus from gaining the sufficient support from across a continuum of green concerns. Thus far, the environmental crisis is merely a crisis of human value. But the fault line here is within Rawls's works, and not Thompson's, for it was Rawls who preserved the idea from *TJ* that his theory would mirror a correct conception

124 *Rawls and the Environmental Crisis*

of humanity's place in the world, and hence why justice as fairness could be taken forward, outward, and inward (much like the process of his principle of just savings that is, to a degree, merely Rawlsian in spirit as it presented by Rawls himself as merely complementary to justice as fairness). This is too comprehensive for proponents of darker green theories of ecological justice, as they, like Read, believe liberal thought itself to be anachronistic given declining global ecological conditions.

Conservatism revisited

We would be well within our rights to leave this whole issue unresolved, and conclude by stating that this contradiction does indeed mean that Rawls's political liberalism is unable to provide a meaningful account of environmental justice, beyond a minimal and shallow instrumentalist theory of dominion. Combined with the motivational discrepancy between the mutual disinterest of parties in the OP, and the implications of the principles of just savings, we may well have reached the end of the line with Rawls given the new and increasingly dismal circumstances of justice. Yet an exploration of the conservative elements of the principle of just savings forces a reappraisal due to the fact that it ultimately expresses a theory of liberalized stewardship in line with the findings of Chapter 4. We have already seen how Thompson looked to the classical, Jeffersonian liberalism versus Burkean conservatism debate as establishing the roots of current discourses on intergenerational justice. A resurgence of conservative green political thought in recent years has much in common with a liberalized concept of environmental stewardship, and provides what could be the missing link between Rawls's notion of mutual disinterest in the OP and his principle of just savings, reliant as it is on a much more demanding transpolitical good of humanity as engaged in a perennial search for justice. It also assists in confronting the separation argument, as well as the question as to how a thicker conception of environmental justice could be more acceptable to holders of darker green concerns.

Both Roger Scruton (2006, 2012) and Katey Castellano (2013) believe that conservative thought has been largely overlooked by green political theory. We have already seen the unequivocal hostility displayed by both Hailwood and Thompson towards a reconciliation of Rawlsian liberalism with the idea of an organic, more conservative green common good. It could be argued that any reluctance to engage with conservatism amongst environmental thinkers is due to modern conservatives' (as a political movement) love for the free market, relentless wealth creation, and hierarchy which are, in fact, the same charges often leveled at liberals within the discourse of green political theory. Moreover, any mention of an organic society, or an appeal to values, traditions, or institutions that are to be ranked above the rights and liberties of the individual, invokes the predictable response of a fear of intolerance, absolutism, or some form of eco-authoritarianism. Yet early conservative discourse presents a timely critique of the separation argument, and modernity more generally, insomuch as by its very nature not only is it committed to intergenerational relationships, but it also embodies a natural theory of environmental stewardship. The question remains as to why the green critique (with the possible exception of Abbey, 2007) fails to recognize that Rawls himself did not rule out an appeal to values beyond the realms of liberalism, when his idea of the well-ordered society, with its just institutions, does nothing *but* appeal to a theory of stewardship.

Key to understanding the inherent conservatism of Rawls's principle of just savings is to consider how it goes against his own defence of the separation argument. By exploring this small body of literature on conservative green thought, and although Castellano and Scruton each interpret Burke differently, it is clear that it offers a welcome critique of the abstraction of human justice from green concerns, but one that does not provide an unrealistic, holistic conception of a green common good that automatically overrides individual rights. Not only this, but it serves as a means of countering the indirectness of both the separation argument and the intergenerational project of humanity central to a liberalized theory of environmental stewardship. Castellano (2013) looks to Burke's 'social ecology' in a holistic interpretation of sustainable living between humans and their environment but for Scruton (2006, 2012), there is an appeal to the basic anthropocentric motivation of a love for one's *oikos* so as to preserve the *heimat*, or home. It should be argued, however, that the most relevant aspect of Burkean thought is what Castellano calls the 'intergenerational imagination' (2013: 16). For Castellano, 'traditionalist' Burkean thought encourages contemporary citizens to be more 'mindful' of their environment, and for Scruton there is an inherent theory of 'trusteeship' in Burke.

Scruton's work is aware of the significance of Burkean intergenerational thought to wider environmental ethics and green political theory, claiming that these disciplines have failed to account for the genuine human motivation that, if harnessed, would encourage individuals to exercise self-restraint, and even to sacrifice their own interests, for wider nature. Scruton first rejects attempts made to either extend established theories of justice to environmental problems (as has been the case with Rawls) or, even worse, to design new theories of citizenship that inspire a metaphysical shift in ecological consciousness, much like Black's approach outlined in the previous chapter (187). For Scruton, '[w]e solve environmental problems not by appointing someone to take charge of them, but by creating incentives that will lead people to solve them for themselves' (97). What is needed is an appeal to human nature as it exists, and not a transformation towards what we 'ought' to think regarding our environment and relationship with wider nature. It is a question of motivation for Scruton, for as soon as the normative or ethical reasons for preserving our environments are handed to 'experts', whether bureaucratic, political, academic, or otherwise, policies and initiatives become distant from the 'real' concerns of ordinary citizens. Two things stand out here: first, that any theory of environmental or ecological justice must be built on principles and attitudes already widely held within a citizenry, and secondly, that only a conservative

126 *Rawls and the Environmental Crisis*

approach to tapping into this motivating force will suffice. Much like the second part of the green critique, Scruton's approach is one that looks to the role of the self-appointed steward, as opposed to an elite serving as a guardian class of masters, thus perpetuating a premodern theory of dominion.

Scruton's conservative thought does make reference to Rawls and his just savings principle, but as with utilitarianism, deep ecology, or Kantian ethics, such 'contractarianism' is flatly ruled out as a consistent principle of motivation for conserving one's environment. This is because, Scruton argues, debates within green political theory 'are largely normative, concerned with what we *ought* to think . . . They do not tell us what ordinary people think, and rarely do they touch on questions of motivation that should be considered by anyone who is looking for policies that would protect future people' (207, emphasis in original). Conservative thought, like the account of liberalized environmental stewardship set out in the previous chapter, is seen as a more individualistic, bottom-up and grass roots theory of citizenship. Technocrats, scientific experts, and academics cannot dupe citizens into believing that there is a need for seismic metaphysical shifts so as to lead them to a correct understanding of their place in the world. Like Michael Oakeshott's (1962) 'rationalist', able to solve any problem placed before them, so, too, are any normative attempts by green political theorists to correct our relationship to wider nature doomed to failure.

Scruton himself draws on Burke's model of intergenerational trusteeship as a challenge to the separation argument that embodies three core principles: 'respect for the dead', the 'little platoon', and the voice of 'tradition' (Scruton, 2012: 215). Taking each of these points in turn, citizens would find themselves committed to an intergenerational chain of connection through *love*. For Scruton, motivation comes from the fact that we cannot know the needs of future persons but 'the past is known, and the dead, our dead, are still objects of love and veneration' (216). Scruton continues that there is a 'line of obligation that connects us to those who gave us what we have; and our concern for the future is an extension of that line'. We care, then, for what is 'ours' and we preserve such goods out of 'gratitude'. Crucially, we belong to a transgenerational *community*. For Scruton, Burke's condemnation of the eighteenth-century French revolutionaries centred on the fact that 'they assumed the right to spend all trusts and endowments on their own self-made emergency' and thus 'systematically destroyed the stock of social capital', including long-established political institutions (217). These institutions, however, are owned fleetingly by trustees who not only have an 'indefinite burden of responsibility' but also 'all the duties of ownership without the rights' (217–8). It is the idea that we are fleeting trustees and a language of duties – not rights – that forms the crux of Scruton's analysis of Burke. Like the idea of lifetime-transcending interests – but unlike the outward projection of our present interests – we are to respect that which we have inherited as we are directly tied to such goods through feelings of love. There is a sense here of trusteeship, not just of inherited transgenerational communities that serve as stable chains of connection between the generations, but also of the responsibilities and duties owed to our predecessors.

Burke's famous idea of 'little platoon' ties in with Scruton's hope for the 'conservative environmentalist'. The rise of statism, or the myth propounded by Black in the previous chapter, replaced the humble *volunteer* and replaced the need (or the desire) for citizens to act for themselves. Just as trustees are held accountable to beneficiaries, volunteers, too, are directly responsible for their own actions to their peers, or colleagues, or for whomever they work. Statist or collective solutions leave little room for individual citizenship, especially within the theory of liberalized environmental stewardship as it has been presented in the preceding chapter. These little platoons also form a store of practical knowledge and are a source of traditions and consequently 'answers' to 'enduring questions'. Scruton summarizes his view of Burke by arguing that these ideas serve as the 'primary *motives* on which enduring societies are built, and it is in terms of them that any believable solution to problems of environmental management must be expressed.' If we sever the context of the potential plight of future persons from the past, it 'merely cuts us off from the only motives that we have to regard those future people as *ours*' (221, emphasis in original). Burke appeals to the duties of the inheritors, of those to whom we are attached through the intergenerational imagination, as opposed to the motivation of extending rights to a previously excluded, and abstract, group of individuals.

Scruton's work invokes a model of environmental trusteeship and citizenship that alludes to the importance of institutions such as the home, trusts, the commons, corporations, or the family *in conjunction with* the self-interest of the individual citizen. Established traditions and enduring institutions embody a natural and thus correct way of organizing human societies, but the key motivating force behind the need for citizens to act as temporary custodians of wider nature is not only the love for the intergenerational community of which they are a member, but also their love for their home, or *heimat*. The key point to make here is that Scruton stumbles upon the separation argument, by merging self-interest (individuals' love of their community and home), with a sense of custodianship over the institutions that they have inherited. Yet can these two ideas be reconciled quite so straightforwardly? Can a theory of environmental stewardship, which appeals to the voluntary care for inherited goods, institutions, and practices, be sustained by an appeal to the self-interests of individuals seeking to protect their home? This is a difficult position to maintain given that the appeal to self-interest can soon slip into the protection of environments only indirectly, and again, for shallow instrumentalist reasons alone. For this to work, a much closer relationship between conservative trusteeship and liberal self-interest needs to be established. This is either a straightforward case of Rawls *versus* Scruton, or together, they could represent two sides of the same coin as they both are concerned with the maintenance of just institutions from one generation to the next, with liberalism providing the idea that this forms part of a much more profound transpolitical, and enduring,

128   *Rawls and the Environmental Crisis*

search for justice by humanity, and conservatism focussing more on the duties and obligations of the free citizen.

Castellano, too, argues that although the reconciliation of green concerns and liberalism forms the centrepiece to green political thought, and if modernity is to be 'characterized by a progressive vision of knowledge, time, and humanity', then the conservative 'revitalization of the intergenerational imagination emerges as a counter-narrative to the optimistic telos of progress' (2013: 4). She therefore identifies Romantic Burkean conservatism, or the conservative traditionalist stance, as being juxtaposed to the liberal individualist strand of post-Reformation thought. Castellano's account goes much further than Scruton's, and provides a stronger challenge to the separation argument in examining 'the nascent social ecology' in the work of Burke which states 'that the fate of humans and their environment are inseparable' (7). Like Scruton, Castellano draws on the idea that 'whether we take responsibility for it or not, human beings are attached to previous and future generations through our shared habitat and modes of habitation' (12). Castellano examines the idea of intergenerational connection based on the ongoing shared experience of living in the environments into which we are born, and not just in the sense that they provide the external circumstances of justice necessary to sustain life, or as a benign background to the more important fact of reasonable pluralism as the internal circumstances of justice.

Conservative values add much-needed motivating qualities of *citizenship* to a theory of liberalized stewardship by way of an appeal to Burke's notion of 'life-renters' and 'temporary possessors'. For Castellano, this represents a point of departure between liberal stewardship and conservative trusteeship, with the latter offering a much deeper degree of *humility*. Her expression for this is 'epistemological modesty' (32), and it derives from the core belief of conservative thought that humans are imperfect. When extended to the issue of humanity's association with wider nature and those once excluded from justice, 'prejudices, habits, and dispositions create social and environmental stability', hence they become virtues (33). Unlike simply taking forward liberal toleration to an intergenerational setting, via a concept of humanity accompanied by the notion of lifetime-transcending interests, Castellano believes Burke's work exemplifies a 'proto-ecological fear' that 'a crumbling society into atomistic individuals suggests that the fate of the political, moral, social, economic, and environmental systems cannot be separated from each other . . . the conservation of the social ecology of established human habits and traditions is of foremost importance in modernity' (35). As such, the individual must learn to see him or herself 'as always merely a "life-renter" − of culture, land, and community − who stands between past and future generations'. Castellano's analysis of conservative green thought, with her focus on humility and the fleeting presence of individual humans, provides the very crux of a theory of environmental stewardship and associated qualities of citizenship that are currently missing from the liberalized idea of humanity as engaged in an intergenerational cooperative endeavour: that we are tied to our habitats by a social ecology of mutual dependence. This is obviously very far removed from Hailwood's more neutral view of 'nature as other' due to its indifference to human existence.

So, Castellano agrees with Burke that the divorcing of the past from the future causes problems, and her analysis is contextualized within the wider critique of modernity. She writes: 'if modernity is characterized by the disassociation between past and future, then Burke's conservation of relationships with the dead attempts to counter that disassociation by constructing traditional communal continuity between the past and future' (25). Early conservative thought, then, resists this 'hallmark of modernity'. Like Scruton, though, 'habitat' is central to the 'proto-ecological fear'. This is another strength of Castellano's view of Burke in that she captures a 'politics of anxiety' in conservative thought – an anxiety that pushes the individual to want to prevent abrupt changes and preserve any progress already achieved. This, undeniably, has much in common with the aims of any Rawlsian liberal who, again in the words of Wissenburg and Levy, seeks to preserve the gains of liberalism. Crucially, Castellano's interpretation of Burkean conservatism is that the social ecology of his thought provides the roots of a much stronger commitment to wider nature that does not view it as a peripheral concern, as is the case with liberalized accounts of environmental stewardship, or Scruton's love of the homestead. The indirectness that results from the preservation of the separation argument can only be overcome by an appeal to conservative values, or at least the admittance that there are serious limits to the motivational force of the mutual disinterest of citizens, and the self-interest of preserving one's homestead, when it comes to sustaining a political agreement and the just institutions of a well-ordered society. There is also the recognition here that central to maintaining the just institutions needed for the liberal, intergenerational agreement of reasonable principles of justice is a strong sense of humility in respect of a citizen's fleeting and temporary role in this wider, transpolitical project of humanity.

The conservatively liberal well-ordered society

Rawls's well-ordered society, as the *what* of intergenerational justice, means that a conservative reading of his work becomes difficult to avoid, based on Scruton's and Castellano's idea of trusteeship, humility, and social ecology. Indeed, such an interpretation even becomes desirable if we are to consider his political liberalism as appealing also to a theory of liberalized environmental stewardship, and to a language beyond the rights and opportunities of the individual citizen. What was missing from the liberalized account of environmental stewardship is again the thicker, and less instrumentalist, reasons for citizens agreeing to sacrifice their own self-interests for a transpolitical good that will move it from the shallow to the slightly darker, and more enlightened, shades of green. As such, the conservative values of humility and the sense of fleeting custodianship contribute to the idea of individuals serving as

130   *Rawls and the Environmental Crisis*

liberal stewards. In doing so, however, how do we avoid the idea of an intergenerational project of cooperation, and an enduring search for human justice, embodying too thick a vision of an exclusionary political *community*? Returning to our overarching question of political liberalism, how are we to retain the freestanding status of justice as fairness? Thompson's notion of lifetime-transcending interests dictates that a citizen's conception of the good exists prior to, during, and after his or her own existence, and that such goods are communicated transgenerationally through *groups and communities*. Likewise, both the conservative and the liberal intergenerational imaginations view such communities and institutions as transmitters of human cooperation from one generation to the next. From this, it is possible to infer that overlapping generations are bound to one another via what Gardiner identifies as a 'chain-connection' and what Gauthier calls the 'chain of interaction' (Gardiner, 2009; Gauthier, 1986, respectively). There are, therefore, links between generations that extend beyond human life, and they exist as a result of the continuation of communities. In a similar vein, the discussion of Rawls's well-ordered society composed of just institutions, and an overlapping consensus, alludes to a politically liberal *community* of justice that comes to exist before, during, and after the lives of individual, future citizens. Such institutions represent (and act as a vehicle *towards*) a transpolitical good of humanity devoid of the outside support of a deity, but as engaged in a perennial search for justice through reasoned political agreement nonetheless. The values embodied within the institutions of a well-ordered society, including, for example, reasonableness, a scheme of liberties, and equality of opportunity, are thus distributed (or taken forward) from one generation of a community of justice to the next, in an overlapping fashion. Liberal values are, therefore, distributed *to* a liberal community *by* a liberal community.

Prima facie, the well-ordered society sounds like an example of just such a substantive liberal, transgenerational community. Being composed of the just institutions, it embodies a commitment to the two principles of justice and forms part of an enduring project of humanity. Yet Rawls, as outlined in Chapter 2, argues against the idea of just such an organic entity: 'political society itself is not a good, but at least a *means* to individual or associational good' (2001: 198, emphasis added). Further, political liberalism must not be seen as a vehicle for the discovery of a *summum bonum*. Rawls expands on his earlier affirmation in *PL* that '[l]iberalism rejects political society as a community because . . . it leads to the systematic denial of basic liberties and may allow the oppressive use of the government's monopoly of (legal) force.' (*PL*: 146, fn.13). Rawls continues: '[o]f course, in the well-ordered society of justice as fairness citizens share a common aim, and one that has high priority: namely, the aim of insuring that political and social institutions are just'. Later, he would arrive at a quite different, yet definitive account of community, in the form of unity around a political conception of justice: 'political society *is* a community if we now mean by a community a society, including a political society, the members of which – in this case citizens – *share certain final ends to which they give very high priority*, so much so that in stating before themselves the kind of person they want to be they count their having these ends as essential' (Rawls, 2001: 200, emphasis added). The means/ends distinction is clear, as the well-ordered society is now both a freestanding end in itself *and* a means to the individual self-authorship of the good – the two are no longer mutually exclusive.

Given the idea that Rawls is acutely aware of the need to steer a careful course between a thick, substantive vision of a community affirming one and the same comprehensive doctrine and a thin, almost meaningless, neutrality between competing conceptions, how does this embody a liberalized theory of environmental stewardship? Again, we see a shift in gear with political liberalism, as the just institutions of a well-ordered society become our *what* (and thus, 'good') of intergenerational justice. So although such a political society was once merely, in Rawls's words, a means to the liberal ends of liberty and equality, much stronger duties of citizenship start to emerge in his mature theory that can only be fulfilled by an appeal to traditional conservative values. It is a community of shared ends held in common by all reasonable citizens, regardless of their own view of the good. Rawls's model seeks to preserve the liberal institutions that will govern the basic structure of society from one generation to the next, and so the liberal political community, or society, can be said to exist independently of its members who are now but temporal and fleeting within the wider project of human cooperation. Here, then, citizens must take seriously the 'epistemological modesty' and humility inherent to conservative thought, and recognize their fleeting custodianship of a wider liberal project of political cooperation embodied in the just institutions they have inherited. Once these institutions are established, Rawlsian notions of intergenerational justice become an exercise in preserving this basic structure of a well-ordered society. Liberal citizens are therefore to become *stewards* of a liberal polity. Citizens of a well-ordered society are to be custodians, trustees, or managers of the just institutions bequeathed to them, and the social ecology that makes them dependent on both the internal and external circumstances of justice, allowing them to pursue their self-penned visions of the good life. They are, as outlined in the previous chapter's account of environmental stewardship, to be managers of their own behaviours, and especially of those ecologically ruinous dispositions that may compromise the 'nascent' social ecology of the well-ordered society, humanity, and wider nature. The liberal overlapping consensus epitomizes this cooperative endeavour and serves as a chain of connection, therefore, that links past, present, and future generations. Rawlsian citizens are thus obliged to both promote and preserve the just institutions of the well-ordered society, not solely for reasons of political recognition and the tolerance of the 'certain final ends to which they give very high priority'.

As already stated, Rawls dropped the Aristotelian motivations that were present in *TJ*, and still hopes to build a theory of intergenerational justice largely on the 'mutual disinterest' of parties in the OP. This is then taken forward and outward to a concern for future generations and non-human species,

132 *Rawls and the Environmental Crisis*

respectively, as they appreciate transpolitical goods only because it is in their own best interest to do so. The argument that citizens of a well-ordered society are inevitably to become stewards of the just institutions they have inherited and from which they benefit, as well as the wider, perennial search for justice that is central to the meta-concept of humanity in the modern period, calls forth the need for political virtues above and beyond the modern liberal view that a polity can be sustained by an appeal to self-interest alone. Preserving the just institutions of the well-ordered society may come into conflict with immediate, and contemporaneous, interests, and so sacrifices may be demanded for the greater good of humanity engaged in an enduring search for justice.

So far, we could say that Rawls's theory of justice is *conservatively liberal* but it is also potentially *liberally conservative*. The political virtues required of liberal stewards seem much more conservative in nature, but how transferable is the concept to the idea of a liberalized account of environmental stewardship? Key to this point is that liberal stewards will not only recognize their duty to maintain the liberal order for future generations, but that they will also acknowledge their increasingly fleeting presence independent from the continued existence of the well-ordered society. This is premised on Rawls's own belief that an overlapping 'consensus achieves compliance by a concordant fit between the political conception and the comprehensive views together with the public recognition of the great political values of the political virtues' (*PL*: 171). Rawls argues, and borrowing from the writings of J.S. Mill, that they are 'the very groundwork of our existence' and 'hence not easily overridden' (*PL*: 139). Not only this, but they 'are expressed by the principles of justice for the basic structure: among them, the values of equal political and civil liberty; fair equality of opportunity; the values of economic reciprocity; the social bases of mutual respect between citizens'. In post-OP stages of democratic deliberation, and public enquiry, the great values and associated virtues are embodied in the spirit of 'public reason' with its 'reasonableness and fair-mindedness'. The political virtues, then, are said to include 'toleration and mutual respect, and a sense of fairness and civility' (*PL*: 122) and will, over time, Rawls argues, develop into a practical 'spirit of compromise and a readiness to meet others halfway' (*PL*: 163). The spirit of these virtues is, in turn, realized in the overlapping consensus.

The political virtues required for a life led under just institutions demand that liberal citizens must humbly accept their duties as liberal stewards. This happens in three ways. The first – and the most liberal aspect of the role – is that they are to be stewards of the liberal political virtues themselves, at an individual level. As part of their psychological makeup, as humans, and as part of the historical, post-Reformation internal circumstances of justice that lead citizens to see themselves as both free and equal, citizens are born with an innate capacity for a *sense of justice*, manifested in – and reflected by – the great political values. Living under just institutions naturally brings out the chief virtues of Rawls's political liberalism: toleration and trust. As free and equal beings, they tolerate other reasonable views of the good, including both comprehensive and partially comprehensive, transgenerational green concerns. They also trust that fellow citizens will exhibit this sense of justice by fulfilling the duties needed to sustain political society, and in managing their destructive human tendencies that could undermine the very circumstances of justice. Rawls envisages this trust as transforming into something more than an aggregation of citizens' desires to live under fair conditions, as the just institutions that serve as a vehicle for the realization of the citizen's view of themselves as 'self-authenticating sources of valid claims' (*PL*: 32) start to exist beyond their lives. This is in line with Castellano's idea of a social ecology, as there is greater integration between the individual, the liberal community, humanity, and wider nature.

This leads to the second element of citizens as stewards, but this time in a much more *conservatively* liberal manner. The established just institutions will come to exist beyond the temporary, fleeting lives of the individual. The enduring search for justice *sans* outside support is to be embodied in a transpolitical, transgenerational, and almost organic entity – a natural growth of the modern search for political unity around principles of justice. As the well-ordered society becomes more established, it is bequeathed to future citizens who may be called upon to defend its institutions. Undoubtedly, this will sometimes require citizens to sacrifice their own interests for the sake of the wider project of humanity busily engaged in a search for justice. The duties of citizenship that originate from citizens' own moral duties to serve justice mean that they are required by the principle of just savings to maintain the institutions of a well-ordered society. Like the previous point, and the one made in the previous chapter by both Di Paolo and Welchman, stewardship could more generally be considered as the management of one's own behaviours, including those that are damaging to the social ecology between humanity, the well-ordered society, and wider nature. This is an individual, self-imposed duty and not one that is bestowed upon them from on high. Such stewardship is thus liberal by virtue of its individualistic egalitarianism, and conservative in its rejection of a rationalistic or elitist imposition on the free citizen.

The third feature of the new liberalized concept of environmental stewardship, that is this time more conservative than liberal, becomes apparent when revisiting Bell's analysis of Rawls's commitment to citizenship education. Rawls argues that the 'state's concern with their education lies in their role as future citizens, and so in such essential things as their acquiring the capacity to understand the public culture and to participate in its institutions . . . and in their developing the political virtues, all this from within a political point of view' (2001: 157). This takes us back to the question of the pervasiveness of the basic structure, and thus the 'main political, social and economic institutions' as a 'unified system of social cooperation from one generation to the next' (*PL*: 11). Recall also that 'nor is it true that the aim of political justice is not an important part of their noninstitutional, or moral, identity' (*PL*: 146 fn.13). The basic structure, for Rawls, is the 'primary subject' because

134 *Rawls and the Environmental Crisis*

of its 'profound and pervasive influence on the persons who live under its institutions . . . it is there that they will lead a complete life' (2001: 55). The basic structure, therefore, 'answers to the public role of educating citizens to a conception of themselves as free and equal' (57). One particular institution that is not part of the basic structure is the family, yet in order for just political and social institutions to be sustained, it too must 'must fulfill this role in appropriate numbers to maintain an enduring society' (163). Rather, Rawls sees it as an 'association' – something not *directly* governed by political principles. The status of family members as free and equal citizens, however, does indeed constrain the internal workings of family life, especially with regards to the equal status of members of minority groups and/or the least advantaged in a liberal society. Rawls explains, however, that as with other associations (churches, universities, businesses, trade unions, etc.) 'we see the need for the division of labor between different kinds of principles' (165). So although there is a certain separateness between the political and political–public life of the citizen, and their non-political public and private life as part of a plurality of associations, Rawls concludes that if 'the so-called private sphere is a space alleged to be exempt from justice, the there is no such thing' (166). Simply put, the principles of justice and the inviolability of equal liberty and fair opportunity pervade all associations and domains of a well-ordered society.

We now have an answer as to influence Rawls envisaged the political would have on the non-political public and private lives of the citizens of a well-ordered society. The virtues needed to uphold this fixed political identity, built on the two principles of justice, are by no means trivial and demand also a language of duty and obligation. These virtues, once we think of his theory as an intergenerational and enduring faith in the just institutions of a well-ordered society, are needed more than ever as the world enters an increasingly dark and uncertain ecological future. Crisis or no crisis, the faith in a citizenry acting as stewards of modern liberal institutions that strive to defend the inviolable liberty and equality of each individual for the good of humanity now lacking divine guidance will inevitably have to protect wider nature with a degree of humility, for the sake of the continuity of this enduring search for justice. The great political values mean that sacrifices will have to be made for the trans-political good of the well-ordered society. The social ecology of the politically liberal community, bound as it is by the constraints and opportunities provided by wider nature, means that this is not simply an indirect obligation. Trust, fair-mindedness, and toleration all point to a recognition of something bigger than the individual – of a perennial search for justice in the name of humanity, since the world lost its outside support during the Reformations. The political virtues necessary for the stewardship of the well-ordered society are far removed from the motivation of mutual disinterest between citizens who view themselves as free and equal. If such a community is at risk from deteriorating ecological conditions, which form an integral part of its existence, then it would be necessary for citizens to subordinate their own interests (lifetime-transcending or otherwise) to the good of an enduring belief that reasoned agreement on principles of justice is possible in the modern period.

Conclusion 135

So after what by now must seem to the reader a laborious exercise in extensionist green political thought, it appears we have only been able to move Rawls's theory of environmental justice from the very light, shallow instrumentalist shades on a continuum of green concerns to a moderately enlightened and more humble ground. The tension between liberal thought and conservatism, exposed in both parts of the green critique, is not something that we should immediately seek to remedy, as they both point to a modern faith in humanity as engaged in meaningful and enduring cooperation from one generation to the next. It also offers a serious reappraisal of Rawls's role as perhaps the most significant *conservative-liberal*, or even *liberal-conservative*, thinker of the late twentieth century. The gains of liberalism, if they are to be protected, require a conservative appeal to virtues now more than ever, a point not missed by Rawls. It is clear, however, that it is not currently a political priority for liberalism to embrace darker green concerns or stronger theories of ecological justice. Nor, perhaps, should it be, given the awful state of affairs humanity has got itself into, ecologically speaking, because even a very instrumentalist light greening of liberal societies in both theory and practice would be a truly radical step and certainly not something to be derided. In a world trapped by the modern Hobbesian belief that political society can reach agreement built only on the self-interest of the individual, now crowned as a little god on earth, a reinvigoration of the age-old theory of stewardship offers a much-needed buffer against human arrogance and our shallow instrumentalist attitude towards wider nature. Yet if it can be judged that this monograph has failed to green justice as fairness in a meaningful way, and should we wish to conclude that it is impossible to develop a theory of liberalized environmental stewardship that successfully navigates between a substantive vision of community and the impartiality of a freestanding political agreement, whilst avoiding a traditional Christian Ages ethic of dominion, then the last word should go to Rawls himself: '[p]erhaps we simply lack the ingenuity to see how the extension may proceed' (*PL*: 21).

Note

1 This could be seen as a development of Rawls's concern for 'marginal cases' (see, for example, *TJ*: 443).

Bibliography

Abbey, R. 2007: 'Rawlsian Resources for Environmental Ethics', *Ethics and the Environment* 12 (1) (pp. 1–22).

Achterberg, W. 1990: 'Ethiek en Duurzame Ontwikkeling', in CREN (RMNO), *Duurzame Ontwikkeling*, Rijswijk, Report no. 40 (pp. 39–47).

Achterberg, W. 1993: 'Can Liberal Democracy Survive the Environmental Crisis? Sustainability, Liberal Neutrality and Overlapping Consensus', in Dobson, A. and Lucardie, P. (eds.) *The Politics of Nature: Explorations in Green Political Theory*. London: Routledge.

Ackerman, B. 2004: 'Political Liberalisms', in Young, S. (ed.) *Political Liberalism: Variations on a Theme*. New York: State University of New York Press.

Barry, J. 1999: *Rethinking Green Politics*. London: Sage.

Beckman, L. 2008: 'Do Global Climate Change and the Interests of Future Generations Have Implications for Democracy?', *Environmental Politics* 17 (4) (pp. 610–624).

Beetham, D. 1993: 'Liberal Democracy and the Limits of Democratisation', in Held, D. (ed.) *Prospects for Democracy: North, South, East West*. London: Polity Press.

Bell, D. 2002: 'How Can Political Liberals be Environmentalists?', *Political Studies* 50 (pp. 703–724).

Bell, D. 2004a: 'Environmental Justice and Rawls Difference Principle', *Environmental Ethics* 26 (pp. 287–306).

Bell, D. 2004b: 'Environmental Refugees: What Rights? Which Duties?', *Res Publica* 10 (pp. 135–152).

Bell, D. 2006: 'Political Liberalism and Ecological Justice', *Analyse & Kritik* 28/2008 (pp. 206–222).

Berlin, I. 1962: 'Does Political Theory Still Exist?', in Laslett, P. and Runciman, W.G. (eds.) *Philosophy, Politics and Society*. Oxford: Blackwell.

Berman, M. 1983: *All That Is Solid Melts into Air: The Experience of Modernity*. London: Verso.

Berry, J. (ed.) 2006: *Environmental Stewardship: Critical Perspectives, Past and Present*. London: Continuum.

Black, J. 1970: *The Dominion of Man. The Search for Ecological Responsibility*. Edinburgh: Edinburgh University Press.

Black, J. 2006: 'The Dominion of Man', in Berry, J. (ed.) *Environmental Stewardship: Critical Perspectives, Past and Present*. London: Continuum.

Burke, E. 2004: *Reflections on the Revolution in France*. London: Penguin.

Caney, S. 2005: 'Cosmopolitan Justice, Responsibility, and Global Climate Change', *Leiden Journal of International Law* 18 (pp. 747–775).

Carruthers, P. 1992: *The Animals Issue*. Cambridge: CUP.

Bibliography 137

Castellano, K. 2013: *The Ecology of British Conservatism, 1790–1837*. London: Palgrave Macmillan.

Crutzen, P. 2002: 'The Anthropocene', *Journal de Physique* 12 (10) (pp. 1–5).

De-Shalit, A. 1995: *Why Posterity Matters: Environmental Policies and Future Generations*. London: Routledge.

De-Shalit, A. 2000: *The Environment between Theory and Practice*. Oxford: Oxford University Press.

Di Paola, M. 2013: 'Environmental Stewardship, Moral Psychology, and Gardens', *Environmental Values* 22 (4) (pp. 503–521).

Dobson, A. 1998: *Justice and the Environment*. Oxford: Oxford University Press.

Dobson, A. (ed.) 1999: *Fairness and Futurity: Essays on Environmental Sustainability and Social Justice*. Oxford: OUP.

Dobson, A. 2003: *Citizenship and the Environment*. Oxford: OUP.

Dobson, A. 2007: *Green Political Thought*. 4th Edition. London: Routledge.

Dobson, A. and Bell, D. (eds.) 2006: *Environmental Citizenship*. London: MIT Press.

Dobson, A. and Saiz, A.V. (eds.) 2005: *Citizenship, Environment, Economy*. London: Routledge.

Eckersley, R. 2004: *The Green State: Rethinking Democracy and Sovereignty*. Cambridge: MIT Press.

Elliot, R. 2006: 'Normative Ethics', in Jamieson, D. (ed.) *A Companion to Environmental Ethics*. Oxford: Blackwell.

Figgis, J.N. 1960: *Political Thought from Gerson to Grotius: 1414–1625*. 2nd Edition. New York: Harper & Brothers.

Forst, R. 2004: 'Foreword', in Young, S. (ed.) *Political Liberalism: Variations on a Theme*. New York: State University of New York Press.

Fortin, E. 1995: 'The Bible Made Me Do It: Christianity, Science, and the Environment', *Review of Politics* 57 (2) (pp. 197–223).

Freeman, S. 1999: *John Rawls: Collected Papers*. Cambridge, MA: Harvard University Press.

Gardiner, S. 2009: 'A Contract on Future Generations', in Gosseries, A. and Meyer, L. (eds.) *Intergenerational Justice*. Oxford: Oxford Scholarship Online.

Gardiner, S. 2011: 'Rawls and Climate Change: Does Rawlsian Political Philosophy Pass the Global Test?', *Critical Review of International Social and Political Philosophy* 14 (2) (pp. 125–151).

Garner, R. 2003: 'Animals, Politics and Justice: Rawlsian Liberalism and the Plight of Non-Humans', *Environmental Politics* 12 (2) (pp. 3–22).

Gaspart, F. and Gosseries, A. 2007: 'Are Generational Savings Just?', *Politics Philosophy and Economics* 6 (pp. 193–227).

Gauthier, D. 1986: *Morals by Agreement*. Oxford: Clarendon Press.

Gillmor, D. 1996: 'The Ecological Crisis and Judeo-Christian Religion.' *Studies: An Irish Quarterly Review* 85 (339) (pp. 261–270).

Gosseries, A. and Meyer, L. (eds.) 2009: *Intergenerational Justice*. Oxford: Oxford Scholarship Online.

Hailwood, S. 1999: 'Towards a Liberal Environment?', *Journal of Applied Philosophy* 16 (3) (pp. 271–281).

Hailwood, S. 2004: *How to be a Green Liberal: Nature, Value and Liberal Philosophy*. Chesham: Acumen.

Hailwood, S. 2005: 'Environmental Citizenship as Reasonable Citizenship', in Dobson, A. and Saiz, A.V. (eds.) *Citizenship, Environment, Economy*. London: Routledge.

Hailwood, S. 2006: 'Political Reasonableness and Nature's Otherness', *Analyse & Kritik* 28 (pp. 173–189).

138 *Bibliography*

Harlow, E. 1992: 'The Human Face of Nature: Environmental Values and the Limits of Anthropocentrism', *Environmental Ethics* 14 (pp. 27–42).

Harrison, P. 2006: 'Having Dominion: Genesis and the Mastery of Nature', in Berry, J. (ed.) *Environmental Stewardship: Critical Perspectives, Past and Present*. London: Continuum.

Hayward, T. 1998: *Political Theory and Ecological Values*. Cambridge: Polity Press.

Heyd, D. 2009: 'A Value or an Obligation? Rawls on Justice to Future Generations', in Gosseries, A. and Meyer, L. (eds.) *Intergenerational Justice*. Oxford: Oxford Scholarship Online.

Hobbes, T. 1996: *Leviathan*. Oxford: OUP.

Holden, B. 1988: *Understanding Liberal Democracy*. London: Philip Allan.

Horstkötter, D. 2004: 'Sustainability and Plurality: From the Moderate End of the Liberal Equilibrium to the Open End of a Situated Liberal Neutrality', in Wissenburg, M. and Levy, Y. (eds.) *Liberal Democracy and Environmentalism: The End of Environmentalism?*. London: Routledge.

Jamieson, D. (ed.) 2001: *A Companion to Environmental Philosophy*. Oxford: Blackwell.

Kassiola, J. 2015: 'The "Tragedy of Modernity": How Environmental Limits and the Environmental Crisis Produce the Need for Postmodern Values and Institutions', in Kassiola, J. (ed.) *Explorations in Environmental Political Theory: Thinking about What We Value*. London: Routledge.

Kay, J. 1995: 'Human Dominion over Nature in the Hebrew Bible', *Annals of the Association of American Geographers* 79 (2) (pp. 214–232).

Kenehan, S. 2015: 'In Defense of the Duty to Assist: A Response to Critics on the Viability of a Rawlsian Approach to Climate Change', *Critical Review of International Social and Political Philosophy* 18 (3) (pp. 308–327).

Koselleck, R. 1988: *Critique and Crisis: Enlightenment and the Pathogenesis of Modern Society*. Oxford: Berghahn.

Koselleck, R. 2002: 'Some Questions Concerning the Conceptual History of "Crisis" ', in Witoszek, N. and Trägårdh, L. (eds.) *Culture and Crisis: The Case of Germany and Sweden*. New York: Berghahn.

Larmore, C. 1990: 'Political Liberalism', *Political Theory* 18 (3) (pp. 339–360).

Laslett, P. (ed.) 1967: *Philosophy, Politics and Society*. Oxford: Basil Blackwell.

Lercher, A. 2006: 'Liberty of Ecological Conscience', *Environmental Ethics* 28 (pp. 315–322).

Levy, Y. 2004: 'The End of Environmentalism (As We Know It)', in Wissenburg, M. and Levy, Y. (eds.) *Liberal Democracy and Environmentalism: The End of Environmentalism?*. London: Routledge.

Litfin, K. 2010: 'The Sacred and the Profane in the Ecological Politics of Sacrifice', in Maniates, M. and Meyer, J. (eds.) *The Environmental Politics of Sacrifice*. London: The MIT Press.

Locke, J. 1965: *Two Treatises of Government*. Cambridge: CUP.

Lovelock, J. 2001: *Gaia: A New Look at Life on Earth*. Oxford: OUP.

Lovelock, J. 2006: 'The Fallible Concept of Stewardship of the Earth', in Berry, J. (ed.) *Environmental Stewardship: Critical Perspectives, Past and Present*. London: Continuum.

Manning, R. 1981: ' "Environmental Ethics and Rawls" Theory of Justice', *Environmental Ethics* 3 (pp. 155–165).

McCormick, H. 2009: 'Intergenerational Justice and the Non-Reciprocity Problem', *Political Studies* 57 (pp. 451–458).

Meadow, D., Randers, J. and Meadows, D. 2004: *Limits to Growth: The 30-Year Update*. London: Earthscan.

Mill, J.S. 1972: *Utilitarianism*. London: Orion Publishing Group.

Mill, J.S. 2008: *On Liberty*. London: Bedford.

Moon, J.D. 2004: 'Political Liberalism: Agency, Rights and Tragic Conflicts', in Young, S. (ed.) *Political Liberalism: Variations on a Theme*. New York: State University of New York Press.

Naess, A. 1973: 'The Shallow and the Deep, Long-Range Ecology Movement: A Summary', *Inquiry* 16 (pp. 95–100).

Neefjes, K. 1999: 'Ecological Degradation: A Cause for Conflict, a Concern for Life', in Dobson (ed.) *Fairness and Futurity*. Oxford: OUP.

Norton, B. 1991: *Toward Unity among Environmentalists*. Oxford: OUP.

Nussbaum, M. 2007: *Frontiers of Justice: Disability, Nationality, Species Membership*. Harvard: Harvard University Press.

Oakeshott, M. 1962: *Rationalism in Politics and Other Essays*. London: Methuen.

Ogg, D. 1952: *Europe in the Seventeenth Century*. London: A & C Black.

O'Neill, J., Holland, A. and Light, A. 2008: *Environmental Values*. Oxon: Routledge.

Osborn, D. 2006: 'Environmental Stewardship Needed for the Core Mission of Public Bodies', in Berry, J. (ed.) *Environmental Stewardship: Critical Perspectives, Past and Present*. London: Continuum.

O'Sullivan, N. 1976: *Conservatism*. London: J.M. Dent & Sons.

Page, E. 2007: 'Intergenerational Justice of What: Welfare, Resources or Capabilities?', *Environmental Politics* 16 (3) (pp. 453–469).

Palmer, C. 2006. 'Stewardship: A Case Study in Environmental Ethics', in Berry, J (ed.) *Environmental Stewardship: Critical Perspectives, Past and Present*. London: T&T Clark.

Palmer, J. and Neal, P. 1994: *The Handbook of Environmental Education*. London: Routledge.

Parfit, D. 1984: *Reasons and Persons*. Oxford: Clarendon Press.

Partridge, E. 2001: 'Future Generations', in Jamieson, D. (ed.) *A Companion to Environmental Philosophy*. Oxford: Blackwell.

Passmore, J. 1974: *Man's Responsibility for Nature*. London: Duckworth.

Plumwood, V. 1991: 'Nature, Self and Gender: Feminism, Environmental Philosophy, and the Critique of Rationalism', *Hypatia* 6 (1) (pp. 3–27).

Rawls, J. 1963: 'Constitutional Liberty and the Concept of Justice', *Nomos VI, Justice* (pp. 281–305). Reprinted in Freeman, S. (ed.) *John Rawls: Collected Papers*. Cambridge: Harvard University Press.

Rawls, J. 1980: 'Kantian Constructivism in Moral Theory', *Journal of Philosophy*, 77 (pp. 515–572). Reprinted in Freeman, S. (ed.) *John Rawls: Collected Papers* (pp. 286–302). Cambridge: Harvard University Press.

Rawls, J. 1985: 'Justice as Fairness: Political Not Metaphysical', *Philosophy and Public Affairs* 14 (pp. 223–252) – Reprinted in Freeman, S. (ed.) *John Rawls: Collected Papers*. Cambridge: Harvard University Press.

Rawls, J. 1999a: *A Theory of Justice*. Revised Edition. Cambridge, MA: The Belknap Press of Harvard University Press.

Rawls, J. 1999b: *The Law of Peoples*. Cambridge, MA: Harvard University Press.

Rawls, J. 1999c: *The Idea of Public Reason Revisited*. Cambridge, MA: Harvard University Press.

Rawls, J. 2001: *Justice as Fairness: A Restatement*. Cambridge, MA: Harvard University Press.

Rawls, J. 2005: *Political Liberalism*. New York: Columbia University Press.

Read, R. 2011: 'Why the Ecological Crisis Spells the End of Liberalism: Rawls' "Difference Principle" Is Ecologically Unsustainable, Exploitative of Persons, or Empty." *Capitalism Nature Socialism*. 22 (3) (pp. 80–94).

140 Bibliography

Regan, T. 1983: *The Case for Animal Rights*. London: Routledge & Kegan Paul.

Reichenbach, B. and Anderson, E. 2006: 'Tensions in a Stewardship Paradigm', in Berry, J (ed.) *Environmental Stewardship: Critical Perspectives, Past and Present*. London: T&T Clark.

Routley, R. and Routley, V. 1982: 'The Nuclear Train to the Future', in Regan, T. and Vande Veer, D. (eds.) *And Justice for All: New Introductory Essays in Ethics and Public Policy*. Totowa, NJ: Rowman and Littlefield.

Rowlands, M. 1997: *Animal Rights: Philosophical Defence*. Basingstoke: MacMillan.

Sagoff, M. 1988: *The Economy of the Earth*. Cambridge: CUP.

Schuppert, F. 2011: 'Climate Change Mitigation and Intergenerational Justice', *Environmental Politics* 20 (3) (pp. 303–321).

Scruton, R. 2006: 'Conservatism', in Dobson, A. and Eckersley, R. (eds.) *Political Theory and the Ecological Challenge*. Cambridge: Cambridge University Press.

Scruton, R. 2012: *Green Philosophy: How to Think Seriously About the Planet*. London: Atlantic Books.

Shklar, J.N. 1957: *After Utopia: The Decline of Political Faith*. Princeton: Princeton University Press.

Singer, B. 1988: 'An Extension of Rawls Theory of Justice to Environmental Ethics', *Environmental Ethics* 10 (pp. 217–231).

Singer, P. 1993: *Practical Ethics*. 2nd Edition. Cambridge: CUP.

Skinner, Q. (ed.) 1985: *The Return of Grand Theory in the Human Sciences*. Cambridge: CUP.

Smith, M. 1998: *Ecologism: Towards Ecological Citizenship*. Buckingham: Open University Press.

Steiner, H. and Vallentyne, P. 2009: 'Libertarian Theories of Intergenerational Justice', in Gosseries, A. and Meyer, L. (eds.) *Intergenerational Justice*. Oxford: Oxford Scholarship Online.

Stephens, P. 2001a: 'Green Liberalism: Nature, Agency and the Good', *Environmental Politics* 10 (3) (pp. 1–22).

Stephens, P. 2001b: 'The Green Only Blooms Amid the Millian Flowers: A Reply to Marcel Wissenburg', *Environmental Politics* 10 (3) (pp. 43–47).

Strauss, L. 1989: 'The Problem of Socrates: Five Lectures', Reprinted in Pangle, T.L. (ed.) *The Rebirth of Classical Political Rationalism: An Introduction to the Thought of Leo Strauss*. London: The University of Chicago Press.

Thero, D. 1995: 'Rawls and Environmental Ethics: A Critical Examination of the Literature', *Environmental Ethics* 17 (Spring) (pp. 93–106).

Thompson, J. 2009: 'Identity and Obligation in a Transgenerational Polity', in Gosseries, A. and Meyer, L. (eds.) *Intergenerational Justice*. Oxford: Oxford Scholarship Online.

Thompson, J. 2013: *Intergenerational Justice. Rights and Responsibilities in an Intergenerational Polity*. London: Routledge.

Vanderheiden, S. 2008: *Atmospheric Justice: A Political Theory of Climate Change*. New York: OUP.

Vincent, A. 2004: *The Nature of Political Theory*. Oxford: OUP.

Welburn, D. 2013: 'Rawls, the Well-Ordered Society and Intergenerational Justice', *Politics* 33 (1) (pp. 56–65).

Welburn, D. 2014: 'Rawlsian Environmental Stewardship and Intergenerational Justice', *Environmental Ethics* 36 (4) (pp. 387–404).

Wenz, P.S. 1988: *Environmental Justice*. Albany: State University of New York Press.

Weston, A. 1999: *An Invitation to Environmental Philosophy*. Oxford: OUP.

White, L. 1967: 'The Historical Roots of Our Ecological Crisis', *Science* 155 (3767) (pp. 1203–1207).

Wissenburg, M. 1998: *Green Liberalism: The Free and the Green Society.* London: Routledge.

Wissenburg, M. 1999: 'An Extension of the Rawlsian Savings Principle to Liberal Theories of Justice in General', in Dobson, A. (ed.) *Fairness and Futurity: Essays on Environmental Sustainability and Social Justice.* Oxford: OUP.

Wissenburg, M. 2001: 'Liberalism Is Always Greener on the Other Side of Mill: A Reply to Piers Stephens', *Environmental Politics* 10 (3) (pp. 23–42).

Wissenburg, M. 2004: 'Little Green Lies: On the Redundancy of "Environment"', in Wissenburg, M. and Levy, Y. (eds.) *Liberal Democracy and Environmentalism: The End of Environmentalism?* London: Routledge.

Wissenburg, M. 2006: 'Liberalism', in Dobson, A. and Eckersley, R. (eds.) *Political Theory and the Ecological Challenge.* Cambridge: Cambridge University Press.

Wissenburg, M. and Levy, Y. (eds.) 2004: *Liberal Democracy and Environmentalism: The End of Environmentalism?* London: Routledge.

Young, S. (ed.) 2004: *Political Liberalism: Variations on a Theme.* New York: State University of New York Press.

Index

Abbey, R. 77–8, 84, 125
Achterberg, W. 56–9, 64; environmental justice 61; hidden green concerns 75; intrinsic value 60; new principles of justice 61, 71, 72, 80; OP designed to a certain outcome 75; public culture 86
Ackerman, B. 19
Anderson, E. 95
apologia 1, 2, 16, 25, 37, 43, 75, 84, 91
Aristotle 18
Aristotelian motivations 18, 19, 77, 131
autonomy 19, 20, 21, 60

background justice 45, 53n5, 54n6
Barry, J. 8
basic liberties 17, 30, 32, 48, 130
basic rights 33
basic structure of society 12, 13, 17, 29, 32, 34, 39, 41, 44, 45, 46, 47, 48, 51, 52–3, 53n2, 53n5, 54n6, 55, 56, 58, 61, 66, 69, 70, 71, 72, 79, 80, 81, 82, 81n1, 89, 131, 132, 133–4
Bayle, P. 24
Beetham, D. 119n6
beginnings 1–3
Bell, D. 43–4, 64–72, 76, 79, 82, 86, 89, 90, 94, 111, 133
Berlin, I. 22
Berry, R. J. 93
Black, J. 97, 98, 99–100, 105, 106–7, 125, 127
burdens of judgement 27, 65
Burke, E. 111, 124, 125, 126–9

Cambridge revolution 1
capitalism 83–4
Carruthers, P. 74
Castellano, K. 124, 125, 128–9, 133
catch-all ideology 5, 92
'categorical imperative' 49

Catholicism 20, 22, 24
Christian stewardship 92–6, 97
citizenship 15, 39, 104, 118, 121, 125, 126, 127; duties 59, 131, 133; education 69, 71, 133; qualities 128; requirements 92; virtues 52
community of justice 67, 130
comprehensive environmental ethic 62, 63
conception of advantage 44
conservatism 113, 118, 124–9, 135
conservatively liberal well-ordered society 129–35
constraint principle 49, 50, 51, 58, 111, 112
constitutional consensus 29–30

democracy 65, 119n6; concept 119n6; development 108; liberal 7, 57–8, 86; property-owning 83
Dobson, A.: compatibility 8; 'immanent critique' 39; liberalism, justice, and green concerns 6, 8; non-anthropocentrism 10; political justice 7; 'second-division' political theory 62, 75; 'terms of reference' 11
difference principle 18, 40, 41, 43, 44, 45, 48, 57, 70–1, 84, 85, 114, 115
Di Paola, M. 100, 106–7, 108, 133
dominion 12, 14, 85, 88, 91–2, 93, 94, 95, 96, 97, 99–100, 101, 102, 105, 108, 118, 119n5, 121, 122, 124, 126, 135
Dutch Constitution 57

ecological justice 2, 4, 7, 9, 10, 11, 14, 23, 25, 27, 32, 37, 38, 39, 41, 43, 55, 57, 58, 59, 61, 63, 64–5, 66, 68, 69, 71, 74, 77, 78, 79, 82, 84, 86, 88, 90, 101, 103, 115, 117, 123, 124, 125, 135
ecosocialism 82–3
Enlightenment 7, 19, 25, 94, 119n4
environmental primary goods 71

144   *Index*

extensionism 1, 6, 13, 27, 34, 38, 40, 41, 42, 43, 56, 61, 62, 64, 71, 72, 73, 77, 78, 81, 82, 85, 86, 91, 105, 112, 115, 119n7, 135
external circumstances of justice 71, 102, 114, 122, 128, 131

Fall, the 94, 95, 96
Figgis, J. N. 34n2
first principles of justice 16, 18, 19, 24, 40, 41, 66, 71, 73, 81, 86, 103
Forst, R. 24–5
Fortin, E. 93
freestanding justice/liberalism 11, 12, 18, 19, 20, 23, 26, 27, 31, 32, 33, 34, 35, 42, 48, 51, 52, 53, 53n1, 55, 58, 59, 61, 63, 65, 66, 69, 73, 75, 76, 80, 81, 82, 86, 90, 92, 100, 102, 103, 104, 114, 118, 135
fundaments of justice 47, 53n1, 89

Gardiner, S. 53n3, 130
Garner, R. 74–7, 79, 82
Gillmor, D. 93, 94–5
global justice 53n3, 115
God 14, 67, 90, 91, 92–5, 96, 97, 98, 116, 119n5
good life 83; conception of the 4, 8, 9, 10, 17, 18, 22, 36, 40, 70, 75, 80, 101, 103; individual pursuits 113; self-authorship 25, 26, 34, 65, 71, 74, 84, 91; visions 23, 24, 34, 80, 84, 89, 118, 131
green concerns 35–54; justification of the separation argument 37–9; liberalism versus 3–8; light versus dark green political theory 8–11; metaphysical concept of human/non-human relations 39–42; principle of just savings 2, 13, 36, 43–51, 52, 53n4, 65, 72, 88, 89, 90, 96, 113, 114, 118, 122, 124, 125, 126, 133; remaining questions 51–3; sentientism 13, 36–7, 38, 39, 41, 46, 123
green critique 55–87; freestanding exploitation 79–85; light green, interim ethic 62–72; non-human species question 72–9; third principle of justice 55, 56–61, 62, 87n2, 103, 104
green critique, second 88–120; beyond mutual disinterest 89–92; Christian stewardship 92–6; liberal rights extension 116–18; nature as independent 101–6; stewardship liberalized 96–101; Thompson's 'lifetime-transcending interests' 110–16; wider nature 101–10 (*see also* wider nature)
guardianship 100, 106

Hailwood, S. 64, 87n4, 88, 118, 119n3, 124; basic structure of society 61; *How to be a Green Liberal* 105; internal circumstances of justice 107, 122; nature as independent 61, 86, 101–6, 109, 110; nature as other 59, 60, 92, 102–3, 104, 105, 110, 117, 121, 129; new principles of justice 61; separation argument 59; self-standingness nature 59; stewardship 108; valued objects 116
Harrison, P. 93, 100
Hobbesian: *modus vivendi* 19; political society can reach agreement on self-interest of individual 135; theory of modernity 119n1
Holden, B. 119n6
Horstkötter, D. 79, 80, 81–2, 86
human dominion 12, 14, 85, 88, 91–2, 93, 94, 95, 96, 97, 99–100, 101, 102, 105, 108, 118, 119n5, 121, 122, 124, 126, 135
human flourishing 8, 13, 18–19, 23, 67

ignorance, veil of 12, 17, 29, 40–1, 46, 48, 49, 74, 84, 86n1
indirectness 'Rawlings-inspired' OP 118, 121–4, 125, 129
intergenerational justice 15n2, 35, 43, 44, 45, 46, 47, 48, 49, 50, 51, 52, 79, 88, 94, 99, 109, 110, 112, 113, 114–15, 116, 120n8, 121, 122, 124, 129, 131

justice, internal circumstances of justice 101, 103, 107, 122, 128, 132
justice, strict 27, 36, 44, 60, 62, 66, 71, 75
justice as fairness 1, 6, 11, 12, 14, 16, 17, 18, 19, 27–9, 31, 32, 33, 34, 36, 37, 38, 39, 40, 41, 42, 43, 44, 45, 46, 51, 52, 53n2, 56, 58, 59, 61, 62, 63, 64, 66, 69, 70, 71, 72, 73, 74, 75, 77–8, 79, 80, 84, 85, 86, 86n1, 89, 90, 91, 92, 103, 105, 108, 109, 112–13, 117, 118, 121, 122, 123, 124, 130, 135
just savings 2, 13, 36, 43–51, 52, 53n4, 65, 72, 88, 89, 90, 96, 113, 114, 118, 122, 124, 125, 126, 133

Kantian influence 11, 16, 18, 19, 25, 49, 108, 126
Kassiola, J. 119n1
Kay, J. 93
Koselleck, R. 20–1, 28

'landscaped' nature 59
Larmore, C. 19, 119n4
Laslett, P. 21

Law of Peoples, The 40
least advantaged 18, 41, 45, 48, 70, 71, 84, 114, 134
Lercher, A. 4, 107
level of benefit 44
Levy, Y. 5, 6, 7–8, 9, 81, 96, 105, 129
liberalized theory of environmental stewardship 3, 14, 91, 95, 118, 122, 125, 131
liberal pluralism 80
liberal rights 78, 108; extension 116–18
lifetime-transcending interests 110–16, 117, 121, 122, 123, 126, 128, 134
Limits to Growth Thesis 83, 85
Litfin, K. 89, 90
Lovelock, J. 38, 95, 106

Manning, R. 49, 86n1
Marshall,: *Berman* 119n1
mature theory 11, 53n1, 91, 131
McCormick, H. 50, 51
Meadows, D. 83
metaphysics 3, 5, 11, 18, 26, 28, 29, 30–1, 32, 36, 37, 52, 59, 60, 62–3, 65, 72, 78, 86, 122, 125, 126; concept of human/non-human relations 39–42, 68; crisis 90
Mill, J. S. 8, 132; *Utilitarianism* 21–2
Millean classical liberalism 19
moral agents 6, 29, 70, 123
'moral person' 17, 75
moral pluralism 75
moral powers 36, 45, 48, 70, 82, 86n1
mutual disinterest 15, 29, 34, 35, 38, 49, 50, 51, 53n4, 62, 63, 84, 112, 117, 118, 124, 129, 131, 134; beyond 89–92

nature as other 60, 61, 102–3, 104, 105, 110, 129
Neal, P. 69
neutrality 8, 11, 19, 20, 25, 32, 34, 36, 38–9, 53n2, 56, 75, 80, 92, 102–3, 116, 131
non-human species question 6, non-human species question 72–9
Nussbaum, M. 5–6

Oakeshott, M. 126
Ogg, D. 24
O'Neill, J. 10
original position (OP) 12, 13, 16, 17–18, 19, 26–34, 38, 40, 47–8, 49, 50, 51, 52, 55, 56, 57, 58, 61, 62, 63, 64, 65, 72, 73, 74, 75, 77, 78, 84, 85, 86n1, 88, 117, 118, 131; indirectness 121–4; post- 41, 46, 66, 69,

71, 76, 79, 82, 89, 121, 132; single-issue 112–13, 122
O'Sullivan, N. 119n2
outside support 20–1, 28, 42, 89, 90, 91, 116, 118, 130, 133, 134
overlapping consensus 18, 26, 28, 29, 30, 31, 33, 55, 56, 57, 59, 65, 66–7, 69, 73, 79, 80, 81, 82, 85, 86, 103, 115, 130, 131, 132

Page, E. 43–4
Palmer, C. 95
Palmer, J. 69
Parfit, D. 98
Passmore, J. 59
perennial search for justice 90, 121, 124, 130, 132, 134
Plato 22
Platonic: belief 93, 109; virtue 100
pluralism: liberal 80; moral 75; reasonable 18, 23, 24, 27, 28, 31, 47, 81, 101, 103, 105, 107, 109, 128; religious 107; simple 30
political conception of justice 12, 20, 27, 28, 29, 30–1, 32–3, 38, 39, 58, 74, 85, 76, 81, 86n1, 102, 103, 114, 130, 132
Political Liberalism (PL) 19, 29–30, 31, 36, 38–9, 40, 42, 49, 52, 58, 59, 63, 72–3, 74, 77, 78, 101, 102, 111, 112, 114, 130
political liberalism 16–34; early 24–6; original position 26–Rawls's 16–20; Reformations as the birth 20–3
polluter pays principle 45
post-Reformation: degeneration 21; human condition 122; liberalism 22, 25, 29, 92; modernity 20; thought 128
prima facie 5, 36, 64, 90, 130
principle of just savings 2, 13, 36, 43–51, 52, 53n4, 65, 72, 88, 89, 90, 96, 113, 114, 118, 122, 124, 125, 126, 133
Protestantism 22, 24, 34n2
public-political culture 33, 34, 72, 81, 86
public reason 30, 38, 66, 67, 68, 81, 87n3, 132

Read, R. 2, 15n1, 82, 83, 84–5, 117, 124
reasonable pluralism 18, 23, 24, 27, 28, 31, 47, 81, 101, 103, 105, 107, 109, 128
Reichenbach, B. 95
religious pluralism 107
Routley, R. 57
Routley, V. 57
Rowlands, M. 72–5, 77

Schuppert, F. 123
Scruton, R. 124, 125–8, 129

146 *Index*

second-division political theory 7, 39, 62
self-standingness 57, 59
sense of justice 17, 18, 19, 31, 33, 36, 37, 48, 50, 70, 74, 76, 86n1, 104, 109, 132, 133
sentientism 13, 36–7, 38, 39, 41, 46, 123
separation argument 3, 7, 12, 13, 14, 16, 26, 27, 32, 34, 35, 36, 43, 44, 51, 55, 56, 58, 59, 60, 62, 64, 65, 66, 72, 74, 75, 77, 78, 80, 85, 86, 88, 91, 96, 98, 101–2, 103, 107, 108, 117, 119, 123, 124, 125, 126, 127, 128; justification 37–9; neglect of environmental injustice 63
shallow instrumentalist 2, 3, 7, 9
Shklar, J. 21
simple pluralism 30
Singer, B. 86n1
Skinner, Q. 22
social contract 18, 40, 41, 63, 72
'speciesism' 7, 101
Spinoza, B. de 24
Stephens, P. 42, 90
stewardship 3, 14–15, 26, 38, 55, 89, 90–2, 104–9, 118, 121–35; Christian 92–6; liberalized 88, 91, 96–101, 107, 122, 124, 126, 127, 128, 129, 131; religious 67; self 110; 'things' 117
Strauss, L. 22
strict justice 27, 36, 44, 60, 62, 66, 71, 75
summum bonum 21–2, 23, 46, 90, 130

Theory of Justice, A (TJ) 1, 17, 18, 19, 21, 22, 29, 31, 36, 41, 42, 43, 47, 48, 49, 50, 52, 53, 53n1, 53n4, 56, 59, 62, 68, 73, 74, 77, 78, 87n2, 91, 101, 111, 112, 119n7, 123–4, 131
Thero, D. 49, 56, 62–3, 68, 70, 72, 77, 86n1; comprehensive environmental ethic 62, 63

third principle of justice 55, 56–61, 62, 87n2, 103, 104
Thompson, J.: 110–16, 118, 120n8, 121, 122, 123, 124, 130
TJ see A Theory of Justice
tolerance 22, 34, 59, 104, 107, 117, 124, 131
transmission principle 57

veil of ignorance 12, 17, 29, 40–1, 46, 48, 49, 74, 84, 86n1
Vincent, A. 34n1

Welchman, J. 92, 105–9, 110, 119nn5–6, 133
'well-ordered society' 2, 11, 12, 15, 16, 17, 18, 19, 20, 23, 29, 33, 35, 41, 43, 44, 47–8, 51, 52, 53n1, 58, 66, 68, 76, 80, 81, 82, 88, 103, 117, 120n8, 121, 125, 129; conservatively liberal 129–35
Wenz, P. S. 86n1, 112; *Environmental Justice* 119n7
White, L. 92–3, 94, 96
wider nature 2, 3, 4, 5, 7, 9, 10, 11, 12–14, 26, 27, 34, 35, 36, 37, 38–9, 41, 42, 46, 51–2, 53, 57, 58, 61, 71, 77, 115, 116, 117, 125, 131, 133; human dominion 12, 14, 85, 88, 91–2, 93, 94, 95, 96, 97, 99–100, 101, 102, 105, 108, 118, 119n5, 121, 122, 124, 126, 135; humanity's relationship 62, 63, 68, 72, 76, 78–9, 82, 88, 90, 91, 92, 93, 94, 95–6, 127, 128, 133, 134; 'independence' 59; indifference 101–10; justice as fairness 64; theory of dominion 85; social ecology 129; valuing 86, 100, 118, 123
Wissenburg, M. 5, 6, 7–8, 9, 10, 50, 51, 81, 105, 114, 129

Young, S. 19